Signs of Life

Royal Free and University College Medical School
UNIVERSITY COLLEGE LONDON

DEPARTMENT OF PRIMARY CARE & POPULATION SCIENCES

Royal Free Campus
Rowland Hill Street, London NW3 2PF

Tel: +44 (0)171 794 0500
Direct: +44 (0)171 830 2239
Fax: +44 (0)171 794 1224

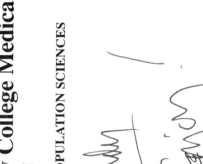

With Compliments

WORLD HEALTH ORGANIZATION COLLABORATING CENTRE

Signs of Life

Cinema and Medicine

Edited by Graeme Harper and Andrew Moor

 **WALLFLOWER PRESS**

LONDON and NEW YORK

First published in Great Britain in 2005 by
Wallflower Press
4th Floor, 26 Shacklewell Lane, London E8 2EZ
www.wallflowerpress.co.uk

A catalogue for this book is available from the British Library.

ISBN 1-904764-16-9 (pbk)
ISBN 1-904764-17-7 (hbk)

Printed by Antony Rowe Ltd., Chippenham, Wiltshire

Contents

Acknowledgements

Many thanks are due to Linda Jones, Research Administrator in the English Department at the University of Wales, Bangor, for her skilled contribution, to the BFI Stills Department for their kind assistance, to Greg Thorpe for helping at the proofing stage, and to Yoram Allon for his constant support and enthusiasm. A great many thanks also to Sir Kenneth Calman for showing interest, even during his busy schedule, and for taking time to write such a lively foreword to this book. Thanks also to Brian Glasser for the invitation to join in a lively dicsussion at UCL. GH would also like to thank Andrew Moor; it has been a real pleasure to work with you on this one, Andrew, from start to finish. Sincere thanks. And sincere thanks, finally, to each and of all our contributors, whose work has made this book what it is.

Notes on Contributors

Bruce Babington is Professor of Film at the University of Newcastle upon Tyne. He is the author of *Launder and Gilliat* (Manchester University Press, 2001) and has co-authored *Blue Skies and Silver Linings: Aspects of the Hollywood Musical* (Manchester University Press, 1985), *Affairs to Remember: The Hollywood Comedy of the Sexes* (Manchester University Press, 1989) and *Biblical Epics* (Manchester University Press, 1993), and is the co-editor of *The Trouble With Men: Masculinities in European and Hollywood Cinema* (Wallflower Press, 2004).

Timothy M. Boon is Head of Collections Development at the Science Museum, London. He has worked on several galleries and exhibitions, including *Making of the Modern World* on the history of technology since 1750, *Health Matters* on twentieth-century medicine and *Treat Yourself* on health consumerism. His doctoral thesis, 'Films and the contestation of public health in interwar Britain' (University of London) was completed in 1999. Publications include papers discussing the cinematic representation of smoke abatement, nutrition, planning and industrial history, and on the place of history in science museum curatorship. His continuing research focuses on several aspects of the cultural history of documentary films, public health and everyday life.

Lucy Fischer is Professor of Film Studies and English at the University of Pittsburgh where she serves as Director of the Film Studies Program. She is the author of *Jacques Tati* (G. K. Hall, 1983), *Shot/Countershot: Film Tradition and Women's Cinema* (Princeton University Press, 1989), *Imitation of Life* (Rutgers University Press, 1991), *Cinematernity: Film, Motherhood, Genre* (Princeton University Press, 1996), *Sunrise* (British Film Institute, 1998), *Designing Women: Art Deco, Cinema and the Female Form* (Columbia University Press, 2003) and the co-editor of *Stars: The Film Reader* (Routledge, 2004).

Brian Glasser has a background in comparative literature and medical sociology. He is a teaching fellow in the Centre for Medical Humanities at the Royal Free and University College Medical School, and Patient Information Programme Officer at the Royal Free Hampstead NHS Trust. He is author of a book about Europe's most important jazz musician, entitled *In a Silent Way: A Portrait of Joe Zawinul* (Sanctuary Books, 2001).

Julia Hallam teaches film and television studies at the University of Liverpool; she has written widely on questions of identity and representation including *Nursing the Image: Media Culture and Professional Identity* (Routledge, 2000). She is co-author of *Realism and Popular Cinema* (Manchester University Press, 2000), co-editor of *Medical Fictions* (Liverpool John Moores University Press, 1998) and is currently writing a book on Lynda La Plante.

Graeme Harper, formerly Director of the Centre for Creative and Performing Arts at the University of Wales, Bangor, is Professor and inaugural Head of the School of Creative

Arts, Film and Media at the University of Portsmouth. He is the author of *Swallowing Film* (DVDX, 2000), *Comedy, Fantasy and Colonialism* (Continuum, 2002) and *Dancing on the Moon* (Eclipse, 2003), and the co-editor of the international journals *Studies in European Cinema* (Intellect) and *New Writing* (MLM).

M. Roy Jobson uses poetry in his teaching of clinical pharmacology at the Medical University of Southern Africa. Dr Jobson is a Family Physician by training, and has also trained as an educator of adults. He is a member of the Clinical Trials and Pharmacovigilance Committees of the South African Medicines Control Council. As a recipient of a Hubert H. Humphrey Fellowship, he spent a year at the University of Minnesota. He is a published poet and has written health education materials for both radio and television.

Donna Knapp van Bogaert is Senior Lecturer in Bioethics in the Faculties of Medicine and Dentistry at the Medical University of Southern Africa and Senior Lecturer in Research and Environmental Ethics at the University of Pretoria School of Public Health. Her M.Phil thesis focused on visual and literary representations of disability and difference in eigtheenth-century Britain.

Kenneth MacKinnon is Professor of Film at London Metropolitan University. He has several play translations (from modern Greek), articles on both Classics and Film Studies, as well as seven academic film books published, including *The Politics of Popular Representation: Reagan, Thatcher, AIDS, and the Movies* (Fairleigh Dickinson University Press, 1992).

Andrew Moor lectures in film and literature at the University of Wales, Bangor. He is the author of *Powell and Pressburger: A Cinema of Magic Spaces* (I. B. Tauris, 2004), and has published various essays on Derek Jarman, Anton Walbrook and Neil Jordan.

C. A. Morgan III is Associate Professor of Psychiatry, and Research Affiliate, History of Medicine at Yale University. He is a recipient of the Stephen Fleck Award at Yale for clinical teaching, and the Lucia P. Fulton Award for his work in the History of Medicine. He is also the director of the Human Performance Laboratory at the Clinical Neuroscience Division of the National Center for Post-Traumatic Stress Disorder.

Tom Shakespeare has researched and taught sociology at the Universities of Cambridge, Sunderland, Leeds and Newcastle. He has written or edited six books and many papers in the areas of disability studies, medical sociology and bioethics. He is a member of the board of Northern Film and Media, a former board member of the Tyneside Cinema, and has written and presented several television documentaries on disability.

Jackie Stacey is Professor of Women's Studies and Cultural Studies in the Department of Sociology at Lancaster University. She has been a co-editor of *Screen* since 1994 and is the author of *Star Gazing: Hollywood Cinema and Female Spectatorship* (Routledge, 1994) and *Teratologies: A Cultural Study of Cancer* (Routledge, 1997) and co-author of *Global Nature, Global Culture* (Sage, 2000). She is currently working on a book entitled *The Cinematic Life of the Gene.*

Foreword

Some of my earliest memories relate to film. In the 1940s and 1950s, before television took over, a trip to the cinema was a major event whether on Saturday afternoons for *Hop Along Cassidy* or Laurel and Hardy or on special occasions to see the new Christmas Disney release; the magic was the same. I see fewer movies on the big screen now and though the small screen versions are not as good, they keep me up-to-date. Indeed I was surprised at how many films I had seen which are covered in this volume. Cinema therefore has always had a special place in my own life and imagination.

But the study of the cinema is a serious topic and deserves to be disconnected from my crude and diminishing childhood memories. Film provides a fascinating and powerful medium to consider issues of life and death and a wide range of emotions in illness and health. This immediately raises an important issue to consider at the outset: whether or not films need to be related to 'medical' or 'health' themes to be relevant to health professionals. Many of the lessons and implications that arise from film need not have a clear health theme to initiate discussion and debate. This issue came up early in our initial work on literature and medicine. It became clear that while medical or health-related books acted as triggers to discussion on values and beliefs they were also limited in that they did not always reflect a wide enough range of emotions and values. I suspect it is the same with cinema. While 'medical' movies illustrate some issues, they have limitations.

Such films, however, have a very specific role in setting the context of health care and providing a visual reminder of what things were like, more vividly than using the written word. Even films produced ten years ago are likely to seem dated – not from the point of view of the values or emotions displayed but from the technology used, the dress, the treatments and the settings. In particular they can be used to consider, and illustrate, the relationship between the major actors (used here in sociological terms) in the film, especially as doctors, patients and nurses. For example, the relationship between the patient and the doctor has changed considerably over the last two decades and film can be used to track such changes, part of the changing role of the doctor. They also illustrate the changing professional relationships that have occurred. Thus the nurse/doctor relationship, portrayed generally as the nurse as handmaiden of the doctor, and the gender always being fixed as male-medical and female-nurse. More recent films have portrayed this in a quite different way and cinema provides an excellent medium for the analysis of such changes. In addition, the public perception and expectations of medicine and health care can be significantly influenced for good or for bad. Television, with its multiple series on health care has had a special role in this.

There is little doubt that such 'medical' films can have a significant effect on those who might wish to become doctors or nurses. Those films with a biographical perspective provide role models and give depth and perhaps meaning to particular career pathways. Medical students, and I confess to being one a long time ago, can learn a great deal from such films. But here the question must be as to whether what is learned is appropriate. Knowledge and skills can be learned in a very limited way from commercial films (as opposed to films made specially for a medical audience) but attitudes can be transmitted, and role models reinforced. To trivialise for a moment, Sir Lancelot Sprat, the autocratic surgeon in the 'Doctor' films, was certainly a character, but perhaps not the only role model for a young person looking for a career in medicine, particularly surgery.

Of more general interest is whether or not cinema adds to the written word, or detracts from it. Is the book better than the film? I suspect it is a mixture of both. Some stories lend themselves to cinematographic treatment, and the visual impact can be profound, portraying emotion and feelings in a very personal and identifiable way, the skill of the actor and the director combining to create something new and special: a reinterpretation of the original.

Storytelling is therefore at the heart of the process whether by the written or spoken word or by visual images. It is the story that creates the atmosphere and the drive to produce something different. There is a fascinating resurgence in the relationship between the arts and humanities (of which cinema is certainly one) and health and medicine. The recognition that medicine is an art (remember Hippocrates' first aphorism: 'the art is long and the judgement difficult…') which requires judgement and feelings and cannot all be reduced to facts and evidence. There are several reasons why the arts might be important in medicine. Firstly, medicine is full of uncertainty: in diagnosis, in treatment and in what to say to the patient. There is often no 'right' answer and the health professional has to rely on experience, judgement and values. The arts and humanities can help with that by providing illustrations of problems that can occur, and how they can be solved. They once again provide a focus for discussion. Secondly, there is the human dimension to caring for people. They are individuals, not ciphers, and a powerful cinematographic image can enhance the feeling of individuality in the process of care. Thirdly, health professionals have a tough job. They see difficult things and are asked to undertake procedures that are above the call of duty on a regular basis. The arts can allow them to relax, unwind and find refreshment in the creativity of others. Finally, patients can find great solace in the arts and find strength and courage when inspired by others. Hence the increasing use of arts as a method of exposing health professionals to different ways of thinking and allowing them to see the world through the eyes of the artist. Cinema provides an important vehicle for this and this volume illustrates the benefits it can bring.

Sir Kenneth Calman, Former Chief Medical Officer, UK
November 2004

Graeme Harper
and Andrew Moor

Introduction

For over a hundred years now, film has assisted us in circulating and rehearsing ideas about medical science. Today, along with its media compatriot, television, it is one of the most pervasive ways through which representations of illness, medical institutions, medical personnel and medical practices are established and confronted in the lay-community. Representations of medical science in film play a key role in supporting or challenging what Michel Foucault has referred to as ideas about 'normality' (Foucault 1973: 35). 'Normality', that is, not only in relation to what it means to be in need of medical assistance, but also in relation to human practices which might be represented as either 'healthy' or 'unhealthy'. It is important to see these definitions as, at very least, *partially* culturally constructed and, quite often, *actively* socially defined.

With this active social construction in mind, doctors, patients and nurses have accrued stereotyped meanings and clichéd roles, although other health workers (midwives, health visitors, social workers, physiotherapists, occupational therapists, pharmacists, dieticians, opticians, clinical psychologists, counsellors, Samaritans, home-carers and relatives, alternative/lay healers, and so on) have tended to attract less attention. Similarly, ideas about tuberculosis, cancer and AIDS have often provided narrative material; other impairments perhaps less so.

Since the clinical language of the medical-professional-scientific lobby largely defines and detects signs of illness, instances of morbidity are sometimes the occasion for dramatic encounters with a highly empowered subculture. When cinema channels and resolves narratives of sickness, dying or healing, it therefore touches inevitably on politicised issues to do with authority and social control. The culture of health and illness can be, of course, a place of physiological or psychological confrontation between human life expectations and human frailties. But it is also a stage on which social inequalities can be considered, the nature of power and professionalism can be illustrated, and, at most, the nature and limits of the self can be explored.

Into the realms of metaphysics, the cultural perception of medicine, health and illness also touches on the divine and a spirit of religiosity frequently underpins popular medicinal myths. Modernity's representations of medicine may claim a toe-hold in secular empiricism, but they glimmer with intimations of immortality and visionary zeal, partly because medicinal discourse overlays and translates older spiritual ways of understanding, and ultimately because of the cultural need to invest medical science with power over death. Doctors become modern priests and sorcerers; medical discoveries our modern miracles. Popular cinema repeatedly deploys, standardises and stereotypes scenarios of Christ-like healing and sudden, inspired moments of scientific breakthrough. It also finds in medical science opportunities for exploring the coming together of the public face of science with the private face of individual lives. And it makes of medical science an opportunity to question the nature, and strength, of human relationships. If cinema has the power to effect perspective through its multi-layered combination of sight and sound and display, then 'medical cinema' certainly makes much of cinema's attention to our senses.

The strengths and limitations of clinical discourse

Colin Samson, following Foucault, notes how the French philosopher René Descartes (1596–1650) established the modern conception of the body as a discreet entity. Samson places the origin of modern medicinal philosophy in the Cartesian duality of body and mind. In a productive reading, he argues that 'the mind, as a soul in the body, retained its sacred status as the essence of human existence … Descartes' well-known phrase "I think, therefore I am" established the mind as the basis of individual identity … the body, having severed its spiritual links with the soul, not only continued to be profane, but, with developments in scientific method, became a spiritually free-floating physical object, mere matter' (Samson 1999: 4). Modern clinical medicine is premised on a mechanistic, materialist view of this body, shorn of its divinity.

Foucault allies bio-medical ideas about the body, personhood and illness with the Enlightenment project's promotion of rationalism, empiricism and progress, a cluster of ideas circulating around reason's ability to dominate nature, to name and marshal its parts as if it were a machine (feminism has noted how gender intervenes in this process, as women are connoted with nature, and science, technology and culture with men). Foucault's influential *The Birth of the Clinic: An Archaeology of Medical Perception* (1973) sees medicine as a form of discernment which isolates, categorises and catalogues disease. The 'clinical gaze' accrues power through rituals of professional diagnosis that aim to discover 'the truth', that 'truth' composed of some generally agreed principles and foundations and some specifically constructed notions and ideals founded on social and cultural hierarchies. In seeking to delineate the character of the disease itself, the personhood of the patient is bracketed off. 'In order to know the truth of the pathological fact', Foucault argues, 'the doctor must abstract the patient' (Foucault 1973: 8). What Foucault is identifying is the kernel of bio-medical knowledge, whose clinical discourse attempts to mask the presence of psychological and sociological factors in both the doctor/patient encounter and the experience of illness or health.

There are implications here for medical practice, the popular understanding of the health professions and wider issues of identity. Clinical medicine's materialist view of the body – which extends to modern genetics, the genome project and cloning – continues to hold sway, and its highly technologised culture ensures that the discourse retains status and mystique. Genetics may enumerate the body's components, and clinical medicine may understand its pure mechanics, but the Cartesian human entity feels itself to be more than the sum of its parts. Thus, the reification of the 'mind' is concomitant with the depersonalising of the body and its appropriation by the medical professions.

Cinema, which is aimed at the mass market of lay-audiences, has a range of options to hand when interpreting the clinic in illness-narratives. Popular culture translates, reduces and traduces the terms of the clinical encounter by stereotyping the roles of patients and health care workers, or by standardising narratives of disease into familiar patterns and genres, or by placing clinical encounters within the context of 'human progression' or some other teleological narrative in which challenges to a centralised perspective is made to seem almost in opposition to 'what is best for humankind'. Naturally, care is taken to ensure points of medical reference are made clear if the project has any educational or didactic purpose, but these reference points tend to be defined by 'what must be learnt' rather than 'what might be discovered'. Equally, technical jargon may sometimes obfuscate the soundtrack if this assists in shoring up the medical profession's reputation for *pure* science. Purity is itself an important element of defining medical ethics; fuzzy logic is not supported in cinematic narratives concerned with medical practice, however speculative some diagnoses might necessarily have to be.

A less known strand of medical films, one that escapes the disinfected clinic walls, points a camera towards public health. The distinct sub-genre of educational public health documentaries, for example, might be identified as one which perhaps inadvertently places clinical medical practice against raw social reality, leaving the viewer (quite often a medical professional themselves) torn between cinematic revelation and institutional discourse. Within Western feature films, the missionary quality of health workers often emphasises their fight with social problems rather than their lab-bound research suggesting, somewhat against a view of 'pure' science, that society itself is a generator of medical discourse. These social issues are often bound up with deprivation, with poor housing, education and hygiene, and with the squalor of an industrialised working-class (or under-class) life. The link between illness and material deprivation is thus established and the conclusion might well be drawn from this that inequalities caused by the economic system are directly to blame for high morbidity rates (or put another way, in the Western world it is quite possible for Capitalism to make us sick).

With this in mind, it is natural that commercial cinema tends to handle socio-medical perspectives gingerly, shying away from exposing social forces and preferring its dynamic of cause and effect to be generated at the personal level. Personalising medical cinema, however, only heightens the possibility of audience/actor empathy, and the results are often an unease about the missing narratives of social dissolution, or a questioning of the 'back story' in which a character or institution seems somehow out of step with the world of power or privilege around them. This unease is not always resolved in the film's conclusion.

Films about illness are not only drawn to bio-medical storylines, of course, but also to psychological and psychiatric ones. Or, alternatively, to socio-medical perspectives – elements sidelined by the clinical gaze. In fact, any preliminary search of the 'cinema of illness' will return a disproportionately high number of films about mental disorders. Clearly, cinema is fascinated with the mind as a subject, for which a host of explanations can be offered. The post-Romantic narratives which are grist to popular cinema's mill are driven by issues of character motivation and interior depth, and the mysteries of the malfunctioning mind are traditional melodramatic fare, especially when its strangeness can import metaphysical connotations (for example, of 'genius'). Popular cinema (particularly Hollywood) has also tended towards personalised, libertarian or existential aesthetics, and individualism like this is thought to reside in the mind.

The prevalence of psychiatric narratives owes something to the presence of popular Freudianism in mainstream classical Hollywood, an example of immigrant intellectualism from Europe infiltrating American culture. Academic film studies, which embraced psychoanalytic concepts so enthusiastically in the 1970s, have complemented this interest in the workings of the mind rather than in the material operations of the body.

Narratives of illness

In the popular mind, illness has a teleology: (a) I am healthy; (b) I fall ill; (c) (i) I recover; or (ii) I die. These social expectations follow the arc often described by classical narrative: an equilibrium of good health is disrupted; incapacities caused by the illness's symptoms present themselves as obstacles; closure is achieved when the symptoms are eradicated or, if the illness proves fatal, the narrative may engineer a 'good death', a noble end with some consequence, which grasps transcendental values to ensure that death shall have no dominion.

Tending, as it does, to reduce the experience of illness to generically recognisable scenarios, the medical film may be drawn to acute or critical ailments. There is a tendency for mainstream cinema to deal most regularly in clear binary opposites – healthy/sick; alive/ dead; able-bodied/disabled – but this is not how many illnesses are experienced. Chronic illness may be accommodated as a feature of a long and fulfilled life. Shades of disability may suggest a continuum rather than a polarity. The strength of the will to polarise suggests a need to preserve the unstained vitality of 'good health'. A need that might be informed by paranoia about personal illness, by film narrative's projection of a clearly defined 'cinematic space' or even by the assumption of audience identification only with a relatively narrow range of situations, characters and themes. While medicine and illness may appear in any genre, melodrama, biopics, horror and comedy feature strongly.

Melodrama has been seen to be often centred on the family, and to present a central character (often female) who is 'acted upon' by an exterior force ('fate', or unsympathetic ideological pressure) rather than a true 'protagonist' who takes decisive action in the social field and is the agent of her/his destiny. Its structure therefore provides the medical narrative with a static, passive sufferer – a patient – and with the justification to write large the traumatic sentiments often associated with illness. Issues of gender may also be involved. Many medical melodramas have explored issues of masculinity by relying on cultural associations of patient-hood which see it as a dramatic 'un-manning' which robs idealised manhood of its definitional, core attributes: activity, physical strength, autonomy.

In supporting a 'mythological' as well as an 'actual' history of medical developments, the medical film typifies popular culture's wish to celebrate individual achievement. In the medical biopic this means the chronicling of the career of one or more players in a significant scientific discovery, and the narrative landmarks here are easily identifiable: the sense of vocation, a secularisation of religious calling; the early, unrecognised period; the rebellious act in the face of superstition or conservatism; the breakthrough; the recognition. Other careers such as nursing have also been chronicled, tending to idealise the nurse's professionalism, and even to understand it as a displaced, angelic maternalism.

In the genres of comedy and horror the discourse is oppositional. Film comedy works to unearth substrata by alerting the viewer to the possibility of alternative perspectives or by presenting established views, only to deconstruct them via comedic situations or events. The perspectives of comedy are those connected with incongruity or challenges to superiority and the resultant response, which will most often be laughter, not only encourages the viewer to engage at a highly-charged physical level with film, but also to consider their perspective in relation to the perspectives of those around them. The comic film doctor is not simply working against our general ideas about what it is to practice medicine but often declaring themselves, through character traits or actual practice itself, to be 'outside the system' of medicine, to be individuals with well-founded, personalised, senses of medical science.

Horror too, as a film genre, gives room to highly-charged physical responses. It is a genre whose sense of engagement with an audience is linked to the disrupting of world views, to challenging personal safety and unearthing psychologies of voyeurism, to the paradoxes of relations between pleasure and pain, and to revealing occasionally crude purposes in established social interaction. No surprise, therefore, that horror has seen its fair share of medically enlivened films. The social and cultural role of doctors offers substantial opportunities for horror film makers to question centralised social management or, by focusing on medical institutions, to examine the motives of policy makers or, by highlighting the role of 'mavericks', to unearth the philosophies guiding the mainstream practice of medicine.

But fictional film genres are never hermetically sealed and we can see in the slippage between melodrama and biopic, comedy and horror that the themes filmmakers have explored in the realm of medical science have often encompassed both negative and positive representations of medicine, and frequently in the same storyline. The genre of science fiction, for example, located as it often is in notions of human progress, has revealed the inherent human quality of seeing medicine as one way of initiating 'improvement' in humankind, human lifestyles and human expectations, while simultaneously showing medicine as a potential battleground for issues of integrity, self-determination, creativity and, more broadly, human rights.

If some of these issues fail to find their way, overtly, into the genres of the medical documentary or the medical training film, it would be a naïve commentator who did not notice them lurking, however covertly, beneath the surface of many of these non-fiction films as well. And a naïve one indeed who did not note that the issues raised here can often be shown to spread out from the genres of film to that of television, as well as to media representations way beyond this still. Specific genre analysis yields specific, but often closely linked, results and our concentration on cinema in no way suggests what is said here has only cinematic relevance.

Signs of life: our coverage

Readers will find what follows covers a wide range of films and topics in the filmic representation of medicine and the discourses of medical science. We would baulk at any suggestion that this coverage is all-encompassing. However, we have aimed to make it broad-ranging and speculative, adding to our own analyses the expertise of a strong contingent of specialists in both medical history and in film analysis. Each writer has approached the subject in a way they have seen best, and we would alert readers to the multiple analytical perspectives at work here, and to the resultant opportunities for the reader to find comparisons and contrasts.

Here Brian Glasser considers filmic narratives of sickness. Lucy Fischer looks at the film *Rosemary's Baby* (1968) and birth traumas and Kenneth MacKinnon charts the public awareness of AIDS and filmic representations of the disease. Timothy Boon focuses on health education films in Britain in the period 1919–39.

Contrasting *Sick: The Life and Death of Bob Flanagan Supermasochist* (1997) with *Crash* (1996) Tom Shakespeare interrogates issues of disability, sex and death while Andrew Moor considers British films coloured by the institutional ideology of the new National Health Service (and more widely, of the Welfare State).

In Roy Jobson and Donna Knapp-van Bogaert's chapter ideas around medical ethics and cinematic representation are broadly explored. Graeme Harper examines 'medical film comedy' in 1930s Hollywood, looking at the activity of comedic discourse on the social foundations of medical science. Julia Hallam considers the representation of nurses and nursing in cinema, and Bruce Babington compares and contrasts the medical biopic over a 25-year period. Andy Morgan, equally closely, moves through a film history in relation to the understanding of combat fatigue. Finally, Jackie Stacey examines the treatment of genetics in the film *Gattaca* (1997).

In each of these chapters the authors seek out key pointers about the ways in which film has dealt with medicine, but also in relation to how medicine itself has used film for its promotion, its preservation and its presentation of what it sees as medical 'issues'. There is no doubt that the story to be told here is an amalgam of ideas and perspectives. Equally, that medicine and cinema have already shared a considerable history, and are likely to have a further association, regardless of the impact of a range of new media technologies. The focus in this book, of course, is largely on 'Western' representations and we are aware that a similar book might well have been written in relation to the cinemas and medical practices of 'non-Western' regions. That aside, we trust *Signs of Life: Cinema and Medicine* will fill the current gap for concerted, multi-faceted work on the topic of medical science and film, and will greatly value any debate that arises from this study of what we feel is a significantly under-examined area of cinema.

References

Foucault, M. (1973) *The Birth of the Clinic: An Archaeology of Medical Perception*. New York: Vintage.
Samson, C. (1999) 'Biomedicine and the body', in C. Samson (ed.) *Health Studies: A Critical and Cross-Cultural Reader*. Oxford: Blackwell, 3–21.

01

Brian Glasser

Magic bullets, dark victories and cold comforts: some preliminary observations about stories of sickness in the cinema

Broadly speaking, sickness has three possible outcomes: you get better; you get worse and die; or you stay the same and live with the condition for the rest of your life. Adopting these real-life endpoints as markers, this chapter will look at cinematic narratives relating to sickness, and some of the uses to which their ingredients are put.[1]

Magic bullets: the sick recover

Patients rarely get well spontaneously in films – they regain their health thanks to the intervention of someone else, usually a doctor. (This is no doubt in part because minor sickness is not the stuff of screenplays.) In consequence, films in which sick people get better are commonly as preoccupied with the health practitioner and his – for they are rarely women – travails as the patient: early models are the Hollywood medical films of the 1930s and 1940s, where country or hospital doctors (as featured respectively in *Meet Dr Christian* (Bernard Vorhaus, 1939) and *Young Dr Kildare* (Harold S. Bucquet, 1938)) effect heroic cures and are portrayed as kindly saviours (Dans 2000). Sickness is the enemy to be overcome by these men just as crocodiles might be for Tarzan.

The Golden Age of Hollywood corresponded with the Golden Age of (the public perception of) Medicine, but as the *zeitgeist* evolved in the second half of the twentieth century, doctors were no longer always seen through rose-coloured lenses and doctor/patient concordance diminished. We could chart this course approximately by skipping from *Magnificent Obsession* (John M. Stahl, 1935) and *Not as a Stranger* (Stanley Kramer, 1955) through *The Young Doctors* (Phil Karlson, 1963), *The Hospital* (Arthur Hiller,

1971) and *Coma* (Michael Crichton, 1976) to *Critical Care* (Sidney Lumet, 1997). This changing backdrop has not precluded the happy ending: the sick can still recover. *The Doctor* (Randa Haines, 1991) combines elements from both the modern and early eras in its story of eponymous surgeon Jack McKee.

Case study 1: *The Doctor* (Touchstone Pictures, 1991)

The opening (and title) sequence of *The Doctor* is set in an operating theatre, where a young man's life is saved against the odds through the expert efforts of McKee (William Hurt) and his team. The scene is a tour-de-force of full-framing, tight camera angles, sharp dialogue and rapid, rhythmic editing. It is assembled to convey viscerally the notion of 'patient as passive object/doctor as master-technician' and the thrill of the life-saving operation, while at the same time signalling most of the issues that the movie will deal with in the next two hours – for the film proves to be a sustained and substantial critique of the medical model of health care and its practitioners.

The sickness narrative of the patient, though barely explored – he is not seen post-operatively, for instance – is nonetheless pertinent: he is in theatre after attempted suicide, and is consequently patronised while unconscious by McKee, an avowed anti-sentimentalist whose concern for his patients extends no further than his mantra: 'Get in – fix it – get out'. This patient's story, then, appears to be the epitome of the sickness narrative that is little more than raw material for the health practitioner's own story. Yet it is this passivity – an authentic component of sickness, it should be noted – that is the baton which is passed on into the second, central sickness narrative – that of the surgeon-superstar, who discovers he has throat cancer and so is forced to become a patient himself.

In a new role in his own hospital, he experiences the frustrations of being on the receiving end – the passive position – of health service bureaucracy and professional detachment; particularly, the inadequacy of a technically competent but emotionally barren consultation style for someone who is finding out they have cancer. He also strikes up a platonic but intimate friendship with a fellow cancer patient which throws into relief the deficiencies of his marriage and his relations with women. There are no metaphysical connotations to his ill-health, but the doctor's private and professional personae are profoundly affected as he is confronted by the limitations of his *Weltanschaaung* in the face of (potentially terminal) sickness.

The originality of this gamekeeper-turned-poacher story does not twist the conventional narrative tramlines where equilibrium is disrupted and then regained, and heterosexual happy-ever-after is assured: the doctor gets better physically (thanks to another, more humane surgeon's skilled intervention) and mentally (in his new enlightened state, he is reconciled with his wife); and his patients get even better than they used to, as he embraces their need to be treated as people rather than fodder for surgery. The sacrificial lamb is his soulmate-in-sickness, the female patient, who dies approximately two-thirds of the way into the movie – effectively a near-death experience for the surgeon that propels him further down the road to wisdom. *The Doctor* not only shares elements with 'recovery' films but also with our next sub-section of sickness movies, as we shall see.

Dark victories: the sick die

Films that contain the death of their main protagonist are a relative rarity in popular cinema – especially death through sickness, the ultimate objective correlative of a feel-bad factor. The paying public may like closure, but not usually in the form of a coffin lid over the head of the hero or heroine who has passed away because of sickness – an element absent from most weepies (for example, *Anna Karenina* (Clarence Brown, 1935)) or death-knell melodramas (for example, *The Killers* (Robert Siodmak, 1946)), in which the central character dies.

Nonetheless, high-profile exceptions to the rule exist from the silent era onwards – *Camille* (Ray C. Smallwood, 1921), *Love Story* (Arthur Hiller, 1970) and *Terms of Endearment* (James L. Brooks, 1983) being cases in point. However, the 'fatal illness' film took a stigma-breaking step forward with *Dark Victory* (Edmund Goulding, 1939) – the first to use a malignancy as the cause of death. 'You've got to remember that this is the mid-1930s and cancer was a dirty word', the film's screenwriter Casey Robinson has recalled (Robinson 1986: 301). Hithertofore, death had been brought about by the more romantic (at least as fictionally presented!) heart disease or consumption.

Case study 2: *Dark Victory* (Warner Bros., 1939)

Judith Traherne (Bette Davis) is a wealthy young socialite – spirited, wilful and intent on nothing except enjoying a responsibility-free life to the full. One morning when she is riding out on one of the horses from her racing stable a sudden attack of double-vision causes her to fall at a jump. Although she dismisses the problem as trivial and transient, recurrent headaches and dizziness eventually result in her seeking medical advice. A disaffected surgeon, who is about to give up his practice to take up an unglamorous research post, diagnoses a brain tumour. He operates, but finds that extirpation is impossible. The condition is unusual in that Traherne will be able to live a healthy, normal life for several months – in fact until a short time before her death, which will be heralded by a total loss of vision. Traherne and the doctor have meanwhile fallen in love. After a bout of self-destructive high living, occasioned by the misapprehension that her personal secretary has been in cahoots with the doctor, Traherne throws over her former lifestyle in order to support him in his research activities. Their life proceeds idyllically, in a country cottage far from the madding crowd, until the day when Traherne does indeed lose her vision. She conceals this from the doctor, who departs for an important academic conference, and dies alone in her bed having planted flowers with her secretary which she knows the latter, as the doctor's next partner, will watch grow.

Great care was taken to fashion *Dark Victory* around Bette Davis, a star whose screen persona was less straightforward than many of her contemporaries (Dick 1981). She had a dramatic CV that had never settled in one place (sometimes tough, sometimes acquiescent, sometimes passionate, sometimes demure, and so on), and the complex inconsistency of this was the springboard for her role in this film. The sickness narrative acts as a basis for all other developments in *Dark Victory*: Traherne is shown exploring her own sexual behaviour, her assumptions about social values and selfhood, her response to adverse events, all in the light of her imminent demise. This journey to self-awareness – feminist readings of the film notwithstanding – culminates in a paradoxical triumph over death (the 'dark victory' of the title) in the final deathbed scene. The discretion of the direction and screenplay allows the film to wear its authenticity lightly – for instance, there is a close fit with narrative issues identified in recent research with cancer patients (Hunt 2000), and Bernard F. Dick has pointed to the film's organic incorporation of what Elizabeth Kübler-Ross (1970) would later label the five-stage response to dying. One could in fact argue that (like the other films discussed in this section) the movie is a death narrative rather than a sickness one, since for the majority of the film Traherne is known to be going to die but shows few signs of sickness.

The utilisation of the basic story elements found in *Dark Victory* is not confined to mainstream cinema. In a film with art-house credentials, Akira Kurosawa's *Ikiru* (1952), the onset of terminal illness – the film's opening shot is of a chest x-ray showing cancer of the main character's lung – injects dynamism into stasis: a life of little social worth and personal fulfilment is transformed by death foretold, two wrongs (sickness and a wasted life) making a right. In this case, it is a low-ranking civil servant who breaks out of his set ways to bring about significant personal and social change: for example, he develops new kinds of relationships (with his colleagues and others); and he engineers the construction of a park on a site where stagnant water was affecting families' health. Although the sequelae of his actions are a little less tidy than in *Dark Victory*, the central device is identical, namely that 'Nothing in his life so became him as the leaving of it'. In both films, redemption is found not so much in death itself as in the moment that mortality is accepted.

Sickness that ends in death is portrayed in these films as transformative in a positive way, and the logical (and entirely credible) possibility exists of someone who, on being diagnosed with a terminal illness, becomes unsympathetic. Yet such characters are hard to find in non-comedic films, their near-invisibility suggesting that there is a cinematic taboo about this storyline – as if the possibility of a deviant occupation of the sick role needs to be denied and that the perceived negativity of death must always be mitigated.[2] This is supported by the similarly infrequent unsympathetic portrayal of people who are sick but not terminally so. The inference is that the uncongenial sick, like the undeserving poor, would evoke contradictory responses in audiences – do we feel sorry for them or dislike them? – with sickness being too culturally protected a topic to use to elicit ambivalence.

Another common model for death-from-sickness is the death of a prominent supporting character – someone who is less weighty than a co-star but more substantial than a secondary personage. An example has already been mentioned, *The Doctor* – and that character falls at the more lightly-sketched end of the range. Fuller versions exist in a wide range of films – examples include *Shadowlands* (Richard Attenborough, 1993), *Cries and Whispers* (Ingmar Bergman, 1972) and *One True Thing* (Carl Franklin, 1998). In these films, terminal sickness is still used as the springboard to new levels of awareness for the central characters, but it is the terminal sickness of significant others: in *One True Thing*, all is revealed to an (adult) daughter about her parents, as individuals and as a couple, when her mother contracts and (near the end of the film) dies from cancer. Just as in earlier eras, it can be hard to distinguish story arcs between mainstream and art movies: *One True Thing* stars Meryl Streep, William Hurt and Renée Zellweger; *Cries and Whispers* stars many of Bergman's usual repertory company (such as Liv Ullman and Ingrid Thulin). Yet the latter also uses the dying of a family member from cancer as the fulcrum of a story about the legacy of difficult family history, in this case the focus being on the victim's siblings. The approaching death of one sister prompts a family reunion of sorts, during which a variety of long-suppressed feelings are aired. As with *Dark Victory* and *Ikiru*, the (narrative) differences between Hollywood and art-house films are to be found in the flesh on the bones of the storyline – the backstory, the characterisation and so on. In *Cries and Whispers*, acrimony is the key note, even at the end of the film: only the dying woman's maid, an important but secondary character, ends the film with her stock in the ascendant; while the sisters (and others) fail to capitalise on the cathartic situation, and hence remain locked in their psychological prisons. In *One True Thing*, by contrast (and as we might expect), both Hurt's and Zellweger's characters have progressed at the end of the film, having broken the mould of certain important behaviours.

Despite the fact that it is 'based on a true story' – Anthony Hopkins and Debra Winger act as C. S. Lewis and Joy Davidson respectively – *Shadowlands* follows the same rubric as our previous examples, wherein the death of one (fictional) character is balanced by the life-affirming gains made by those most closely associated with them: the pending death from cancer of Davidson (with whom he is having a semi-detached relationship) brings Lewis considerable enlightenment and self-liberation – for instance, he adopts the role of full-blooded lover to her while she is alive, and of parent to her young son when she is dead. Whatever happened 'in real life' to these people, their story has been fitted into a cinematic template. In all these films, terminal sickness acts as a can opener – with the contents turning out to be worms or caviar.

Cold comforts: the sick live on, sickly

'Dès qu'il y a mort, il y a la morale ... Laisser les gens là, ce qui est beaucoup plus dur à la fin' ('As soon as there's death, there's a moral ... Leaving people there, that's actually a much harder thing to do') (Blier 1986: 10). Bertrand Blier's words were not spoken in relation to sickness narratives, but might as well have been, given their resonance with the points being made in this chapter.

If death inevitably attracts moralising on the part of the filmmaker – presumably in the service of the audience – ongoing sickness is a more intractable commodity. Absence of simple closure is a defining feature of chronic sickness, which makes it difficult to represent within the realist tradition (there is an intrinsic mismatch between a film that ends and a sickness that does not). The common solution to this is to engineer peripheral closures to offset central open-endedness. In *The Snake Pit* (Anatole Litvak, 1948), the female lead suffers from nervous breakdowns, out of the shadow of which she emerges only tentatively at the end of the film. However, she has managed to come to terms with certain of her demons with the help of a psychoanalyst, and it is this breakthrough in therapy – a success for the analyst in an institution which is sceptical of his approach, as well as for the patient – and the patient's consequent discharge from the mental hospital, that provides enough closure to enable the film to end. In *Bill of Divorcement* (George Cukor, 1932), the dénouement comprises a daughter relinquishing the opportunity of love and marriage in order to look after her mentally sick father, whose condition she fears may be hereditary. Quasi-closure here comes from her decision to renounce the possibility of personal happiness; and from her mother's second marriage and departure from the family home – both topics which have been the subject of much agonising throughout the film. More recently, *Awakenings* (Penny Marshall, 1990) features a prominent secondary character whose remission from, and subsequent relapse into, chronic sickness serves as a stimulus for changes in his doctor's (that is, the main character's) life: at the end of the film, the doctor is able to take his first tentative step towards a relationship with a woman; and his status and self-belief with regard to his profession are less precarious than at the outset.

These examples highlight the fact that where chronic sickness *is* featured in movies, it tends to be of the mental type – chronic physical sickness is yet another instance of a category that should logically exist but that comes up blank in practice.[3] There are few if any examples of films in which the main or even a secondary character is chronically, physically sick. A film which offers something at least close is *Marvin's Room* (Jerry Zaks,

1996). The title itself suggests that chronic sickness may be the centre of the film – the opening shots are of multitudinous medications for Marvin, who it soon transpires is an elderly man whose sickness confines him to his room. However, Marvin is in fact so sick – his physical ailments render him practically incommunicado – that his role is emblematic, the real drama being played out by surrounding family members. In a story twist not dissimilar to that in *The Doctor*, one of his daughters discovers that she has cancer (which she will die from, although the film ends before that event). It is her sickness, rather than Marvin's, which provides the film's main narrative drive. Hence, although Marvin's condition is a core plot element, and there are several scenes which show his daughter caring for him, it would be stretching a point to claim that the film explores the experience of chronic sickness.

These sundry examples notwithstanding, chronic sickness films constitute a considerably smaller sub-genre than 'death from sickness' films. Why should this be? Why might not a chronic condition allow a main or secondary protagonist to reinvent him- or herself just as the imminence of death does? Might we not propose a story in which the very absence of closure, or more accurately the withholding of the threat of death in the presence of sickness, is the subject under investigation – a purgatory of a Sisyphean nature? In fact these story elements *can* be found – but we have to turn to films about disability for them (such as the post-war tales *The Best Years of Our Lives* (William Wyler, 1946) and *Coming Home* (Hal Ashby, 1978) to do so). Again, one can hypothesise that the uncertainty of chronic sickness – is the person well or sick, for there is no simple binary opposition? – makes it a blunt tool for cracking open a character's morality or other 'human interest' treasure chests. So, in these chronic sickness films the central characters do not experience the epiphany-like process that we noted in our 'death' or 'recovery' films.

Alternative take: *mise-en-scène*

While we have identified storyline similarities in sickness movies with our three-fold typology, it would be misleading to ignore the differences amongst the films. These differences are to be found in formal elements of cinematic expression, such as *mise-en-scène*, although of course it is impossible to separate these from narrative in terms of the impact on the audience.

Case study 3: *Blue* (Channel Four Films, 1993)
Blue (Derek Jarman) is, perhaps, the most striking of examples relating to *mise-en-scène*. Famously, this 'movie' was produced without a camera, being made by painting entire reels of unexposed 35mm film 'Yves Klein' blue. The screened image, then, is a virtually unchanging backdrop – there are random variations due to scratches near reel changes, for example – against which the story of sickness is narrated for the more-or-less standard 80 minutes film-time by director Jarman and a handful of actors. The subject of the film is Jarman's experience of living with – or 'dying from', as he preferred it – AIDS (the film was completed before his death), with particular emphasis given to the blindness which accompanies the sickness as it progresses. The voice-over soundtrack ranges widely in subject matter and tone, the script striking out on almost arbitrary flights of emotional and intellectual fancy. The effect is to make the film one of the most imposing (the viewer, under the reduced visual circumstances, is forcibly bound to the power of the word) and the least reductive of all treatments of terminal illness – an irony given its literally monotonous

screen content. (There is a coincidental parallel with *Dark Victory* – the blindness caused by Judith Traherne's cancer mirrors the blindness caused by AIDS in *Blue*. While this might primarily be a plot device in *Dark Victory*, it is central to *Blue*: Jarman originally studied as a painter, and his films had been extensions of this base – in that context, his sight was arguably his most crucial sense, and his banishment of the camera makes the audience share something of his loss. The loss of screen image is also used as a symbol of death in the final shot of *Dark Victory*, in which Traherne's dying moment is signalled by her image slipping out of focus until it is an unrecognisable blur.)

Blue has its basis in the real sickness narrative of a real person. We saw earlier that there are fictional films whose principle character dies, and fictional films in which the sickness/death role is assigned to a significant secondary character. So it is with films in which there are relatively unmediated, non-fictional sickness narratives – films which deal with the actual death of real people other than the auteur, such as *Lightning Over Water* (Wim Wenders/Nicholas Ray, 1980). These might be termed cinematic pathographies as opposed to an autopathography such as *Blue*. Although the directorial credit for *Lightning Over Water* is shared between Wenders and Ray, there are strong arguments (characteristic filming and editing styles, use of then-modern video technology, and so on) for ascribing it to the German's oeuvre rather than to the American's. At any rate, it is a film which charts the last weeks in the life of Ray, who is dying from cancer; and it shares many characteristics of a documentary – for instance, everyone in the film plays themselves (the film's cast consisting mostly of its crew) and it is shot with little cinematic artifice. As such, *Lightning Over Water* is something of a departure from our 'death' template, with its absence of 'revelation when *in extremis*'. Wenders is a participant-observer in the decline and death of Ray: the German director (and by extension the audience) are far from unaffected by Ray's demise, but the documentary-like presentation steers the movie firmly away from the 'four-handkerchief film' zone into the more cerebral territory we encountered in *Blue*.

Two more alternative takes: *caveat* filmgoer, and the march of time

All art may be autobiography – perhaps 'auteur's documentary', in filmic terms – but degrees of mediation vary, and not always along the lines one would predict. Just as we can split off the 'death of a real person' movies such as *Blue*, *Lightning Over Water* and *Shadowlands* and note the *mise-en-scène* differences that ensue when the story passes through the hands of intermediaries (as noted, *Shadowlands* is made with actors and a director who have no direct relation to the subject matter), so we can compare *My Life* (Bruce Joel Rubin, 1993) and an episode from the triptych that makes up *Dear Diary* (Nanni Moretti, 1996).

Case study 4: *My Life* versus *Dear Diary*

These two films are dissimilar in many important ways – the former is made by a Hollywood *metteur-en-scène*, the latter by an Italian auteur – but nonetheless they have an uncanny degree of overlap: in both, the central character contracts cancer (one cancer is fatal, the other is curable); both use the patient's video diary as a central narrative device; both inveigh against the deficiencies of Western medicine (one on the basis of its lack of spirituality, the other on pragmatic 'they don't know what they're doing' grounds); and both stories are based on real-life experiences (one grew out of a dream of the director, the other out of a real medical condition experienced by the director). We could add that one is a semi-comic tragedy, which does not flinch from showing the actual moment of death as experienced by the dying person; while the other is a comic semi-tragedy, with Kafkaesque tendencies. On the basis of this head-to-head description, who would feel confident about assigning one film to America and the other to Europe?[4]

Earlier we noted that the differences between mainstream and art-house movies commonly lie in *mise-en-scène* practice. But these two films, made within three years of each other, jointly act as a further cautionary tale about over-generalising (at least when it comes to sickness narratives). At the same time, they provide rich material for an exploration of cultural similarities and differences: for example, systems of conventional and complementary health care provision, use of consultation styles, and so on, in the USA and Italy.

Although *My Life* is an exception, cinematic sickness is generally presented chronologically. Of the physical sickness films we have considered, only two include flashbacks (*Cries and Whispers* and *My Life*),[5] and any ellipses tend to be uncomplicated and naturalistic. This might be considered surprising, given the tendency of the (cinematic) sickness experience to prompt soul-searching on the part of the sufferer – for instance, the remembrances in *My Life* (couched as dream sequences) usually concern the cancer victim's childhood relationship with his father and brother.

One can surmise that the progress of sickness supplies a natural crescendo, resulting in the film's climax of death or recovery, which is irresistible and (judged to be) immutable. The effect of accepting this imperative is to reinforce the concept of stable entities of disease, and by extension the medical model of sickness. The narrative disruption plunges the films' protagonist into a new state (sickness), but not into something which is in itself unknowable to the audience. This relatively fixed, new reference point then serves as a basis for the metaphorical journeys the character takes. Were the reference point to be a sickness which had no label, and which was fluid and ill-defined, audience and filmmaker would have to expend continual energy attending to it in various ways; and would then be distracted from the task-in-hand of the main storyline. Or so the argument might go… *Mise-en-scène* strategies can go some way to offsetting this predictability (as in *Blue*); but they tend not to obliterate it altogether.

Celluloid sicknesses

Cinematic epidemiology is an underdeveloped field, but even within the potentially unrepresentative limits of this chapter, patterns start to emerge. *Dark Victory* was credited as the first high-profile movie to feature cancer, but nowadays it seems to be the cinematic sickness of choice, as the films discussed thus far attest. This trend echoes the progression described in Susan Sontag's *Illness as Metaphor* (1978), which demonstrates how cancer displaced tuberculosis as the dread disease of literature. And just as Sontag updated and reworked her treatise to include AIDS, so should we: for since its advent as global health issue in the 1980s, AIDS has come to occupy a comparable cultural space to cancer (see Sontag 1988), and both mainstream and independent films have reflected this (for example, *Longtime Companion* (Norman René, 1990), *Philadelphia* (Jonathan Demme, 1993) and *Drôle de Félix* (Olivier Ducastel/Jacques Martineau, 2000). The pre-eminence of these diseases is only partially representative of modern-day league tables of causes of death in the Western world, AIDS getting a higher profile in films than it deserves and heart disease a lower one. The global resurgence of tuberculosis may yet revive its movie career!

Epidemics and plagues have also featured in films (for example, *Panic in the Streets* (Elia Kazan, 1950); *Outbreak* (Wolfgang Petersen, 1995); *The Horseman on the Roof* (Jean-Paul Rappeneau, 1999)). However, these movies are better classified as 'disease narratives', since almost no attention is given to the subjective experience of sickness. Despite the small but significant number of films that deal with mental sickness, no particular condition features recurrently – and indeed the somewhat undifferentiated diagnoses in the majority of these films perhaps reflect the general ignorance of filmmakers and public alike with regard to mental health.

Reflections

'Who wants to see a movie about a girl that dies?' said studio head Jack Warner, on hearing the pitch for *Dark Victory* – but box-office success and three Academy Award nominations suggest that the rhetorical question had an answer, which was: 'Lots of people, if the material is handled in a certain way.' (Certainly the concept of a 'good death', however defined (Walter 2003), appears to be a *sine qua non*, especially in Hollywood movies. In the films we have considered, only the death in *Cries and Whispers* is shown as unhappy.)

Sickness narratives are perennial subject matter in both the mainstream and art-house sectors. It is easy to see why – they provide many of the staple ingredients of popular narrative: they are of timeless and universal interest (we all get sick, and we all die eventually); they have considerable built-in emotional potential (sickness – either in ourselves or in people we know – can be a major life event in itself, as well as a *memento mori*); and they can include non-violent life-or-death situations that are credible, and so offer ready-made closure. (Of course, the scope of this chapter's informal survey has been restricted to films that have been on relatively general release in the first world, a selection criterion which is fraught with cultural connotations. Further work could usefully be done investigating, for instance, sickness movies made for Chinese or Indian audiences.) Sickness narratives have at least one turning point, the onset of illness that sits easily in the realistic tradition, as does the biographical disruption, so beloved by narratologists of all disciplines, that stems from it.

With these monumental building blocks in place, most sickness films content themselves with fiddling around at the edges of the story, investing the particulars with novelty rather than the superstructure. This is in contrast to literature: Howard Brody (1987) suggests that there are at least seven possible literary stories of sickness – and only three or four of them occur in films. For example, there seem to be no films in which sickness is adopted as a career, the victim abandoning their original life-plan entirely. A film like *Drunken Angel* (Akira Kurosawa, 1948), in which a doctor and his patient are both sick, and bound together in a complex relationship around their sicknesses, is rare in its originality (of premise and outcome). Cinematic sickness is not often allegorical, or imbued with cultural significance (except perhaps for the 'disease narratives' mentioned earlier, the most obvious example being films about AIDS, which usually have a strong sexual-political agenda) – an orientation perhaps traceable back, in the mainstream at least, to cinema's predilection for character-driven narratives.

We have seen that the cinematic portrayal of sickness is very often paradoxical: in physical terms, it is shown to be less desirable than good health (in that it causes pain and discomfort); and yet existentially, diverse benefits can flow from it (to either the sick person or a significant other or both, depending on who needs them). The epiphanies engendered by a sickness are in proportion to its severity, pending death being a particularly 'privileged point of destabilisation' (Russell 1995: 4). Indeed, in a contemporary, secular world under-written by Thanatos and Eros, it has been suggested that sickness and death are the vehicles that enable people to re-enact the repentance of sinners (Hydén 1997: 60). Perhaps size matters: because the cinema screen (as opposed to television) shows images that are bigger than life, the sickness subject matter needs to be drawn from the tip of the clinical iceberg: one or two of the Big Diseases are featured at the expense of the far greater amount of minor morbidity people suffer – although in real life, intimations of mortality can result from almost any diagnosis, no matter how apparently trivial. Television is not only con-structed on a different scale – it fits into a living room – it can also act cumulatively: the consideration of chronic sickness is much more viable in a TV series than a one-off film. This bias also has the effect of emphasising a medical model of sickness in the cinema: sicknesses always stick to the recipe in the International Classification of Diseases, and the 'Why me? Why now?' questions that many real-life patients ask themselves are rarely posed on screen. Non-compliance, iatrogenesis, dissimulating disorders – the sorts of things that medicine finds hard to contend with – slip almost entirely through the cinematic net.

Nor are the proposed healing properties of sickness stories for the teller in real life (Riessman 2002) commonly an element in movie sickness, *My Life* being an exception. This may be because films are not unproblematically 'told' by one person (Bordwell 1986: 12). Nonetheless, the audience may gain the healing benefit, if we allow that films enable us to experience life events vicariously and in do-able doses. In this light, watching sick-ness movies is like going for an inoculation; and part of what Clive Seale has called the 'resurrective practice' by which we bolster our sense of security in the face of the perpetual possibility of death (Seale 2000: 36).

The duality associated with cinematic sickness parallels Talcott Parsons' (1951) classic elaboration of the sick role, and its rights and obligations. His framework established the principle that sickness is a privileged state, and consequently that a return to health might be unwelcome. It has recently been suggested that people may seek a safe haven from life's difficulties by retreating into the sick role (Malleson 2002). However, in the cinema there are few examples where physical sickness is seen as being worth prolonging, despite the benefits it has brought in its wake; whereas mental ill-health is often depicted as being in many ways a superior state to normality (for example, *One Flew Over the Cuckoo's Nest* (Milos Forman, 1975) and *Morgan: A Suitable Case For Treatment* (Karel Reisz, 1965), with Nicholas Ray's *Bigger Than Life* (1956) straddling the fence), in an artistic tradition that can be traced back through the idiot savant to the Shakespearean fool, if not further.

This chapter has taken a broad-brush approach to sickness narratives in cinema – exceptions to the various 'rules' abound, and detail has inevitably been sacrificed on the altar of forward momentum. I hope nonetheless to have created a basis for further discus-sion. We have seen the collapse of one possible distinction – that art films are of an entirely different timbre to mainstream ones – at least when it comes to sickness narratives; we have seen that the sickness narratives that most properly constitute a genre in their own right are actually death narratives; and we have also seen that, however we may experience it in real life, sickness in the cinema is, above all, paradoxical.

Notes

1   A word about terminology: in this chapter, I shall observe the widely-used subjective/objective distinction between illness and disease – the former being something a person

has on the way to the doctor's surgery, the latter being what he has on the way home. In this context, sickness is a conveniently neutral term to describe the phenomenon of being unhealthy, however that may be culturally defined.

2   Consider as an example, in contrast, the sick and tyrannical mother in *Throw Momma From the Train* (Danny De Vito, 1987) who is placed safely in a humorous context and not killed by sickness.

3   As before, one has to have recourse to comedy to find an example – perhaps *The Odd Couple* (Gene Saks, 1968)?

4   If you have not seen the films, the first clause in all the above comparisons relates to *My Life*.

5   As usual, films dealing with mental illness have conventions that include reference to Freud and so frequently employ flashbacks (for example, *Spellbound* (Alfred Hitchcock, 1945)).

References

Blier, B. (1986) 'Les mots et les choses: entretien avec Bertrand Blier' (interview by Pascal Bonitzer and Serge Toubiana), *Cahiers du Cinéma*, 382.

Bordwell, D. (1986) *Narration in the Fiction Film*. London: Routledge.

Brody, H. (1987) *Stories of Sickness*. Yale University Press: London.

Bury, M. (1982) 'Chronic illness as biographical disruption', *Sociology of Health & Illness*, 5, 2, 168–95.

Dans, P. E. (2000) *Doctors in the Movies: Boil the Water and Just Say Aah*. Bloomington: Medi-Ed Press.

Dick, B. F. (ed.) (1981) *Dark Victory*. Wisconsin: University of Wisconsin Press.

Greenhalgh, T. and B. Hurwitz (eds) (1998) *Narrative Based Medicine*. London: B. M. J. Books.

Hunt, L. M. (2000) 'Strategic suffering: illness narratives as social empowerment among Mexican cancer patients', in C. Mattingly and L. G. Garro (eds) *Narrative and the Cultural Construction of Illness and Healing*. London: University of California Press, 90.

Hydén, L.-C. (1997) 'Illness and narrative', *Sociology of Health and Illness*, 19, 1, 48–69.

Kübler-Ross, E. (1970) *On Death and Dying*. London: Tavistock Publications.

Lothe, J. (2000) *Narrative in Fiction and Film*. Oxford: Oxford University Press.

Malleson, A. (2002) *Whiplash and Other Useful Injuries*. Montreal and Kingston: McGill-Queen's University Press.

Murray, S. A., K. Boyd, M. Kendall, A. Worth, T. F. Benton, H. Clausen (2002) 'Dying of lung cancer or cardiac failure: prospective qualitative interview study of patients and their carers in the community', *British Medical Journal*, 325, 929–32.

Parsons, T. (1951) *The Social System*. Glencoe, IL: Free Press.

Riessman, C. K. (2002) 'Illness narrative and performance', unpublished presentation given at 'Narrative and Health Workshop', 14 November 2002, King's College, Cambridge.

Robinson, C. (1986) 'Casey Robinson: master adaptor' (interview with Joel Greenberg), in P. McGilligan (ed.) *Backstory: Interviews with Screenwriters of Hollywood's Golden Age*. Berkeley: University of California Press, 301.

Russell, C. (1995) *Narrative Mortality: Death, Closure and New Wave Cinemas*. London: University of Minnesota Press.

Seale, C. (2000) 'Resurrective practice and narrative', in M. Andrews, S. D. Sclater,

C. Squire and A. Treacher (eds) *Lines of Narrative: Psychosocial Perspectives*. London: Routledge, 36.

Sontag, S. (1978) *Illness as Metaphor*. New York: Farrar, Straus and Giroux.

_____ (1988) *AIDS and its Metaphors*. New York: Farrar, Straus and Giroux.

Walter, T. (2003) 'Historic and cultural variants on the good death', *British Medical Journal*, 327, 218–20.

18

02

Birth traumas: medicine, parturition and horror in *Rosemary's Baby*[1]

Prologue: Multiple births

> Any effort at redefining motherhood must include some consideration of child-birth's meaning. (Daly & Reddy 1991: 4)

Though a natural bodily process (and not an illness), pregnancy and childbirth often require medical intervention. As we know, developed countries have far lower infant and maternal mortality rates than do non-industrialised nations, largely because of the availability of pre-natal care – most often administered by nurses, doctors and other health professionals. Furthermore, most deliveries in the First World take place within a hospital setting. There, routine vaginal births are often assisted by various medical devices (such as foetal heart monitors), as well as by the administration of drugs and anaesthesia (for example, Pitocin or epidural analgesia). More complex births often require an operation – a Caesarean section – a procedure which has become common in the post-Second World War era. Now, harried expectant mothers who have no biological 'need' for such a measure schedule it, nonetheless, simply for their own convenience: a fixed delivery date (consonant with business commitments) and a predictable visiting plan for out-of-town relatives. Furthermore, the issue of pregnancy and childbirth has recently entered the realm of high-tech science. We now speak of 'reproductive technologies' by which we mean a series of synthetic techniques through which individuals who cannot conceive or carry babies can be helped to do so. Thus we talk of *in vitro* fertilisation, donor eggs, surrogate mothers, sex selection, sperm banks and the post-mortem germ cell 'harvesting'. One day the newspaper

birth traumas: medicine, parturition and horror

reports that a European woman in her sixties has given birth to a baby; the next, it asserts that a French laboratory has proclaimed the birth of a human clone.

For all these reasons, the site of pregnancy and childbirth has become highly charged. On the one hand, traditional and sentimental images remain. In the supermarket, the slick cover of *Working Mother* presents a radiant television personality who is 'Pretty and Pregnant'. *Newsweek* flaunts a responsible expectant couple purchasing Mass Mutual Insurance. *Parent* pictures a postpartum madonna gazing wondrously at her infant – nursing now, but planning to use Gerber Baby Formula.[2] In the local video store, the self-help aisle is stocked with reassuring instructional tapes: *Your First Baby* and *Childbirth Preparation*. The neighbourhood book shop features *Pregnant and Lovin' It*, a guide to 'one of the greatest, most pleasurable events of life' (Curtis & Caroles 1985: 4).

On the other hand, contemporary popular cinema has proffered alternate views of maternity – ones that reflect the public's growing concerns. Some works have imagined the birth of an archetypal monster. *It's Alive!* (Larry Cohen, 1974) opens with a woman in labour, trying to quell a premonition that something is dreadfully wrong. The sequence ends with bloodied doctors evacuating a delivery room where they have inadvertently birthed her murderous progeny. This eerie scenario is extended in the film's two sequels: *It Lives Again* (Larry Cohen, 1978) and *It's Alive III: Island of the Alive* (Larry Cohen, 1987). In *The Brood* (David Cronenberg, 1979) a female mental patient incubates heinous foetuses in external belly sacs; *Embryo* (Ralph Nelson, 1976) and *Eraserhead* (David Lynch, 1978) pursue this theme of malevolent extrauterine conception.[3] Other films take an extraterrestrial spin on the subject. In *Biohazard: The Alien Force* (Shinji Mikami, 1995), a company spawns a genetically-engineered creature. When its host mother escapes the compound and gives birth to the child in the outside world, it wreaks havoc on the unsuspecting masses. In *The Unnameable* (Jean-Paul Ouellette, 1988) and *The Unnameable II: The Statement of Randolph Carter* (Jean-Paul Ouellette, 1993), a fiend birthed by a woman in the 1800s is suddenly unleashed on some modern college students. Finally, in *The Astronaut's Wife* (Rand Ravich, 1999), a pregnant woman becomes uneasy when her pilot husband begins to act strangely following his last space mission. She suspects that the alien force that has transformed her spouse has also mutated his unborn child.

Our reflex is to keep these diverse impressions of childbirth separate: to deem some idyllic and others grotesque, some accurate and others apocryphal, some objective and others subjective, some benign and others perverse. But scholarly work on the horror genre is sceptical of such binary oppositions. Caryn James sees horror as evoking 'universal' terrors (1990: 15); Dennis L. White notes its roots in 'the common fears of everyday life' (1987: 16). For many writers, such trepidations involve cultural tensions. Dana Polan finds common domestic strife in *The Howling* (Joe Dante, 1981) (1984: 202–8), and Serafina Bathrick decodes familiar forms of sexual fright in *Carrie* (Brian De Palma, 1976) (1977: 9–10). Andrew Tudor locates a 'trend toward family-oriented horror' in recent works of the genre (1989: 128). Hence, in its social register, horror constitutes an expressionistic 'allegory of the real'.[4]

It is from this perspective that I will view Roman Polanski's *Rosemary's Baby* (1968), a movie that heralds both the birth of horror and the horror of birth in the modern cinema (Carroll 1990: 2, 107). Though the film is certainly an odious fable of parturition, it is also a bizarre 'documentary' of the medical, societal and personal turmoil that has regularly attended female reproduction. While for Rhona Berenstein the film reflects the 'horrifying status of motherhood in American patriarchal culture' (Berenstein 1990: 55), I will read the film against that grain, for its utterance of women's private experience of pregnancy.

The 'gynaecological gothic'[5]

> Last night I dreamed I gave birth to a monster. Are you that menacing creature I saw in my dream? My monster, myself ... *Maybe it's Rosemary's baby in there.* (Chesler 1979: 36, 33, my emphasis)

Rosemary's Baby is the story of Rosemary and Guy Woodhouse (Mia Farrow/John Cassavetes), newlyweds who rent an apartment in the Bramford, a Victorian high-rise reputed to have been haunted by witches.[6] Guy, an actor, is consumed with his career. Rosemary, a traditional homemaker, wants to start a family. Once the Woodhouses move in, their eccentric, elderly neighbours, Roman and Minnie Castevet (Sidney Blackmer/ Ruth Gordon), insinuate themselves into the couple's life. At first, Guy resists them, while Rosemary urges him to socialise. But after a dinner party (in which Roman claims a certain influence in the theatre world), Guy seems bent on befriending the Castevets. Soon, he expresses his willingness to have a child. Gradually, Rosemary becomes wary of the Castevets: she wonders why the previous tenant barricaded a door leading to their apartment; she hears strange chants emanating through their adjoining wall; a young female guest of the Castevets suddenly commits suicide; Minnie gives Rosemary a foul-smelling amulet to wear.

Rosemary becomes pregnant and, despite her reservations, allows Minnie to advise her – to administer herbal medicines and to enlist Dr Abraham Sapirstein (Ralph Bellamy). Rather than thrive, Rosemary sickens and fears that something is amiss. When her friend, Hutch (Maurice Evans), warns her that the Castevets are demons, he mysteriously dies, willing her a volume on witchcraft through which she learns the terrible facts. She tries, frantically, to escape the clutches of the Castevets, who have ensnared Guy with the promise of stage stardom. When Rosemary seeks refuge with her own obstetrician, Dr Hill (Charles Grodin), he thinks she is crazed and calls Dr Sapirstein and Guy to retrieve her. Rosemary flees and gives birth to a baby in her home, but the infant is taken from her and she is told it is dead. As the film ends, she follows the sound of a baby's cry to the Castevets' apartment where a coven is celebrating the arrival of the devil-child. Though at first repulsed, Rosemary soon approaches the cradle to comfort the infant.

Significantly, Rosemary gains access to her child through a door that conjoins the Woodhouse and Castevet abodes – a geographic proximity that has doomed her pregnancy. This trope of contiguity will also inform my methodology, as I read the film in the 'space' of various neighbouring cultural discourses on childbirth: the sacred, the mythic, the obstetrical, the psychiatric, the therapeutic and the artistic. By juxtaposing such diverse textual 'locales' (medical and otherwise), their complex boundaries will be outlined. For, as Stuart Hall has noted, the study of popular culture 'yields most when it is seen in relation to a more general, a wider history' (Hall 1981: 230).

False labour

> One might say that the true subject of the horror genre is the struggle for recognition of all that our civilisation *re*presses or *op*presses. (Wood 1986: 75)

As multifarious visions of childbirth have proliferated, so have competing discourses, each seeking to explain and contain it. Despite this apparent vocalism, the dialogue has generally disempowered woman or relegated her to virtual silence. Religious thought has elided her from the birth act (as in Eve's appearance from Adam's rib, Athena's creation from the forehead of Zeus, or Aphrodite's formation from the phallus of Uranus). Traditional obstetrics has denied her agency, configuring the parturient woman as a passive patient. Psychiatry 'damns her with faint praise' for successfully achieving maternal maturity by sublimating her penis envy.

No wonder that in the plethora of voices many sense a mutism. Iris Marion Young is not 'surprised to learn that discourse on pregnancy omits subjectivity', and that 'the specific experience of women has been absent from most of our culture's discourse about human experience' (Young 1984: 45). Myra Leifer corroborates this insight: 'Although for many years researchers have been interested in the effect of the trauma of birth on the newborn … strikingly less attention has been given to its impact upon the mother' (Leifer 1980: 117). It is important that Leifer (writing in 1980) uses the term 'trauma'; for in the decades immediately preceding her statement, voluntary, middle-class pregnancy was regarded more romantically. As Eva Zajicek remarks, 'In the 1930s and 1940s, when views of women were more obviously stereotyped … it was considered important for them to experience only the rewarding, fulfilling aspects of pregnancy and motherhood'. Any deviance from this was regarded as 'a sign of maladjustment' (Zajicek in Wolkind & Zajicek 1981: 32, 35). Even a manual from the 1980s promises expectant women a purely 'joyful' pregnancy, urging them to 'be free of fear and full of confidence' (Curtis & Caroles 1985: 4).

The feminist movement of the 1970s spurred a reconsideration of parturition in two contradictory ways. On the one hand, reproduction was further glorified by the proponents of woman-centred, natural childbirth. Suzanne Arms deems this the 'most profound, personal experience a woman can have' and claims that if woman finds it 'dangerous, risky, painful and terrifying', it is only because the male medical system has made it so (Arms 1975: xiii, 23). On the other hand, the era saw a lifting of taboos concerning childbirth. In a satiric attack on the Lamaze method, Nora Ephron complains that it 'never crossed (her) mind that (she) would live through the late 1960s and early 1970s in America only to discover that in the end what was expected of (her) was a brave, albeit vigorous squat in the fields like the heroine of *The Good Earth* [Sidney Franklin, 1937]' (Ephron 1978: 88). On a darker note, Adrienne Rich admits that pregnancy is not only an exquisite phenomenon, but one characterised by 'anxiety, depression [and] the sense of being a sacrificial victim' (Rich 1986: 153). While the bleak side of parturition represents just another rival discourse on the subject, its admission stands as a corrective to more ubiquitous sanguine views. Released in 1968, *Rosemary's Baby* announces this discursive disturbance, and the film's malign *mise-en-scène* bespeaks a return of the repressed.

In considering the film, we might first examine the work's chilling atmosphere (the threatening Bramford, its repugnant tenants, the rumours of savagery, the nightmare imagery). As Diane Waldman has noted, the narrative has all the earmarks of the Gothic mode (the naïve young heroine, her opaque husband, the awesome mansion, the supernatural events (Waldman 1981: 308–25)). As such, it might well be dismissed as mere phantasmagoria, but it is more challenging to query the film's relevance to childbirth lore. (James Twitchell finds all horror related to themes of 'sex and reproduction' (Twitchell 1985: 66).)

In 1945, Freudian psychiatrist Helene Deutsch acknowledged maternity's disquieting aspects, despite her conviction that it was woman's sublime calling. In one passage, she spoke of pregnancy as having an 'abnormal psychic charge', and employed the term 'horror' to characterise delivery. She resorted to the same phrasing to describe women with postpartum problems: 'Something has happened during childbirth to disappoint [them] and fill them with *horror*' (Deutsch 1945: 135, 251, my emphasis). More recently, in Leifer's interviews with primiparous women, subjects related the 'horror stories' they had heard (Leifer 1980: 45).

Such tales are not entirely fictional. As Ann Dally has stated, 'throughout history, until recent times, motherhood was always close to death'. This obtained for the newborn, in periods of high infant mortality. (In England and Wales of 1885, 14–16 per cent of babies died during their first year.) But childbirth was also 'one of the greatest hazards that adult women had to face' (Dally 1983: 26, 31). Among the chamber of maternal horrors was puerperal fever, which reached epidemic proportions between the seventeenth and nineteenth centuries. Most ghoulish was its transmission by doctors, who, unaware of sepsis, went directly from dissecting cadavers to delivering babies. As Julia Kristeva remarks: 'here is a fever where what bears life passes over to the side of the dead body' (Kristeva 1982: 159).[7] Another potential medical crisis was obstructed labour, for which physicians used tortuous tools (reminiscent of those in *Dead Ringers* (David Cronenberg, 1988)) to extract (or decapitate) the baby. Sheila Kitzinger describes such a delivery scene (evocative of a sequence in *Alien* (Ridley Scott, 1979)): 'a long ... labour may be terminated by rupture of the uterus and death of the baby and mother, and to those helping it must look really *as if the baby has burst up out of the womb*' (Kitzinger 1978: 85–6, my emphasis).

Beyond such parallels between the macabre and childbirth, what else can we read from the supernatural aura of *Rosemary's Baby*? Rich speaks of female reproduction as conventionally assigned 'malign occult influences', as being 'vulnerable to or emanating evil' (Rich 1986: 163–4). Kitzinger talks of parturition as a 'ritual state' necessitating the intervention of shamans, priests and priestesses (Kitzinger 1978: 71). Both associate pregnancy with 'possession'. For Kitzinger, this means 'being taken over by an unknown and even hostile stranger' (1978: 78); for Rich, it connotes being dominated by labour's painful contractions. Both remark on the uncanny sense of 'doubling' and 'splitting' in reproduction – the former at conception; the latter at delivery.[8] Hence, pregnancy is a 'liminal' or 'marginal' state (Kitzinger 1978: 67). While such characterisations are, clearly, pernicious, Grete Bibring wonders whether, by banishing 'magical and superstitious customs surrounding pregnancy', science has 'removed certain concepts and activities which ... help in organising and channeling the intense emotional reactions of the pregnant woman' (Bibring 1959: 113–21).

But what of *Rosemary's Baby*'s specific references to witchcraft? What social or psychic echoes reverberate here? It is necessary to recall the history of childbirth prior to the ascendancy of the male physician, when care of the pregnant woman was entrusted to a midwife – often a poor, older, peasant woman with little standing in the community. Frequently, such individuals were thought to bear evil spirits, capable of inducing female fertility or male impotence (Deutsch 1945: 206; Rich 1986: 135ff). Consequently, midwives were often accused of witchcraft, and were cited in the *Malleus Maleficarum*, the primary reference volume of the era. As Thomas Rogers Forbes writes: 'Because midwives so often were in bad repute, even an innocent practitioner might be accused of witchcraft if the delivery had an unhappy outcome' (Forbes 1966: 5; see also Ehrenreich 1973: 13).

When the birth was successful, midwives might still be charged with selling an infant's soul to the devil. In the *Compendium Maleficarum* of 1626, Guaccius writes:

> When [witches] do not kill the babies, they offer them [horrible to relate] to the demons in this execrable manner. After the child is born the witch-midwife … pretends that something should be done to restore the strength of the baby, carries it outside the bedroom, and elevating it on high [offers] it to the Prince of Devils. (Forbes 1966: 128)

In recent decades, feminists have challenged liturgical discourse – reclaiming the figure of the midwife-witch. By rereading it, they have seen her as the repository of patriarchal fears of female strength, and as a scapegoat for the emergent obstetrical profession. As Rich notes: 'men gradually annexed the role of birth-attendant and thus assumed authority over the very sphere which had originally been one source of female power and charisma' (1986: 129).

In this light, it is tempting to recast Minnie Castevet as an ersatz modern midwife, shrouded in misogyny. From her first entrance into the Woodhouse apartment (when she asks if Rosemary will have children), she is overly concerned with her neighbour's reproductive life, and when Rosemary becomes pregnant, it is Minnie who administers homeopathic potions (filled with 'snails and puppy dog tails'). Like the ancient midwife, she must transfer her power to a male physician (Dr Sapirstein), who, nonetheless, relies on her expertise. Significantly, rumours of the Bramford's haunting centre on the Trench sisters' cannibalism toward babies. The historical roots of the midwife-witch, is consonant with Minnie's naturalistic presentation, a touch that caught critics off guard. Robert Chapetta complains that the demons in Polanski's film are 'not frightening, but an absurd lot, rather like a small far-out California religious sect' (Chapetta 1969: 38).

Hysterical pregnancy

> The key to monster movies … is the theme of horrible and mysterious psychological and physical change … which is directly associated with secondary sexual characteristics … and with … erotic behavior. (Evans 1984: 54)

Although some unsettling elements of the film are explained by the actual linkage of witchcraft and childbirth, it is equally fruitful to place them within a psychological frame. For much of what passes for Rosemary's 'demented' musings are consonant with representations of woman's ordinary experience of parturition. The birth process starts with conception and, in *Rosemary's Baby*, the primal scene is overlain with terror. One night, Guy reveals his sudden desire to father a baby, whereupon he choreographs a candlelight dinner. The meal is interrupted by the arrival of Minnie, who brings her special chocolate *mousse*. Though Rosemary dislikes its 'chalky undertaste', Guy urges her to eat it.

Within moments of eating, Rosemary collapses and Guy carries her to bed. Rosemary suffers a perverse delirium: she sails on a ship; Guy rips off her clothing; she gazes up at religious paintings; she walks through flames; a monster's hand maims her; hags tie her down and paint her body; she begs the Pope for forgiveness. 'This is not a dream', she shouts; 'this is really happening!' The next morning, when Rosemary notices scratches on her skin, she asks Guy what has transpired. He says that, despite her faint, he had not wanted to 'miss baby night', and confesses that sex had been fun in a 'necrophilic sort of way'.

This warped rape fantasy reverberates with cultural clichés of woman's sexual position. With female eroticism conventionally conceived as 'the embodiment of guilt', it is logical that Rosemary seeks the Holy Father's blessing (Rich 1986: 164). That she is unconscious during intercourse, mocks woman's 'designated' coital stance: passive and undemanding. That Guy is uninvolved with her impregnation, evokes primitive beliefs that human males are removed from procreation. Finally, the devious dénouement of Rosemary's pregnancy assigns her blame. It is *she* who has most wanted a child. (Even in her drugged stupor, she pleads to 'make a baby'.) It is *she* who has arranged to live in the Bramford (despite its chilling reputation). It is *she* who has pushed intimacy with the Castevets. (Guy originally warned: 'If we get friendly with an old couple ... we'll never get rid of them.') Thus, the New Eve is charged with Original Sin.

Louise Sweeney found viewing *Rosemary's Baby* 'like having someone else's nightmare' (Sweeney 1968: 6). In truth, dreams have long been linked to the horror genre and Noël Carroll sees the form as fraught with 'nightmare imagery' (Carroll 1981: 16). Significantly, researchers have also noted the importance of dreams to pregnancy. Psychiatrist Deutsch deems the nine-month period a quasi-oneiric state, since women must attend to an abstract being within them. She also finds women prone to reverie in this condition, and records some patient dreams that are reminiscent of Rosemary's. Certain fantasies occur involving water (conjuring the amniotic fluid); others offer scenarios of harassment:

> In such dreams wild beasts chase the dreamer, or a sharp claw or tooth is plunged into some part of her body. She tries to flee, but her persecutors run after her from behind while she faces another danger in front. (Deutsch 1945: 233)

As Rosemary's pregnancy progresses, its baroque narrative constructs a distorted projection of quotidian experience. Almost immediately, she is consumed with angst: she is uneasy when Dr Hill requests a second blood sample; she develops insomnia upon overhearing the Castevets' voices next door. When Rosemary visits Dr Sapirstein, she reveals that she fears an ectopic complication. Though, within the story, there is an unearthly rationale for Rosemary's concerns, her state of mind is not untoward. Leifer notes a 'growing sense of anxiety' accompanying pregnancy, along with a feeling of 'emotional liability' (Leifer 1980: 31). In the past, such nervousness was often regarded as hysterical, and its admission was discouraged. Recently, however, scholars have seen such tension in a positive light as 'a significant reflection of the developing maternal bond' (Leifer 1980: 47). Rosemary, however, is almost paranoid – understandable given the assumptions of the plot. Again, we find that ordinary pregnant women can approach this state. As Leifer notes: 'Women commonly beg(in) to view the outside world as potentially threatening. They bec(ome) more cautious in their activities, fear(ing) that they might be harmed or attacked' (Leifer 1980: 49). For Leifer, this is not a pathological symptom but a protective stance that reflects 'realistic concerns' for safety.

The premise of *Rosemary's Baby* is that the heroine germinates a devil-child; but worries of an abnormal foetus are common in normal pregnancies. Deutsch mentions the 'painful idea that [the baby] will be a monster, an idiot, a cripple' (Deutsch 1945: 151). And Leifer reports that: 'Women typically ... vividly imagine a variety of deformities that they had either read about or seen' (Leifer 1980: 47). Some women perceive the foetus as a foreign being: Deutsch admits that it can be seen as a 'parasite' which 'exploits' the maternal host (Deutsch 1945: 131). Interestingly, a 1968 pregnancy manual uses this precise language, characterising the 'tiny parasite of a foetus' as appropriating the body of its 'mother-host' for 'his own purposes' (Liley & Day 1968). Even the cool discourse of modern science casts the foetus in an eerie light. Three years before the release of *Rosemary's Baby*, Lennart Nillson published his shocking, groundbreaking photographs of embryos in *Life* magazine. As ontogeny repeats phylogeny the embryo is seen to resemble an aquatic being (what poet Summer Brenner calls 'the prince of whales'). Genetics catalogues the foetus's sequential organ development, informing us when it acquires what. (We are reminded that, for Carroll, monsters suffer from 'categorical incompleteness' (Carroll 1990: 33).)

While women have been told to purge such disturbing thoughts (to deny pregnancy's 'chalky undertaste'), Leifer argues for their validity: 'These concerns often represen(t) realistic apprehensions about a variety of unknown events' (Leifer 1980: 47). Patriarchy has its own reasons for eliding female ambivalence. While man has traditionally imagined the *mother* as 'abject' – associated as she is with menstrual blood and infantile excrement (Leifer 1980: 115–16, 99–100), he rejects the thought that she might find abjection in *him* (the beloved child). Such inversion constitutes a narcissistic wound to one who refuses to see the 'Other' in himself.

Along with a case of 'nerves', Rosemary suffers illness, a fact which surfaces cultural confusion about the status of pregnancy. On the one hand, history has amassed a compendium of medical disorders that collectively mark the state a 'disease' – from eclampsia, to toxaemia, to varicose veins. Yet, with the threat of physiological harm abated, women have challenged institutionalised paternalism – claiming recognition for the pregnant woman's health, strength and fortitude. Ironically, while physicians have made the parturient woman an Imaginary Invalid, they have often disregarded her justified complaints. In *Rosemary's Baby*, the heroine's discomforts are consistently minimised, as though 'pain, like love, [were] embedded in the ideology of motherhood' (Rich 1986: 157). Guy ignores her ailments, and Dr Sapirstein implies that they are psychosomatic. In 1939 a study showed morning sickness to be a sign of neurosis, entailing the repudiation of femininity; in 1943 another found queasiness prevalent in women 'who had an unconscious desire not to be pregnant' (Wolkind & Zajicek 1981: 77, 76). Though Guy and Dr Sapirstein have devious reasons for slighting Rosemary's grievances, most doctors and husbands ostensibly do not.

Following the trajectory of documented pregnancies, Rosemary's discomfort and fear temporarily lessen at the moment of 'quickening'. As Leifer notes: 'The almost universal reactions to this event [are] immense relief ... and a new feeling of confidence' (Leifer 1980: 78). However, when Rosemary shouts 'It's Alive!', the contemporary audience is struck by the intertextual irony of her words.

As Rosemary's term continues, she becomes appalled by her pallid and wasted appearance. While her condition results from demonic poisoning (and not morning sickness), and stands in *inverse* relation to the usual plenitude of pregnancy, some expectant women dread their corporeal transformation. Leifer claims that many regard their swelling bodies as 'ego-alien', and view them in fantastic terms:

> The rapidly growing abdomen, continued to evoke anxiety, and women reported feeling like Alice in Wonderland, upon taking the magic pills; growing and growing with no end in sight ... losing control over their bodies. (Leifer 1980: 34–5)

Consumed by her fears of possession, Rosemary refuses to see friends – mimicking the pregnant woman's alleged 'increased self-preoccupation and … decline of emotional investment in the external world' (Leifer 1980: 43). As Rosemary's worries multiply, she even grows wary of her husband: she is puzzled by the scratches he has made on her body; she searches for cult markings on his shoulder; she is perplexed that he can no longer return her gaze; she wonders why he is suddenly a popular actor, whose 'break' comes at the expense of another's welfare. While Rosemary's doubts are explained supernaturally, such behaviour can occur in ordinary circumstances: 'Anxiety about losing one's husband … was expressed by more than half of the [pregnant] women [questioned]' (Leifer 1980: 49–50).

For these myriad reasons, expectant women may feel a loss of control, a challenge to their physical and spiritual autonomy. For Zajicek, pregnancy is 'a period of emotional stress' with a 'high potential for psychiatric breakdown'. Despite a certain tendency toward solitude, women do seek external support out of a desire 'to be cared for and protected' – a fact that mirrors Rosemary's unwise turn to Minnie Castevet (Wolkind & Zajicek 1981: 60; Leifer 1980: 54). The film chronicles this dependency, as Rosemary passively 'transfers' stewardship of her pregnancy to others. Though she has wanted a child, it is Guy who orchestrates conception. One friend sends her to Dr Hill; then, Minnie reroutes her to Dr Sapirstein. Since the latter is a 'front', Minnie engineers Rosemary's care behind the scenes. Both Guy and Sapirstein attempt to keep Rosemary ignorant, cautioning her against reading. In a drugged delivery (fraught with childbirth 'amnesia') her baby is stolen from her in recompense for Guy's Faustian pact.

An alternate title for the film might read: *Whose Baby is it Anyway?*

I cannot remember the birth. Cold white rooms, cleanliness the colour of nothing. Sometimes a woman dreams that she's given birth to a litter of piglets attached to her breasts like pink balloons. When I look in the crib there is no baby… (Maxine Chernoff, in Chester 1989: 93)

The arrival of Rosemary's child is one of the most ghastly scenes in the film. Pursued by Guy and Sapirstein from Dr Hill's office, she returns to her apartment, where she falls on the floor in the throes of labour. A hallucinatory sequence unfolds in which a coven of witches gag her, tie her down, sedate her and deliver of her a male child whom they steal away. On one level (divested of the occult), the scene can be read as a dramatisation of old-fashioned home birth – with a female midwife present. The feigned death of Rosemary's child stands in for the real infant mortality which obtained until the modern era. (In justifying his evil sacrifice to the Castevets, Guy even asks Rosemary: 'Suppose you had had the baby and lost it – wouldn't it have been the same?') Rosemary, however, suspects that her 'dead' child is living. She becomes alarmed when she hears a muffled infant's wail next door, and when she perceives that one of Minnie's friends saves milk extracted from the maternal breast.

On another tier, the birth scene superimposes upon the site of midwife delivery the malevolent mythology of witchcraft – of Satanic beings stealing babies for the devil. On a final plateau, the vignette subjectively replicates woman's experience of traditional hospital birth – of being physically restrained, anaesthetised and summarily separated from her baby (who is taken to a nursery). Here is how poet, Diana Di Prima, portrays such an event in 'Nativity':

Dark timbers of lost forests falling into my bed.
My hairs stirring, not asleep. Did they fetter me
with cat's paw, rock root, the beard
(o shame) of woman? They fettered me
w/ leather straps, on delivery table. I cd not
cry out. Forced gas mask over mouth,
slave. I cd not
turn head. Did they fetter me
w/ breath of a fish? These poison airs? I cd not
turn head, move hand, or leg
thus forced. They tore child from me. Whose?
(Di Prima, in Chester 1989: 107)

Even Rosemary's response to her demon-child suggests a real mother's contradictory emotions toward her infant. Bibring finds frequent 'disturbances in the earliest attitudes of the young mother toward her newborn baby' (Bibring 1959: 14); Deutsch remarks that many women first view their child as a 'rejected alien object' (Deutsch 1945: 251). Rosemary's vacillation between love and hate should not surprise us in a genre structured by the 'conflict between attraction and repulsion' (Carroll 1981: 17). Such a magnetic field sustains the tension of *Rosemary's Baby* which acknowledges parturition as a bliss and a blight. Like most social groups, the Castevets' coven harnesses guilt to prod Rosemary toward parental bonding. 'Aren't you his mother?' they ask; 'Be a mother to your baby.' Maternal 'instinct' eventually triumphs, and her initial ambivalence is quashed.

It seems significant that, as Rosemary rocks the cradle, we never fully glimpse her infamous baby, who remains forever, off-screen.[9] On one level, this visual denial foregrounds Carroll's notion that monsters are 'inconceivable' (Carroll 1990: 21). But, on another, it addresses horror's appropriation of the quotidian – since it never gives us an other-worldly creature to view. In accepting her loathsome offspring, Rosemary acknowledges her *own* demons – the fears of motherhood that society wants hushed. Thus, in some respects, Rosemary's baby is her double. (In a diary, Phyllis Chesler once called her foetus 'my monster, myself' (Chesler 1979: 101)). Similarly, Polan notes an introspective trend in contemporary *grand guignol*, which suggest(s) 'that the horror is not merely among us, but rather part of us' (Polan 1984: 202).

If *Rosemary's Baby* assumes a certain 'banality' to horror, it replays that thesis on the level of style. With the exception of the dream/hallucination sequences, the work is crafted with conventional cinematic verisimilitude: long-shot/long-take format, standard lenses, location shooting, continuity editing, credible costume and decor. For Beverley Houston and Marsha Kinder, *Rosemary's Baby* 'create(s) the impression that never … were things so clearly seen, so concrete, so "real"' (Houston & Kinder 1968–69: 18).

Afterbirth

A pointing finger always accompanies the classic text: the truth is thereby long desired and avoided, kept in a kind of *pregnancy* for its full term, a *pregnancy* whose end, both liberating and catastrophic, will bring about the utter end of the discourse. (Barthes 1974: 62, my emphasis)

Early on in *Rosemary's Baby* we learn that the Woodhouse and Castevet apartments were once a single residence, which was later subdivided. The Woodhouses now live in the 'back rooms' of the original lodging. Significantly, at the film's conclusion, Rosemary opens the barricaded door that conjoins the two habitations. Sensing that her attendants are sequestering her child, she goes to her hall closet and removes the rear shelves. Like Alice, she peers through a hole into her neighbours' caballic abode (Wexman 1987: 41). Grasping a knife, she traverses the space – leaving home for a Satanic Wonderland. (As Julia Kristeva has noted, abjection involves an ambiguity of 'borders' (Kristeva 1982: 67).)

Clearly, Rosemary's trajectory has implications beyond the physical, for it replays (in navigational terms) the thematic project of the film. While contemporary discourse (be it patriarchal or feminist) has often idealised childbirth and suppressed its disturbing terrain, the film negotiates the geography that connects these ideological quarters. In journeying to the Castevets' suite, Rosemary links woman's conscious and unconscious pregnancies, her ecstatic and despondent views, modern and ancient medical practices, scientific and mystical beliefs, realistic and supernatural portrayals. In unleashing the horrific, Rosemary has un-'shelved' the Maternal Macabre – has reclaimed its 'back rooms' – has forced it out of the cultural and cinematic 'closet'.

In 1968, many middle-class expectant mothers were enrolled in uplifting Lamaze classes where they dutifully viewed graphic movies of labour and delivery. (On the same page as Andrew Sarris's *Village Voice* critique of *Rosemary's Baby* is a notice for a screening of an instructional childbirth film.) Here is how Margaret Atwood depicts such a session in the short story *Giving Birth*:

> They have seen the film made by the hospital, a full-colour film of a woman giving birth to, can it be a baby? 'Not all babies will be this large at birth,' the Australian nurse who introduces the movie says. Still, the audience, half of which is pregnant, doesn't look very relaxed when the lights go on. ('If you don't like the visuals,' a friend of [hers] has told her, 'you can always close your eyes'). (Atwood 1990: 139)

Such Lamaze devotees may well have avoided Polanski's thriller, fearing the distress it could engender. Retrospectively, however, one wonders *which* women were most 'prepared' for parturition: which saw the horror film and which the documentary?

Notes

1 I am using the term 'parturition' here to refer to numerous aspects of the female reproductive experience (for example pregnancy and delivery).

2 I am referring to material in *Newsweek* (14 May 1990) and *Working Mother* (June 1989). The precise issue of *Parent* is not known.

3 For a further discussion of some of these films see also: William Paul, *Laughing Screaming: Modern Hollywood Horror and Comedy* (New York: Columbia University Press, 1994), 354–80; Barbara Creed, *The Monstrous Feminine: Film, Feminism, Psychoanalysis* (London and New York: Routledge), 1993: 43–58.

4 Dana Polan coined this term for me in a discussion of the paper, but let me elaborate on its use. Allegory is commonly understood to be an extended narrative that carries a second meaning along with the surface story. As Gay Clifford points out in *The Transformations of Allegory* (London and Boston: Routledge and Kegan Paul, 1974:

11, 25), 'allegorical action often takes the form of a … quest, or a pursuit' exposing a 'credible and realistic hero to a journey through an extraordinary allegorical world'. Often, as in the case of *Frankenstein* or *The Trial* (both cited by Clifford), though the narrative universe is fantastic, it invokes a real social order (moribund and irrational bureaucracy in *The Trial*; the perils of technological invention in *Frankenstein*). It is this sense in which I apply the term to *Rosemary's Baby*. While on one level, Rosemary's journey proceeds as a hyperbolic fiction, on another it charts the psychological and historical 'realities' of quotidian pregnancy. According to theorists, allegory can either apply to the process by which an author creates a fiction or to the strategy by which a critic reads it. It is this latter sense I invoke, and make no claims for allegorical intentionality on the part of Ira Levin or Roman Polanski.

5   This term was used by Penelope Gilliatt in her review of *Rosemary's Baby* ('Anguish Under the Skin', *The New Yorker* (15 June 1968), 87–9).

6   The film is based on Ira Levin's 1967 novel of the same title.

7   On this issue, see also Barbara Creed (1986) 'Horror and the Monstrous Feminine – an Imaginary Abjection.' *Screen*, 27, 1, 44–71.

8   See also Iris Marion Young (1984) 'Pregnant Embodiment: Subjectivity and Alienation', *The Journal of Medicine and Philosophy*, 9, 46.

9   Though we do not see the baby in this sequence, there is an earlier moment (after Rosemary has first approached the cradle) when she is horrified by the child's appearance and asks, 'What have you done to his eyes?' Later, when she learns that her son is the devil's child, she shouts, 'It's not true', and her image is superimposed with a shot of the creature's eyes. These eyes are possibly her child's eyes or those of the devil; it is unclear.

References

Arms, S. (1975) *Immaculate Deception: A New Look at Women and Childbirth in America*. Boston: Houghton Mifflin.

Atwood, M. (1990) 'Giving birth', in W. Martin (ed.) *We Are the Stories We Tell*. New York: Pantheon, 134–49.

Bathrick, S. K. (1977) 'Ragtime: the horror of growing up female', *Jump Cut*, 14, March, 9–10.

Barthes, R. (1974) *S/Z: An Essay*, trans. Richard Miller. New York: Hill and Wang.

Berenstein, R. (1990) 'Mommie Dearest: *Aliens*, *Rosemary's Baby* and mothering', *Journal of Popular Culture*, 24, 2, 55–73.

Bibring, G. L. (1959) 'Some considerations of the psychological process in pregnancy', *The Psychoanalytic Study of the Child*, 14, 113–21.

Carroll, N. (1981) 'Nightmare and the horror film: the symbolic biology of fantastic beings', *Film Quarterly*, 34, 3, 16–25.

_____ (1990) *The Philosophy of Horror or Paradoxes of the Heart*. New York and London: Routledge.

Chapetta, R. (1969) '*Rosemary's Baby*', *Film Quarterly*, 22, Spring, 35–8.

Chesler, P. (1979) *With Child: A Diary of Motherhood*. New York: Thomas V. Crowell.

Chester, L. (ed.) (1989) *Cradle and All: Women Writers on Pregnancy and Childbirth*. Boston and London: Faber and Faber.

Clifford, G. (1974) *The Transformations of Allegory*. London and Boston: Routledge and

Kegan Paul.

Creed, B. (1986) 'Horror and the monstrous feminine: an imaginary abjection', *Screen*, 27, 1, 44–71.

_____ (1993) *The Monstrous Feminine: Film, Feminism, Psychoanalysis*. London and New York: Routledge.

Curtis, L. R. and Y. Caroles (1985) *Pregnant and Lovin' It*. Los Angeles and San Francisco: Price/Stern.

Dally, A. (1983) *Inventing Motherhood: The Consequences of an Ideal*. New York: Schocken.

Daly, B. O. and M. T. Reddy (eds) (1991) *Narrating Mothers: Theorizing Maternal Subjectivities*. Knoxville: University of Tennessee.

Deutsch, H. (1945) *The Psychology of Woman*, Vol. III. New York: Grune and Stratton.

Ehrenreich, B. (1973) *Witches, Midwives, and Nurses: A History of Woman Healers*. Old Westbury, NY: The Feminist Press.

Ephron, N. (1978) 'Having a baby after 35', *New York Times Magazine* (26 November), 28–9, 86, 88–9.

Evans, W. (1984) 'Monster movies: a sexual theory', in B. K. Grant (ed.) *Planks of Reason: Essays on the Horror Film*. Metuchen, NJ and London: Scarecrow Press, 53–64.

Forbes, T. R. (1966) *The Midwife and the Witch*. New Haven and London: Yale University Press.

Gilliatt, P. (1968) 'Anguish under the skin', *New Yorker* (15 June), 87–9.

Grant, B. K. (ed.) (1984) *Planks of Reason: Essays on the Horror Film*. Metuchen, NJ and London: Scarecrow Press.

Hall, S. (1981) 'Notes on deconstructing "The Popular"', in R. Samuel (ed.) *People's History and Socialist Theory*. London and Boston: Routledge and Kegan Paul, 227–40.

Houston, B. and M. Kinder (1968–69) 'Rosemary's Baby', *Sight and Sound*, 38, 1, 17–19.

James, C. (1990) 'The high art of horror films can cut deep into the psyche', *New York Times* (27 May), Section 2, 1, 15.

Kitzinger, S. (1978) *Women as Mothers*. New York: Random House.

Kristeva, J. (1982) *Powers of Horror: An Essay on Abjection*, trans. Leon S. Roudiez. New York: Columbia University Press.

Leifer, M. (1980) *Psychological Effects of Motherhood: A Study of First Pregnancy*. New York: Praeger.

Levin, I. (1967) *Rosemary's Baby*. New York: Random House.

Liley, H. M. and B. Day (1968) 'The inside story of your baby's life before birth', *Expecting* (A Guide for Expectant Mothers Published by *Parent's Magazine*) (Fall).

Nillson, L. (1965) 'Drama of life before birth', *Life*, 58, 17, 30 April.

Paul, W. (1994) *Laughing Screaming: Modern Hollywood Horror and Comedy*. New York: Columbia University Press.

Polan, D. (1984) 'Eros and syphilization: the contemporary horror film', in B. K. Grant (ed.) *Planks of Reason: Essays on the Horror Film*. Metuchen, NJ and London: Scarecrow Press, 201–11.

Rich, A. (1986) *Of Woman Born: Motherhood as Experience and Institution*. New York and London: W. W. Norton.

Sarris, A. (1968) (review). *The Village Voice*, 25 July, 37.

Sweeney, L. (1968) 'Polanski's satanic parody', in *Christian Science Monitor* (Western edition; 22 June), 6.

Tudor, A. (1989) *Monsters and Mad Scientists: A Cultural History of the Horror Movie*.

Oxford: Basil Blackwell.

Twitchell, J. B. (1985) *Dreadful Pleasures: An Anatomy of Modern Horror.* New York and Oxford: Oxford University Press.

Waldman, D. (1981) *Horror and Domesticity: The Modern Romance Film of the 1940s.* PhD dissertation, University of Wisconsin-Madison.

Wexman, V. W. (1987) 'The trauma of infancy in Roman Polanski's *Rosemary's Baby*', in G. Waller (ed.) *American Horrors: Essays on the Modern American Horror Film.* Urbana and Chicago: University of Illinois Press, 30–43.

White, D. L. (1987) 'The poetics of horror: more than meets the eye', *Cinema Journal*, 10, 2, 1–18.

Wood, R. (1984) 'An introduction to the American horror film', in B. K. Grant (ed.) *Planks of Reason: Essays on the Horror Film.* Metuchen, NJ and London: Scarecrow Press, 164–200.

_____ (1986) *Hollywood from Vietnam to Reagan.* New York: Columbia University Press.

Wolkind, S. and E. Zajicek (1981) *Pregnancy: A Psychological and Social Study.* London: Academic Press.

Young, I. M. (1984) 'Pregnant embodiment: subjectivity and alienation', *Journal of Medicine and Philosophy*, 9, 45–62.

03

Kenneth MacKinnon

The mainstream AIDS movie prior to the 1990s

At first sight, the title of this chapter must seem highly eccentric. Is there, it could fairly be asked, any such thing as a mainstream English-language AIDS movie before Norman René's *Longtime Companion* of 1990, the same decade as produced the far higher-profile and star-bedecked *Philadelphia* (Jonathan Demme, 1993)? If there is not, cinema contrasts in this respect with other media.

Certainly, television evidences awareness of the syndrome in the 1980s. In late 1983, *St Elsewhere* included a story where a young politician suffered from AIDS-related illness. *An Early Frost* (John Erman, 1985) centred on the crisis produced by a young man's suffering from AIDS. This telefilm seemed to set a pattern, later to some extent reproduced in *Philadelphia*, whereby concerns of the hero's male lover are given less consideration than his family's. The climactic moments are reserved for the son's reconciliation with his father and the closing of ranks by the family. In 1986 *The A.I.D.S. Show* was broadcast; this was a version of the review originally staged by San Francisco's Theatre Rhinoceros. Meanwhile, in the UK, television spoke about AIDS to a narrower and more complicit audience. Channel 4 had broadcast as part of its *Eleventh Hour* series Stuart Marshall's videotape *Bright Eyes*, an attempt to expose and contest the homophobia prevalent in dominant media's representations of AIDS. Further videotapes on AIDS, attempting also to provide images and rhetoric designed to counter those of dominant media, were included in that part of The American Film Institute Video Festival (1987) organised by Bill Horrigan and B. Ruby Rich and called 'Only Human: Sex, Gender and Other Misrepresentations'. Evidence of the media homophobia combated by these videotapes could be found in P.B.S.'s *AIDS: A Public Inquiry*.

The television-viewing public's awareness, however confused, of HIV and AIDS issues seemed to be guaranteed by Rock Hudson's death in October 1985, shortly after he had starred in *Dynasty*. Viewers of *Dallas* and *Dynasty* learned that their stars had undergone blood tests for the presence of HIV and that an executive of the company making *Dynasty* had also died an AIDS-related death (Hancock & Carim 1986: 38). In the theatre of the 1980s, works such as Jeff Hagedorn's *One*, Bob Chesley's *Night Sweat*, Larry Kramer's *The Normal Heart* and William Hoffman's *As Is* centred on AIDS (Altman 1986: 23).

Photography responded to the health crisis in such exhibitions as the British 'Bodies of Experience' of 1989. In this, six photographers took the opportunity to record the effects of HIV infection on their lives. ACT-UP's 'Let the Record Show…' was displayed in 1987 in a window of New York City's New Museum of Contemporary Arts. The text begins with the words: 'By Thanksgiving 1981, 244 known dead … AIDS … no word from the President.' The final entry, after a year-by-year statement of known dead and silence from President Reagan, records that by Thanksgiving 1987 the number of known dead was 25,644 and that the presidential silence was broken at last with the declaration of an inquiry about the 'AIDS virus' to be conducted by the Department of Health and Human Services (Crimp 1988: 7–11).

Some at least of the video, theatre and exhibition work could be thought indirectly to illustrate Douglas Crimp's assertion that art has the power to save lives, though that power is consequent only on the replacement of the 'personal and elegiac' with practices that are 'critical, theoretical and activist' (Crimp 1988: 15). Perhaps it is the split between the personal/elegiac and the critical/activist that helps to explain the invisibility of the 'AIDS movie' in the 1980s. Both sides of the split are represented, as has been stated above, on television. *An Early Frost*, nevertheless, was somewhat unusual in being prime-time viewing. (*Bright Eyes*, for example, was eleventh-hour viewing in more than one sense.)

The film world is not devoid of overtly AIDS-centred work in the 1980s. Two films of 1985 for example – *Buddies* (Arthur J. Bressan Jr.) and *Parting Glances* (Bill Sherwood) – centre on themes of AIDS and gayness. Noticeably, though, these films might not be thought of as movies; that is, they are not made as entertainment for mass audiences. Their address is to those who are both politically aware and 'gay-friendly', a more narrowly conceived and ready-made audience than Hollywood movies could countenance. They are, in other words, preaching to the converted, and are made 'from the inside' for a complicit viewer. The stance of the dominant, entertainment movie has, it would appear, to be 'from the outside'.

There are what amount to fleeting references and oblique allusions aplenty to AIDS and HIV in dominant movies of the 1980s. *Dune's* (David Lynch, 1984) homosexual villain has suppurating sores on his face. In 1987, the Richard Dreyfuss character in *Stakeout* (John Badham) is told, 'I trust you practised safe sex.' That the sex referred to is heterosexual seems to make the remark playful, a joke which suggests rather than its obvious meaning its opposite – these lovers do not have to take the precautions which same-sex male lovers would socially be expected to take by this point in American history. In the same year, the Australian-made comedy *Les Patterson Saves the World* (George Miller) involves a certain Dr Herpes discovering the antidote to a repulsive skin ailment with the acronym of HELP. The fatal illness is exported to the United States by a Colonel Godowni by means of infected toilet seats. There are the usual difficulties in taking a serious stance on knockabout comedy, still more in attempting to estimate the 'message' of such comedy and its likely reception. This one seems to turn on the popular misconception that the syndrome with the new acronym of AIDS is 'merely' sexually transmitted, though the further twist is that it is an STD that can be caught from toilet seats.

Where AIDS resonates powerfully is in the paradoxical silence about it in *Torch Song Trilogy* (Paul Bogart, 1988) and, even in heterosexual terms, *Cocktail* (Roger Donaldson, 1988). The 1970s setting is necessarily foregrounded in both. When no such alibi is offered, as in Blake Edwards's *Skin Deep* of the same year, questions may be raised in the minds of their audiences. Evidence of this is discoverable in Kim Newman's remark in a review of the movie: 'Aside from one jokey and smug reference to AIDS, the film ignores modern sexual mores and assumes that Zach's promiscuity is of vital interest only to himself and to Alex' (Newman 1989: 215). One conclusion suggested by the evasiveness of dominant movies as well as by the complacency with which they suggest that the syndrome is linked exclusively with homosexuality might be that AIDS is treated with a similar nervousness to that which afflicted Hollywood's relation to the war in Vietnam while that war was still being waged. The massacre in the western *Soldier Blue* (Ralph Nelson, 1970) was taken by many contemporary audiences to reference such atrocities as My Lai, and *Little Big Man* (Arthur Penn, 1970) was held to concern the US's relation with the people of Vietnam as much as the white man's with 'redskin' society. Vietnam-era movies were 'read' for their subtexts, taken never overtly to be commenting on the war but often doing so obliquely. Could something analogous be claimed for the elusive 1980s 'AIDS movie'?

Some subtextual evidence

The movie genre which seems most evidently to deal in concepts which could easily be read as relevant to AIDS imagery and popular beliefs about HIV/AIDS is that of horror. The 1980s is, after all, elsewhere recognised for the genre's fascination with 'body horror', and not only in the work of David Cronenberg. Essays by Philip Brophy and Pete Boss, appearing in the same issue of *Screen*, are particularly helpful in this regard (Brophy 1986; Boss 1986). John Carpenter's *The Thing* (1982) centres on the process of body invasion. While the limiting of personnel in the Antarctic setting to men only is clearly motivated within the diegesis, the resultant victimisation of men's bodies by those of other men seems to have connotations beyond that of the overt situation, even if the director links the corporeal invasions only with cancer (not normally conceived as contagious). The movie's test for infected blood notably *precedes* the advent of a test for blood received from blood donors in social actuality. In the same year, *The Beast Within* (Phillipe Mora, 1982) depicts the transformation of a boy in a hospital bed until, echoing *Alien* (Ridley Scott, 1979), a creature erupts from his body.

A prominent feature of body horror is the reduction of the self to the body (Boss 1986: 16). This idea is most fully explored in Cronenberg's *The Fly* (1986). Here, the hero's (Jeff Goldblum) bodily declension (or, more neutrally, transformation – but increasingly into the body and eating habits of a fly!) becomes a central element. This occasions another, the negotiation of disgust between two former lovers. Tellingly, bodily transformation and sexual desire are linked. The hero, once timid about his teleportation experiments, is energised and emboldened to go further with them by his physical relationship with journalist Veronica Quaife (Geena Davis). The conjuncture of desire and bodily danger is found again in Frank Henenlotter's *Brain Damage* (1987). The hero takes his parasite, nicknamed Elmer, into the city. During a kiss with his girlfriend, Elmer darts out of his mouth to consume her brains. (The idea of the transfer of parasites through kisses, as well as coitus, is already to be found in Cronenberg's *Shivers*, 1974.) Chuck Russell's *The Blob* (1988) might be argued to allude to a persistent conspiracy theory about AIDS's genesis from a medical/scientific experiment gone wrong. In the movie, the Blob is born from a disastrous germ-warfare experiment. Then, too, the fundamentalist Rev. Meeker means to bring about 'the Rapture' – the destruction of the sinful world – from fragments of the Blob. By the end of the decade, the linking of casual sex and death is commonplace, occurring in, for example, the non-horror *Sea of Love* (Harold Becker, 1989), where anxiety is created about the potential lethality of one-night stands.

What this itemisation of possible movie references outwards to persistent popular beliefs and anxieties engendered by the pandemic could suggest is that these fears are too controversial and unsettling to be handled 'up-front' even by body horror, just as the social and political divisions to be found in Vietnam-era America seemed not to be capable of being addressed by movie entertainment. If this is a fair hypothesis, then it might be conceded that there are entire movies in this decade which centre on AIDS (while never mentioning the syndrome). *The Fly* seems the most obvious example from those already cited. Another body-horror worth considering in this regard is Brian Yuzna's *Society* (1989). The most obvious thematic is the amorality of the rich and powerful or that of conspicuous consumption – including consumption of human flesh. The climactic sequence has members of 'Society' interchanging body parts as well as fastening their mouths on the naked flesh of victims – 'sucking off' in the movie's own terms – which may be partly assimilated with their own. This visceral horror is topped by another, the 'shunting' sequence, in which a male body is turned literally inside out, by invasion of it via the anus. All the violations of 'human rules' perpetrated within this movie are fundamentally linked with sex. The first element in the attempted shunting of the hero Bill (Billy Warlock) is the planting of the handsome young villain's mouth on his. Yuzna reported that the audience was more upset by teenage boys apparently kissing than by the violence of the full-scale shunting. He asks, 'Why are people more squeamish about sex than horror?' (in Jones 1990: 12). Perhaps he may be missing the obvious here, that sexual dreads often underlie horror motifs. The surprisingly graphic connection between shunting and homosexual practices may precisely illustrate the point. Shunting here represents a lethal assault on the male body by means of anal penetration of it. *Society*'s sucking off and shunting are bizarre, and in the mundane realist terms which are so inappropriate for the sub-genre, impossible acts. Yet, they have a clear basis in culturally taboo areas of sexuality – fellatio and 'fisting', acts to be found within heterosexual practices but culturally projected on to exclusively homosexual subculture, to judge by this movie's evidence alone.

Adrian Lyne's *Fatal Attraction* (1987), categorised as other than a body-horror movie, is yet another. Brian De Palma, in the *Guardian* newspaper (17 December 1987) called it a 'postfeminist AIDS thriller'. The description ought to seem odd, since the movie at no point alludes to AIDS. In realist terms, this itself is odd, since the setting is New York City and one deeply-feared result of weekend playing around is infection with a condition that might then be transferred to a regular partner. The sex here cannot be 'safe'. Why otherwise would the later claim of pregnancy by Alex (Glenn Close) be thought to be so easily credible by Dan (Michael Douglas)? More commentators than De Palma linked the anxieties embodied by the weekend lover with AIDS. Peter McKay in his review of the movie makes a comment as complacent and heterosexist as the most unthinking of 'AIDS movies': 'It does not seem to me that it would put delinquent males off having one-night stands any more than AIDS has done. Sex is rarely subject to rational thought processes'

(McKay 1988: 9). J. Hoberman feels that the absence of specific mention of AIDS is because such mention is unnecessary: 'society has never needed a sexually transmitted killer virus to seek to regulate individual libidos' (Hoberman 1987: 68).

The conceptualisation of AIDS in the 1980s

The claim so far is that body-horror movies and those foregrounding the connection between death and sex, especially sex regarded as deviant by the criteria of political conservatives, have a close relation with AIDS beliefs of the 1980s. Such a claim sounds dangerously close to the reading-off of meaning. It makes good sense, therefore, to pause here to consider medical and more particularly popular belief about the syndrome. Doctors in Manhattan, Los Angeles and San Francisco were aware as early as 1979 of the long-term enlargement of lymph nodes in several gay patients and of the virulence of Kaposi's sarcoma and pneumocystis carinii pneumonia in young men who had been in full vigour before their illnesses. Expert medical opinion believed the underlying cause of these lethal versions of KS and PCP to be a breakdown in the sufferers' immune systems. These facts and interpretations were made public by the breaking of the story in the *New York Times* of 3 July 1981 under the headline 'Rare Cancer Seen in 41 Homosexuals'. Thus, from the beginning, a strong link was suggested between KS and homosexuality (not yet differentiated in terms of particular sexual practices or what might broadly be termed 'gay lifestyle'). KS itself was for a time popularly known as 'gay cancer'. Moreover, the new syndrome was linked with nothing other than male homosexuality in the early days of its advent. A close connection was further suggested between KS, PCP and sexually transmitted disease (see Weeks 1985: 46; Gilman 1988: 247). It may not therefore be surprising that one of the commonest acronyms in the early days of medical inquiry into the complex of KS and PCP was GRID – standing for 'gay-related immunodeficiency'. The acronym AIDS – acquired immune deficiency syndrome – was officially adopted by the Centers for Disease Control in 1982 (Grover, in Crimp 1988: 18–19). We learn from Jeffrey Weeks (1985) that an entire complex of symptoms relating to depressed immune systems was, in the first quarter of 1982, labelled as GRID though by that time it was known that intravenous drug users, haemophiliacs and Haitian immigrants into the United States were to be numbered among the sufferers. The intimacy and near exclusivity of the relationship between the syndrome and a particular sort of sexuality in the early 1980s, coupled with not coincidental public fear of that sexuality and its imagined manifestations, help to explain, though not to excuse, the silence of politicians about the medical catastrophe that was clearly happening. (Over 1,000 cases were reported in the US and Europe within 18 months.) President Reagan did not address the disaster, as has been noted already, until Thanksgiving 1987. As Kevin M. Cahill states, 'Almost without exception public leaders evaded the epidemic, avoiding even the usual expressions of compassion and concern. It was as if the sexual orientation of the victims made any involvement risky, and the politicians directed their courage and energies elsewhere' (Cahill 1983: 2). Furthermore, Cahill accuses the organised medical community of equal evasiveness as long as the connection between the epidemic and homosexuality was believed to be paramount.

It is difficult to tell with hindsight whether the absence of a clear cause or the eventual identification of HIV as causative produced greater panic in the 1980s. It was during 1983 and 1984 that French and American researchers isolated what was termed the human immunodefiency virus (HIV). A conflict continued thereafter for a time between, broadly, those who saw HIV as causative and those who took it as a sign of just another opportunistic infection. For the public, however, the message apparently offered by this identification prominently included notions of infection and contamination. The wish to isolate male homosexuality as having nothing to do with what in the UK was known as 'the general population' may well have been intensified by the fear of forced or surreptitious contagion of the pure by the polluted.

Such fear of contagion seems to give rise to a profound emotional need for a border, a fence behind which the uncontaminated can shelter, removed from alien threats, both foreign and 'other'. The psychological appeal of a border helps to explain the energy that went into the need to balkanise sexualities. Balkanisation beliefs were a means by which heterosexuality could shake off any admixture of the homosexual and clothe itself in pro-family sentiment in a bid to forget the freeing up of sexuality in general. The claimed sexual revolution of the 1960s and 1970s suggested that sex-as-pleasurable-adventure and the concomitant embracing of a measure of promiscuity were possibilities within heterosexuality, whether or not these had been adapted from homosexuality. The memory had to be suppressed if balkanised sexualities were to have any conviction. A wishful amnesia about the 1970s had to envelop much of the American populace.

This wishfulness may explain the President's appeal in the 1980s. The Reagan years were vigorously promoted as a sharp change in direction from those of President Carter. Militancy was to replace alleged softness, reinvigorated family values, so-called, those of years in a sort of sexual and social wilderness. Michael Paul Rogin sees in this President a demonologist, in the sense that a demonologist splits the world in two, investing the bad half with malign magical powers, making it a centre of evil whose dangerous influence has to be met with counter-subversion headed by the demonologist himself (Rogin 1987: xiii–xiv). The metaphorical aspect of cancer as 'alien invasion' has a particular application here. As Susan Sontag puts it, 'Cancer is a demonic pregnancy ... The patient is "invaded" by alien cells which multiply, causing an atrophy or blockage of bodily functions' (Sontag 1978: 18). Significantly, Rogin believes that Ronald Reagan was unique among post-Second World War presidents in separating benignity from malignity in terms of national boundaries and attempting to inspire his country to keep the national borders impermeable by the alien forces of malignancy.[1] 'Even the bodily well-being of the leader was equated with the health of the body politic ... the cancer that had been cut out of the president's body must now ... be excised from "the American mainland" as well' (the reference here being specifically to Nicaragua) (Rogin 1987: xv). In Reaganite thinking, HIV was an invader that might already have penetrated the body's borders to hide within it and become an alien that seemed like part of ourselves (see McGrath 1990: 144).

A writer who, with the hindsight of some twenty years, seems to have given proper weight to the crucial importance of the American socio-political and psychological setting for the emergence of AIDS is Casper G. Schmidt (1984). (Today he might, admittedly, be reckoned to be on the losing side of medical controversy when he is under-impressed with the explanation of AIDS in a viral origin.) Gender dysphoria, Schmidt argues, seems to have been afflicting the nation for years before the advent of AIDS because, for example, of the curbs placed on what he conceives as the phallic assertiveness of nuclear weapons. He gives due weight to far-reaching changes in American family life. He believes that women's demand for orgasm and the growth of recreational sex in the 1970s generated fear and guilt. Evidence for this is claimed in the public outcry for severer punishment for sexual licentiousness, as in the pre-AIDS call for chemical castration, so-called, of rapists.[2]

One of his principal theses is that homosexual males were the containers chosen by the American public for its disavowed impulses. The former, he believes, played the masochists to the sadists embodied by the New Right, turning their aggression inward upon their own bodies. This latter belief of Schmidt's is in line with his emphasis on the damage done to the human immune system by, for example, clinical depression, and his concern that the explanatory value of depression caused by public scapegoating is not given enough attention in the wake of the HIV discovery. The loading of unpalatable guilt on to a section of the public cast into suspicion and dislike because of other factors is seen to be not merely a result of homophobia. Susan Sontag concurs; she highlights 'the utility of AIDS in pursuing one of the main activities of the so-called neo-conservatives, the Kulturkampf against all that is called, for short (and inaccurately) the 1960s. A whole politics of "the will" – of intolerance, of paranoia, of fear of political weakness – has fastened on to this disease' (Sontag 1988: 63).

The pre-AIDS 'AIDS movie'?

The conclusion arrived at by Schmidt and Sontag is that much media and public reaction to AIDS in the early 1980s was explicable as an ingredient in a wider set of reactions. This is particularly useful in part explanation of a curious and initially baffling phenomenon: that some of the most pertinent-seeming movie commentaries on AIDS occur in a period when not even medical experts were as yet aware of the syndrome. Take, for example, David Cronenberg's *Shivers*. The setting is a luxury apartment block, Starliner Towers, situated on an island near Montreal. In it, materially successful Canadians enjoy their lifestyle free from interference from the outside world. Part of that lifestyle appears to be sexual promiscuity. Or perhaps sexual promiscuity is a result of parasite invasion, the movie also suggests. During the residents' sexual activities parasites – the result of a scientific experiment conducted in the Towers to replace organ transplants with parasite implantation – invade human bodies. Their presence seems to act as a powerful aphrodisiac producing more sexual activity and thus more opportunity for the spread of the parasites. They can also use the sanitation system, to creep via the plughole into a woman's body when she is taking a bath, for example, or to leap out of a washing machine. The appearance of the parasites disturbed some contemporary critics. Natalie Edwards likened it to that of a cross between a slug, a leech and 'particularly offensive penis' (Edwards 1975: 44) – fair comment, despite the curious choice of phraseology in the quoted section. Another way of looking at this appearance is that it has both penile and faecal connotations. To cite one of the alternative titles for *Shivers*, 'they came from within': that is, from within the body itself as well as sexual desires. The movie sets up a connection between sanitation and washing as wishful denial and, on the other hand, sex. The parasites by their workings and look mock that wishful denial.

Reviewers of the movie sometimes talk as if the outbreak of contagion has a moral relation with the 'unnatural' lives of the residents. One goes so far as to talk of Starliner Towers as 'already an incubator of deviant forms of behaviour' (Combs 1976: 62). This is echoed in the judgment that the parasites are 'literal embodiments of the general malaise attached to the place' (Leayman 1976: 22). Charles D. Leayman credibly links the parasites with the famous Don Siegel 'pods' of *Invasion of the Body Snatchers* (1956). In *Shivers*, however, it is as if the Towers' residents are already pods, as if the parasite invasion transforms their passionlessness into wild erotic hunger, their passivity into aggressive

the mainstream AIDS movie

activity. While the parasites give their lives a particular and controversial sense of purpose, their end is in destruction. Leayman comments on the version of liberation offered here by the parasites' aphrodisiacal stimulus by quoting from Marcuse's *Eros and Civilisation*: 'Left to pursue their natural objectives, the basic instincts of man would be incompatible with all lasting association and preservation' (Leayman 1976: 22). The British Board of Film Censors at the time opined that 'the permissive society' might be the result of 'this new form of plague' (Walker 1976). Today, this would seem more prescient if cause and effect were reversed. Curiously, Alexander Walker refers to the infestation under the heading of a 'parasitic *virus*' (Walker 1976, my emphasis). Robin Wood, after the Edinburgh Film Festival's exhibition of the movie, objected to its ideology in portraying lesbian acts as 'monstrous'; yet, he also detects 'a sort of perverse wish-fulfilment' as part of its message (quoted in Leayman 1976: 23). So many links with early 1980s AIDS reactions, then: fear of sex getting 'out of control', its 'deviancy' becoming thus linked with infection; that infection becoming equatable with a virus; sexual (and gay/lesbian) liberation so-called having a double-edged quality, of both advancing and threatening society; the virtual plague's origin in a scientific experiment that went wrong, as in so many of the popular mythologies surrounding the genesis of AIDS; even the desire, noted above, for a border echoed in the literally insular and insulated life of Starliner Towers; fears for wholesale destruction of 'the general population' as the consequence of the rampaging deviants' break-out from the island. Yet *Shivers* was released in 1974.

Today, a movie sequence in which a bisexual male infects his long-term female partner after a succession of one-night stands with gay males by exposing her to his blood would almost inevitably be read by worldwide audiences as a reference to HIV infection and transmission. There is no sequence with exactly this content in William Friedkin's 1980 movie, *Cruising*. Yet, one sequence which seemed to make no very obvious sense at the time seems almost prophetic now, if not of the facts of AIDS at least of their perception. The movie centres on the immersion of apparently heterosexual patrolman Steve Burns (Al Pacino) in the world of same-sex sado-masochist clubs and gay bars as part of an attempt by the New York police department to hunt down through his under-cover work a serial killer of apparently homosexual men. *Cruising* shows that the S/M world and that of the NYPD have a great deal to do with each other even outside the serial-killer hunt. This is neatly epitomised in the irony of Burns being denied entry to an S/M bar because he is not wearing police uniform – while all the sadists inside are! The movie suggests that Burns, bored, it would seem, by the predictability of his heterosexual relationship, finds a greater fascination in the teeming under-belly of the city than might be anticipated. Part of this must, in context, be acted. If he is to merge seamlessly into the urban gay life-style imaged by the movie, he has to simulate. Yet, by the end, he seems to have become so dangerously involved with one young man that the final murder is as likely to have been performed by him as by a(nother) serial killer. The infectivity of homosexuality, so often promoted as belief in early AIDS rhetoric, appears to be foregrounded in this narrative.

The sequence of particular suggestiveness in this regard is in the later section of *Cruising*, when Burns returns to his girlfriend Nancy (Karen Allen) in the morning after a night of apparent debauchery (whether real or simulated). He wears his SS leather jacket, presumably as the passport that allows him unquestioned access to the hidden world of gay S/M. Once home, he leaves his jacket off in order to shave. While he is in the bathroom at the mirror, Nancy tries the jacket on and regards her reflection. Crosscut with this moment is another, where Burns nicks his throat with the razor and his blood flows. There are other possible connotations in the relation set up between these two separate events. For example, there seems to be an oblique comment on the way that the feminine is repressed and dressed up to look ultra-macho in leather gear. What would have been opaque, though, to the general public in 1980, the link between infected blood and further contamination, is strongly suggested and would almost certainly be so taken in a post-AIDS viewing context. Robin Wood asks how Nancy could possibly have contracted the 'disease' – of gay sado-masochism? – from him (Wood 1986: 68). By rational logic, she could not have. In the irrational flights of imagination in the heat of AIDS panic, rationality is no longer the criterion, however, and would not be in a post-AIDS reading of the sequence.

The fascinated horror with which 1970s sexual adventurousness and unemotional sexual promiscuity are viewed is excellently illustrated by Richard Brooks' *Looking for Mr Goodbar* (1977). Here, a species of alibi is offered the heroine Teresa (Diane Keaton): fear of transmission of her genetically inherited scoliosis partly explains her retreat from the sort of committed relationship associated with planned child-bearing; in addition, her flight from her Roman Catholic family and particularly father (literally a patriarch) helps to ease the spectator into empathy with her detached, often amused, exploration of the New York subculture of one-night stands. The catastrophe with which her life ends is a brutal and rape-like stabbing – not, though, by one of the many insensitive heterosexual boors that she retreats from in much of the movie, but by a homosexual 'closet case' who punishes what he thinks of as her mockery of his masculinity with her murder. Even before then, *Looking for Mr Goodbar* has repeatedly suggested permeation of the 'straight' world of sexual experimentation with gay elements. The men in the succession of flashes of fun time in bars that forms the background to the credit sequence are coded as, in large part, gay. The soundtrack for some of the movie's disco and bedroom-sex sequences is provided by Donna Summers, diva and gay icon until she suddenly lost that status with her anti-gay Christian Right moralism in the early 1980s. The confusion which accounts for Teresa's picking up what transpires to be a homosexual man in a singles bar seems in this context not just to be a cruel irony. Rather, it is an indication of the proximity of those identifying in the 1970s as sexually liberated to those hitherto excluded from the approved heterosexual lifestyle. It is precisely the horror felt for the possibility of contamination, the guilt for association with licentiousness once putatively confined to the gay world, that Schmidt points to in his explanation for the way that homosexual men were scapegoated in the early days of AIDS panic. If this movie is within a 'sex = death' tradition, it is notable that the sex that seems to call for death in these contexts is popularly considered deviant.

Brian De Palma's *Dressed To Kill* (1980) could be – and has been – identified as another sex = death movie. The punishment inflicted on bored and sexually undervalued housewife Kate (Angie Dickinson) for one afternoon of irresponsible pleasure with a male pick-up seems out of all proportion to the 'sin' committed. The savagery of Kate's murder upset many of the audience, not all of them feminist in sympathy, when the movie was first shown. It stood out as the sort of over-the-top butchering of a woman who has given way to temptation not seen as graphically since 1960's murder of the impulse-thief Marion Crane in *Psycho*. That the killing is executed by a transvestite (not yet successfully transsexual) male is of course also a form of *hommage* to Alfred Hitchcock's esteemed work. Yet once again, the link between heterosexual promiscuity and deviant sexuality is firmly suggested to audiences in 1980 who cannot yet make the obvious connection to AIDS mythology.

Ridley Scott's *Alien* belongs, apparently, to a very different movie tradition. While gender may be a key issue in readings of the movie, sexuality does not seem to be. There could – just – be a strained attempt to see the John Hurt character as coded in terms of sexual deviancy, so that his quasi-pregnancy is less capricious than it might otherwise appear to the less clued-in spectator. Nevertheless, leaving sexuality out of the debate, we could still be struck by the way that parasitic invasion is so emotively linked here with the need for borders to be rigorously policed. It is Ripley herself (Sigourney Weaver) who attempts to follow procedure and take a severe, but correct, line when she is confronted by crisis. One of the party exploring the wilderness beyond the mothership has been assailed by an organism which has attached itself to his helmet (and subsequently finds entry to his body via attachment to his throat). Faced by his likely contamination by an entity of which the space-travellers know nothing, she tries to keep the ship air-locked and pure. She is criticised in the name of humane treatment. Her adamant refusal to admit her sick colleague is rendered void by the action of another who later turns out to be an android. The apparently successful operation thereafter on the crew member rendered unconscious by his contact with the unknown organism is shown to be nothing of the sort in the most famous sequence, when the alien erupts from the belly of its host as he eats ravenously along with the other crew members.

The need for vigilance in the protection of the mothership's healthful purity is economically and frighteningly proved by all the events on her from this point. That need is soon to be given added point in the persistent popular belief that HIV comes from outside national borders, so that if it comes from within then it comes from within external agents' bodies. These bodies may literally come from outside (the nation) or, less literally, from such wishfully denied areas as sexual deviancy and such people as intravenous drug users that society refuses to recognise as within it, as a part of itself.

Conclusion

The silence about AIDS in mainstream movie entertainment of the 1980s is profound. At times, that silence seems to be broken only by giggles about a syndrome which is implied to afflict only an isolated section with which 'the general population' need not concern itself, unless members of it turn away from family life – when they can expect little sympathy and major disaster. It might be easily accepted, on the other hand, that the manifest panics about AIDS and HIV in social actuality are addressed obliquely by body-horror movies and such moralities as *Fatal Attraction*. What would at first consideration appear to damage the credibility of this thesis would be the fair, persuasive objection that body-horror and moral tales about the lethal danger of sexual deviance are by no means exclusive to the post-AIDS-awareness 1980s. Not only are there several prominent examples of these movies in the 1970s, but in many remarkable ways they seem more pertinently to explore aspects of AIDS awareness than their 1980s counterparts.

This is at least curious. We are unlikely to rest satisfied with crediting pre-AIDS movies with the gift of prophecy or a bafflingly random and unconscious prescience. Some more convincing explanation is required. Could it not be that the plague thinking and moral panic which result, in social actuality, from public awareness of AIDS are not new but, rather, old attitudes given a new, sharper focus? The latter 1970s' campaigns against gay rights, for instance – Anita Bryant's activities in the US, Mary Whitehouse's in the UK – suggest more than their overt mission. The zeal with which family values, defined in a particular way by such campaigners, were lauded indicates a wider concern with shaking off the dread inheritance of the 'permissiveness' by which some politicians characterised the 1960s and 1970s. At one level, Reagan's presidency and Thatcher's period of prime-ministerial office are advertised by their administrations as radical breaks with the previous situations, the Carter years being particularly linked with softness and moral laxity. It is almost as if the Western world, and with it its mass entertainment, were gearing itself up for the arrival of AIDS. The new syndrome was difficult enough to come to grips with in medical terms, let alone to attempt to cure. Yet, the connotations of pollution, both corporeal and moral, were easily and swiftly attached to AIDS by popular journalism. These were embraced by a public anxious to create a bulwark between itself and what might as well have been plague-carriers, not only actual but potential.

The dreads that underlie such movies as *Looking for Mr Goodbar*, *Alien*, *Cruising* and which permeate Cronenberg's work in the pre-AIDS period have such power over audience imaginations because they have no easy explanation. Suddenly, with AIDS awareness, the inexplicable becomes readily comprehensible. AIDS is born, as it were, into a world where the very governments have geared themselves up to fight their perceptions of decadence, to draw clear lines between accepted and unacceptable lifestyles, to seek out 'the enemy within'. Is it any surprise that some 1980s movies do not create but rather fit into a tradition – a tradition established in an earlier decade? The fear of the 'other', of the enemy within the human body as well as the body politic, of contagion through contact with the polluted, can suddenly appear less paranoid. It can seem downright reasonable under the umbrella of paranoia.

Notes

1 Unique among presidents, but not among politicians of the Western world: in France, Jean-Marie Le Pen, leader of the extreme Right, called for mandatory nationwide testing and quarantining of those found to be carrying HIV.

2 This moralism and demand for punishment discerned by Schmidt could be detected in other areas not cited by him: in, for instance, the media coverage given to genital herpes in the summer of 1982, and the photographic emphasis of that coverage on the polluted (pretty, but herpes-ravaged, single women, for example) as opposed to 'herpes-free' – and, it has to be said, 'homely' – mothers and wives.

References

Altman, D. (1986) *AIDS and the New Puritanism*. London: Pluto Press.
Boss, P. (1986) 'Vile bodies and bad medicine', *Screen*, 27, 1, 14–24.
Brophy, P. (1986) 'Horrality: the textuality of Contemporary Horror Films', *Screen*, 27, 1, 2–13.
Cahill, K. M. (1983) *The AIDS Epidemic*. New York: St Martin's Press.
Combs, R. (1976) '*Shivers*', *Monthly Film Bulletin*, 43, 506.
Crimp, D. (ed.) (1988) *AIDS: Cultural Analysis/Cultural Activism*. Cambridge: MIT Press.
Edwards, N. (1975) 'The parasite murders', *Cinema Canada*, 22, 44–5.
Gilman, S. L. (1988) *Disease and Representation: Images of Illness From Madness to AIDS*. Ithaca: Cornell University Press.

Grover, J. Z. (1988) 'AIDS: keywords', in D. Crimp (ed.) *AIDS: Cultural Analysis/Cultural Activism*. Cambridge: MIT Press, 17–30.

Hancock, G. and E. Carim (1986) *AIDS: The Deadly Epidemic*. London: Victor Gollancz.

Hoberman, J. (1987) 'The Other, Woman', *Village Voice*, 1 December, 68.

Jones, A. (1990) 'Brian Yuzna's *Society*'. *Starburst*, 140, 9–12.

Leayman, C. D. (1976) '"They Came from Within": Siegel's "Pods" have in fact won out', *Cinefantastique*, 5, 3, 22–3.

McGrath, R. (1990) 'Dangerous liaisons: health, disease and representation', in T. Boffin and S. Gupta (eds) *Ecstatic Antibodies: Resisting the AIDS Mythology*. London: Rivers Oram Press, 142–55.

McKay, P. (1988) 'Fatal Attraction', *Evening Standard*, 7 March.

Newman, K. (1989) 'Skin Deep', *Monthly Film Bulletin*, 56, 215.

Rogin, M. P. (1987) *Ronald Reagan, the Movie, and Other Episodes in Political Demonology*. Berkeley and Los Angeles: University of California Press.

Schmidt, C. G. (1984) 'The group-fantasy origin of AIDS', *Journal of Psychohistory*, 12, 37–78.

Sontag, S. (1978) *Illness as Metaphor*. New York: Farrar, Straus and Giroux.

_____ (1988) *AIDS and Its Metaphors*. New York: Farrar, Straus and Giroux.

Walker, A. (1976) *Evening Standard*, 29 April.

Weeks, J. (1985) *Sexuality and Its Discontents: Meanings, Myths and Modern Sexualities*. London: Routledge and Kegan Paul.

Wood, R. (1986) *Hollywood from Vietnam to Reagan*. New York: Columbia University Press.

04

Timothy M. Boon

Health education films in Britain, 1919–39: production, genres and audiences

Health education films, unlike most of the other cinematic subjects of this book, did not simply represent medicine and health, they were conceived as their instruments: each film was, in one way or another, intended to alter public behaviour to enhance health. The brief compass of this chapter provides space to discuss the first 20 years of the genre in Britain. The films I discuss here have received little serious attention from film historians or members of the film studies community.[1] Scholars usually opt to study better known, or simply better made, examples of the cartoon, melodrama and documentary genres with which they are associated. But the size of the genre is sufficient in itself to demand study and explanation. Between the foundation of the Ministry of Health in 1919 and the outbreak of the Second World War, approximately 350 health films were produced or shown in Britain. For the historian of medicine, this provokes questions: who made these films and why did health education matter so much to them? Why did the films differ so much in style? And who saw them? Fortunately, survival of films is good enough (mainly in the National Film and Television Archive) and just sufficient paper documentation persists in the archives to be able to answer many of these questions.

Most of those responsible conceived of these films as part of a broader health education enterprise. Health education of the public was chosen as a mode of quasi-political activity by groups of activists, very often organised into voluntary health associations. These organisations were an established part of the mixed public/private 'economy' of the interwar public sphere. The CCHE's 1939 *Health Education Year Book* lists 76 such voluntary associations, of which 38 had films in distribution. Most active participants in these associations believed that private-sector delivery of health education

– the arrangement in place before 1919 – was the correct way to deliver the service and that it should continue; for them health propaganda was not the state's business. The heterogeneous groups of people who made up the associations included aristocrats seeking to retain a type of political role in a period of decline; aspirant middle-class professionals – including doctors – making a political place for themselves or asserting a particular view of medicine; and women, before 1928 deprived them of the vote, finding a type of political stage on which to act. The voluntary health associations differed over what they believed mattered to public health; for some it was particular diseases, whilst others worried about the moral state of the population, their uptake of medical services, or their genetic decline. Later, questions of public health became entangled in issues of more general social reform and citizenship.

The effect of these differing concerns was magnified by the policy of the Ministry of Health, whose ministers and officials confirmed in 1920 that practical health education should not normally be undertaken centrally, but should be delegated to these voluntary health associations and to the Medical Officers of Health employed by all local councils. Ministry officials developed a fundamentally hierarchical model of communication, with educated intermediaries sitting between the State and the public. As George Newman, the first Chief Medical Officer, put it: 'governmental action is the outcome of public opinion, and this in turn is formed by the more educated section of the people and by individual exponents' (Newman 1925: 17–18). The voluntary associations were seen as key members of that 'more educated section'. The Ministry allowed for only one potential exception to this delegation model; that in times of crisis, symbolised for them by the influenza epidemic of 1918, the Ministry might take direct charge of health education (Boon 1999: 90–1).

The organisations that assumed a role in health education used a wide range of media in addition to films, for different audiences: lectures, meetings, conferences, books, journals, editorials, newspapers, posters, leaflets and broadcasting. Films were generally conceived as tools of persuasion of the general public. Going to the cinema was a highly significant aspect of British social life, as Jeffrey Richards (1984) has shown, and health educators hankered after a share of that audience. The *Health Education Year Book* stated in 1939 that 'the value of the Film as an impressive visual medium of education needs no emphasis' (CCHE 1939: 111), betraying a commonly held faith that the power of celluloid could be put to use for propaganda purposes. Allen Daley, Medical Officer of Health for Blackburn, speaking about health education lectures, commented that 'practically everywhere audiences of 1,000 to 3,000 can be obtained: the former for lantern lectures, the latter for those where cinema films are shown' (Daley 1924: 308). As films were expensive to make – according to Daley in 1924, even the cheapest were normally beyond the reach of individual local health authorities – the fact that so many were made confirms the high estimate of their propaganda power.[2]

For all groups commissioning health films, there came to be a choice to be made between types of film and filmmaker. Over half of interwar health education titles were made by professional filmmakers, of many complexions, including then well-known companies such as Bruce Woolfe's Gaumont-British Instructional (British Instructional Films before 1933). But large numbers were also made by tiny companies, for instance the National Progress Film Company, which occupied what Rachael Low describes as 'a hinterland of filmmakers and agents, largely unknown to the rest of the film industry, arranging for the production and dissemination of publicity films' (Low 1979b: 128). And, from 1935, the more familiar names of the documentary film movement – including Paul Rotha, Edgar Anstey and Arthur Elton – were increasingly involved as they began to ply their trade in the commercial sector.

The films can be seen as products of occasions of agreement between the organisations commissioning them and filmmakers. This was so at the general level, for example that suppliers of funds made possible the production of films. But it was also so at the level of detailed negotiation of the contents of films and how they were cinematically expressed. Every example where a production archive survives reveals the influence on the final film of many different types of individual: specialist doctors, local government officials, funders and experts of one kind or another. A particularly striking example is the way that nutrition scientist John Boyd Orr rewrote the last third of Paul Rotha's 1943 film *World of Plenty* (Boon 1997). In other words, individual films are cultural artefacts contingent on the extended groups responsible for their production. Similarly, the long-standing generic similarities of the several sub-classes of film were products not only of the adoption of existing genres, but also of long-term relationships between public health organisations and filmmakers. The director Mary Field (1896–1968) for example, who worked for British Instructional Films, sat on the propaganda committee of the British Social Hygiene Council from 1929 for at least a decade. Orr was associated with the documentarists from 1929 to at least 1947. And the instances of agreement that produced films often extended beyond consensus about the form the film should take to shared political and cultural values (Boon 1999: 149, 245–7, 9–12).

Voluntary health associations and 'moral tales'

The majority of health education films, certainly up to 1939, were 'moral tales': fictional stories presented as entertainment films using moral narratives (often featuring sequences of innocence, transgression, punishment and atonement) intended to convey a health implication. This genre drew on traditions in melodrama, themselves deriving from popular theatrical traditions of the nineteenth century, as Raymond Williams has shown (1983: 15–16). It was the voluntary health associations that particularly favoured this genre, from the time of the venereal disease film *Whatsoever a Man Soweth*, in 1918, onwards. The only association consistently receiving substantial central or local government funding, the National Council for Combating Venereal Disease – renamed the British Social Hygiene Council (BSHC) in 1925 – generated, or handled British distribution of, as many as 45 films between 1919 and 1939. Over 130 films were produced by other, privately funded, voluntary associations. The Health and Cleanliness Council (H&CC), responsible for 19 films including the *Giro the Germ* cartoon series, was dependent on concealed commercial funding, from the electrical industry, and probably also from soap manufacturers (Daley 1959: 34). Of local voluntary associations, it was the housing associations that produced the largest numbers of films. Two examples will give a clear idea of the genre.

Deferred Payment, made by Mary Field in 1929, was the first collaboration between BSHC and British Instructional Films. It was described as 'a dramatic film dealing with the need for ante-natal treatment of an infected mother and emphasising the danger of "quack" treatment' (BSHC 1928–29: 34). The film was described as being made with the co-operation of Dr Marjorie Smith-Wilson, Dr Margaret Rorke (Medical Officer in charge of the female VD department at the Royal Free Hospital) and Dr Morna Rawlins (Assistant Director of the equivalent department at Guy's Hospital). Its scenario was approved by the chairmen of the BSHC's propaganda and executive committees and by the senior venereologist Colonel L. W. Harrison.[3] This group produced a film typical of the 'moral tale' genre, as the catalogue description, quoted in full, reveals:

> The story of a wireless officer who, transferred to home service and anxious to marry his old sweetheart with a clean bill of health, visits a quack doctor to whom he makes heavy payments for so-called 'treatment'. Thinking that he is cured, he marries. The wife, when the first baby is expected, attends an ante-natal clinic, where she is informed that she is infected with Syphilis, but that with careful treatment the baby will probably be born healthy. The husband then visits a doctor and also undergoes treatment. A healthy girl is born, but when a second child is expected in two years' time, the husband persuades his wife, in spite of the doctor's advice, that it is not necessary for her to take any more treatment as they are all well. A baby boy is born, who grows up a weakling, and eventually it is ascertained that his eyesight has been damaged by Syphilitic infection. Through treatment the little boy's sight is saved, but so weakened that it will affect his choice of profession. The father realises that the child will continue to pay indefinitely for his fault. (Crew 1935: 42)

This film conforms to Annette Kuhn's (1988) analysis of the mode of address of earlier VD films. Aimed at mixed audiences, men and women each have a figure with whom to identify – Leonard and Gladys Dawson – each of whom is given a speech at the end (on caption boards) expressing their own culpability for their son's condition. Cinematically, the film is similar in kind to earlier VD films, with its limited and literal use of editing and of close ups, and the universal use of static shots. This is an unaffected, literal mode of film style in which Leonard's 'fault', illicit and dangerous sex, is vigorously suggested, but not stated. The literalistic style of filmmaking tends to enhance the moralistic and authoritarian strands in the film relating to medical figures. The representation of the quack doctor first visited by Leonard is in sharp contrast to the doctor at the Maternity and Child Welfare Centre who diagnoses Gladys' syphilis. The quack smokes, wears a bow tie and winks and beckons to his female typist to leave the room when the nervous Leonard arrives. The doctor, on the other hand, white-suited, straight-tied, is represented by his gestures as deeply troubled by the tragedy of VD. His authority is signalled literally by his being filmed standing up looking down on Gladys who looks up at him. When Leonard confesses about the quack, the doctor addresses him as disobedient to medical authority: 'It was foolish and you have lost valuable time, which makes it more difficult to cure you.' *Deferred Payment*, in proposing obedience to medical authority, and a moral regime for the prevention of VD, presented a conservative moral universe of stable marriage, clean of the taint of promiscuity with its necessary concomitant VD.

The four-strong *Giro the Germ* series exemplifies some of the characteristics of H&CC films. Rachael Low sums up the style of these black-and-white films: 'the animation was crude, with passages repeated for the sake of economy, and the lesson was contained in a jingle which appeared as titles in the silent version or was sung in the sound version' (Low 1979b: 152). *Giro the Germ (Episode One)* (1927) has germs ('giros') as imp-like creatures mischievously intent on spreading disease. As the year book says; 'while the audience laugh at this amusing little creature they realise how dangerous he is' (CCHE 1939: 124). Cavorting in an uncovered dustbin, the 'giros' call 'Taxi!' and clutch onto the legs of

Figure 1: *The Road to Health* (Brian Salt, Gaumont-British Instructional, 1938). One of the British Social Hygiene Council's moral tales about venereal disease. BFI Stills, Posters and Designs. Crown copyright – HMSO

passing flies. Landing on a windowsill they reject one house as unsuitable: 'No good! This is a clean house. About turn!' A caption reads: 'If your house is dirty and the house-fly comes and sees, they will bring the Giros – they will bring disease.' They select the house of a character named 'Grimy': 'Said Grimy to the Giro "If this were Friday night, I'd up and go and wash myself and give you all a fright".' Grimy smokes a pipe carrying a 'giro' and his wife drinks from a similarly infected teacup and they both become (instantly) sick. They call the doctor:

> Here comes the wise old Doctor man
> To try to save them if he can.
> And if he does, he's sure to say:
> 'It's Giro's made you ill today!
> Here's the soap and water.
> See the Giros run!
> Now in soapy slaughter
> Giro's day is done!

Here, as in the VD films, it is the doctor, with his authoritative pronouncements, who restores order, and a clear deference to medical authority is implied for the viewer identifying with Mr or Mrs Grimy. The doctor instructs Grimy to cover the bin and his wife to scrub the house. Order is thereby restored. The structure of the film is a fable in which dirtiness is associated with punishment in disease. But it is also redemptive in that it is implied that cleanliness not only brings freedom from disease but also a restoration of moral order.[4]

Other film producers

Although the Ministry of Health placed a responsibility on local authorities to undertake health education, they did not provide funds for filmmaking. The Medical Officers, who were the main players in health education in the public sector, could usually not afford to make films, and, if they did, it was on an amateur basis. The result was that many Medical Officers showed health films, but few made them. There were two main exceptions to this rule. Bermondsey Borough Council made about 18 films as part of their experiment in municipal socialism, often using special projector vans to show efforts such as *Where There's Life There's Soap* in the borough's streets (see Lebas 1995). This film featured the verse, designed for children to chant, 'I'd wash if I'd been born a fish/Or e'en a humble frog./Alas! Alas! my habits are,/the habits of a hog.' The other interesting cluster of local authority films is the five or so made by Medical Officers to promote diphtheria immunisation, at that stage permitted by the Ministry of Health, but not promoted by them. *The Empty Bed*, made in Camberwell in 1935, is an interesting surviving example (Boon 1999: 187–90).

Social problems, health and documentary

From the mid-1930s, the gas industry pioneered a subtle commercial use of documentary film, as they employed it in their public relations strategy. They had the problem that the electricity industry, their main competitor for domestic fuel supply, was promoting itself as an avatar of modernity (Rotha 1973: 155; Luckin 1990: 9–22). Gas fought back, representing itself as a socially-conscious modern industry, using films such as *Housing Problems* (1935) and *Enough to Eat?* (1936) (see Boon 1993). These were not strictly health education films, but documentary films presented as discussions of public health issues *qua* social problems. They were not made by the commercial trade, but by documentarists, ranged on the political left and more or less strongly influenced by the rigours of Russian montage theory. The gas industry's 1939 film catalogue, 'Modern Films on Matters of Moment', asserted that their films were 'dramatic accounts of some of the problems of modern Citizenship in which the general public and the Gas Industry have a common concern … Nutrition, Housing Reform and Public Health'. They stated that the films 'will serve not only to make known the activities of the Gas Industry and the responsibilities which the Industry has taken upon itself in matters of Public Health and general welfare, but also help to articulate the public knowledge in the major social problems' (BCGA 1939: 3). The fact that 'the problems of modern *Citizenship*' were presented as the grounds for discussion by the Gas Industry and the public confirms for us the importance of citizenship as a common ideology when documentary filmmakers were involved.

Enough to Eat? (also known as *The Nutrition Film*) falls into three main sections – on laboratory and social survey research in nutrition; on the activities of local, national and international organisations; and proposed policy for England – with an introduction and a conclusion. The film's soundtrack is dominated by the narration spoken by the biologist and public figure, Julian Huxley, with no music or other sounds. Its visuals have been edited to fit the soundtrack, and are of several kinds: literal, whether synchronised as in the case of Huxley's appearances, or tied to the soundtrack, as when Huxley states, 'here you see the boys of the school being weighed and measured', or literal and specific, as in the use of animated diagrams. There is also substantial use made of figurative visuals, as in the montage of newspaper stories and nutrition publications that starts the film, and the use of suggestive shots to accompany abstract statements on the soundtrack, as for example where the pitch forking of hay is used to accompany a speech from Lord Astor on world trade.

Edgar Anstey, director of *Enough to Eat?*, later described the film as 'a scientific argument deployed by scientists'.[5] According to contemporary categories, it was a descriptive or *reportage* film, as opposed to the more poetic and formalistic impressionistic documentary style (Rotha 1936: 225). It is clear that the adoption of the *reportage* style was a deliberate choice to represent a social and scientific subject in the supposedly more neutral and 'scientific' style of a film lecture. This choice may have been compounded by the controversy surrounding the nutrition question in 1936; those involved had made a deliberate choice to intervene in a politically disputed area, and the adoption of an 'objective' form was a sophisticated move.[6]

Government

The Ministry of Health, because they had delegated health education to the periphery, were directly responsible for the production of very few films in the interwar period. But officials at the Ministry were discussing the possibility of a publicity film *about* its responsibilities from shortly after the reintroduction of an intelligence and public relations infrastructure from 1935, after 15 years in which financial stringency had prevented any such activity. With effect from March 1935, a combined Intelligence and PR Division serving the Ministry of Health and the Board of Education was established, with the civil servant S. H. Wood as its Director. New emphasis on public relations was typical of government in this period. The film historian Paul Swann explains: 'as a consequence of the arrival of universal suffrage and the growing extent to which government departments intervened in the lives of the general public, politicians … were compelled to pay much greater attention to public opinion in Britain than they had previously' (Swann 1989: 2).

Wood was quick to clarify the three different roles of the new division as he saw them: intelligence was ensuring that 'information relating to subjects with which the Department deals is readily available when and where it is wanted'; public relations was the giving of intelligence information on request; whereas publicity was 'the provision of information on the initiative of the Ministry rather than at the request of the public'. It was this last rediscovered role which was performed with new energy in the second half of the 1930s. 'The object of publicity at its best,' he argued, 'is to try to make the work of the Ministry a matter of legitimate interest to ordinary men and women' (Wood 1935).

From 1936 the Ministry had a fortnightly meeting to 'determine from above' what subjects should be publicised. The suggested shortlist of items for discussion at the regular meetings included both films and responsibility for direct health propaganda. Both pre-war Health Ministers, Kingsley Wood and Walter Elliot, viewed the public relations committee as significant enough to chair its fortnightly meetings. It was only with the rise of public relations that the conditions were right for a new mode of health film to come into being. The documentarists, who had been nurtured within government at the Empire Marketing Board and GPO, were creatures of government publicity. And it was their model of film-making that appealed to the officials at the Ministry of Health; Ministry civil servants saw themselves as experts in administration, and they looked to the documentarists as experts in filmmaking.

This eventually produced, on the eve of war, a film called *Health for the Nation*, directed by John Monck, sometime associate of Robert Flaherty. From the start there was agreement that the film should be a film about England, its history, its consequent health problems, and the work of the Ministry in alleviating them. Not tied to a particular campaign or health issue, it was designed to create in the public mind a picture of the concerns of the Ministry of Health; in Wood's terms it was 'publicity'. *Health for the Nation*, in contrast to *Enough to Eat?* is an impressionistic documentary covering its material at a stately pace, constructed following the principles of dialectical montage – structuring via thesis, antithesis and synthesis – enunciated by Sergei Eisenstein and Vsevelod Pudovkin (see Boon 2004). It features lyrical orchestral music, dissolving scenes of English countryside, industrial scenes, people at work and in their everyday lives and sporadic, poetic, commentary spoken by Ralph Richardson. The thesis of the film is the industrial development of the country, an impressionistic cinematic 'English Journey' accompanied by industrial location sounds, introducing the coal, iron, steel districts of England, the textile industry, transport. The closing stanzas of this reel introduce the antithesis, that 'out of iron and coal and steel we've built … slag heaps and smoke, soot upon the fields, forests of chimneys. In a hundred and fifty years we have changed the face of Britain. We have changed it forever.' The antithesis is amplified by a section on 'The people', and the impact of industrialisation on their health. The catastrophic interpretation of industrialisation is then given a forceful expression in an impressionistic sequence of panning shots of industrial areas, accompanied by the score at its most sombre: 'Overcrowded, poor, under the shadow of disease. Into filthy hovels, into ill-ventilated factories and mines was crowded the manpower, the driving force of industry: men, women and children.' The synthesis is introduced by a sequence of the dates and titles of Public Health Acts, culminating in the foundation of the Ministry of Health. The film builds on this with a series of cases, many of them compared with the state of things in the nineteenth century, presented in impressionistic manner with sparse commentary: water supply and drainage, house building, refuse disposal, medical services, infant welfare, school meals and milk, the school medical service, National Health Insurance, pensions. The concluding sections give an upbeat account of progress in responding to the health problems of the previous century. In sum, the film is a portrait of the English nation. Its visual language presents established characteristics of the English Nation, the underlying rurality, a people defined by industrial work. England here is an essentially prosperous modern nation; the achievement of this modernity has had a serious cost in terms of health problems, but these are presented either as already solved or as in process of solution (Boon 1999: 286–300; Boon 2004).

Audiences

The archives, periodicals, histories and biographies can yield a rich picture of the types of health film made during the interwar period, as the first sections of this chapter have sketched. More problematic is the question of who saw the films. For us, who inhabit a world saturated with surveys, focus groups and audience evaluation, the interwar period is a foreign country. It seems that those responsible for these films simply assumed that health education worked. All they asked was that significant numbers saw the films. Data on mainstream cinema-going reveal that 18 million per week went to 'the flicks' (Rowson 1936). For health education films specifically, some specialised archives hold detailed reports. For example, the BSHC's travelling projection outfit visited Southport

Figure 2: The world industrialisation has wrought, from *Health for the Nation* (John Monck, GPO Film Unit, 1939). BFI Stills, Posters and Designs, courtesy The Royal Mail Film Archive.

in September 1922, where a total of 1,700 people saw films at three venues: 'At each meeting the halls were full, many having to be turned away. In many cases it was necessary to admit the public an hour before the beginning of the showing' (BSHC 1922: 29).[7] And, because of the BSHC's policy of targeting some propaganda films separately at men and women, there are disaggregated data about gender split in audiences. So there is some potential to draw up a picture by mapping these geographically-specific reports; for example, at Stoke on Trent in February 1923, 3,834 men and 4,274 women watched VD films in a period of a fortnight.[8] There is sufficient information to make comparisons, but, at best, we can only say how many men and women saw particular films in particular places at particular times. And the records are remarkably short on references to any impact on behaviour.

For a more intimate sense of the impact of these films, we would have to turn to more sociological sources. The first organisation in Britain to apply sociological technique to the cinema audience was Mass Observation, the home-brew social anthropology organisation. A research programme outlined in 1937 directed observers to record details of the size, composition, appearance and behaviour of cinema audiences, reaction to films and overheard conversations. A questionnaire was also circulated to cinema audiences in spring 1938 (Richards and Sheridan 1987: 4). None of this study was directed to health education films, rather it traced responses to the ordinary diet of cinema-goers, which from at least 1925 was 95 per cent Hollywood product (Corrigan 1983: 26). One can be too pedantic of course, and the generality of the responses does give a sense of the context within which audience members might have placed the health education films they saw. For example, the questionnaire responses show that drama and tragedy, into which category we might place the majority of the VD dramas, was the second most popular genre, with 21 per cent of women and 17 per cent of men placing it as their favourite. So we may conclude that the VD film producers had selected a popular genre, but we cannot say that the audiences believed them to be particularly fine examples.

In the absence of detailed contemporary analysis of what films meant to individuals, we are obliged to fall back on what can be said about spectators in general and their relationship to the films. We may say that the different genres of health film we have already encountered, by using different modes of address to their viewers, *asserted* particular relationships to exist between the authority they represented and their audiences. In the case of health education films produced by voluntary associations, the address drew on long traditions of the class authority associated with aristocratic power and nineteenth-century charitable activity. This carried political implications of an older deferential politics. In the case of documentary, the address drew upon a newer professionalised view of how society should be run, and it carried a citizenship discourse in which the films' audiences were invoked as active and responsible members of the state.

The documentary-maker and theorist Paul Rotha touched on the different modes of action of different genres in his landmark text *Documentary Film* (1936). He argued that documentary demands 'from an audience an attention quite different from that of a fictional story. In the latter, the reaction of the spectator lies in the projection of his or her character and personality into those of the actors playing in the story and the ultimate result of a series of fictional complications ... [whereas] in watching documentary, the audience is continually noting distinctions and analysing situations and probing the "why" and the "wherefore"' (Rotha 1936: 141–3). Rotha is here outlining in a partisan way what Bill Nichols' essay 'Documentary theory and practice' later called 'mode of address' (Nichols 1976/77). This mode of analysis has the value of directing our attention to the choices of cinematic technique made by directors and other participants in the production of health films, and to the way that has led to the construction of a cinematic 'voice of public health'. The mode of address of individual health education films embodies the voice of medical authority in public health to potential patients. As such, it is a vehicle of the power relations of medicine. Briefly, in Nichols' formulation, mode of address may be 'indirect', as is found in fiction films such as *Deferred Payment*, where the viewer follows the action of the film through identification with the characters on the screen; footage is generally literal, showing the fictional world the characters inhabit. Alternatively, the mode of address may be 'direct', as is found in most documentary films, *Enough to Eat?* for example, where an individual – sometimes seen on the screen – speaks directly to viewers; visual images are either the literal footage of the speaker or illustrative footage backing up the argument. Each of these modes of address implies a position for the viewer in relation to the film and its authors; passive in the case of indirect address of the fiction film and active in the case of direct address of the documentary. In the context of public health films, filmmakers and their production allies may be seen to be making assumptions about the degree of active engagement in health issues by their choice of film genre; whilst the address of the 'moral tale' fiction-based health education film implies taking the opportunity of the viewer's passive state to convey health 'messages', documentary implies the active engaged citizen.[9]

This approach can take us one stage further with the question of the cinematic voice of public health. Health education films adopting the fictional mode were products, as we have seen, of voluntary associations, members of the private sphere of medical practice and their filmmaking allies, private sector companies. These groups tended to have conservative views about society, as about medicine. In many respects they conform to the organicist model of conservative thought proposed by Karl Mannheim and discussed by David Bloor. Under this view, 'organic images of family unity' dominate, and it is believed that

> rights, duties, obligations and authority ought not to be spread uniformly. They should be unequally distributed according to generation, rank and role. Further-more, justice ... naturally adopts an autocratic but flexible and benevolent form, being gradually adjusted to the changing ages, responsibilities and conditions of its members. (Bloor 1991: 63)

The views of the mass audience held by these groups tended therefore to be hierarchical – perhaps almost literally of 'the great unwashed'. But, for them, the appropriate address to the mass audience was via appeal to them not in the mode of oratory to the group, but intimately, to an audience of individual subjects, each separately identifying with one or more of the film's characters. At the level of simile, we may see this as being like a series of doctor/patient encounters with docile, respectful, social subordinates.[10]

The address of documentaries, on the other hand, is also to the audience as individuals, but in a different mode. The wide groups responsible for the production of these films tended to have liberal or left political affiliations, and assumed that the audience would be as discerning in cinematic technique as it was expected to be in political matters. In their attitudes to the mass audience, they can be seen as exhibiting characteristics of the Enlightenment or 'natural law' style of thought opposing conservative thought style in Mannheim's account:

> [This is] individualistic and atomistic. This means that it conceives of wholes and collectivities as being unproblematically equivalent to sets of individual units ... individual persons are made up of their reasoning or calculating facility and a set of needs and desires, plus, of course, their kit of natural rights. (Bloor 1991: 63)

The oratorical metaphor applies more directly to documentaries; the audience is conceived as a collective of individuals' 'reasoning faculties'. The action proposed for them is col-lective, it is that which 'we' ought to do as members of society. This mode of address resonates with public health as mass intervention via the state.

Conclusion

In the 'Age of the Dream Palace', millions of people every year also went to see health education films in town halls, mechanics institutes and other public venues. Their precise experience of this genre is lost to the historical record, or at least dissipated throughout it at a very low concentration. But, by studying the surviving films, the written records and contextual evidence that persist in libraries and archives, it is possible to recognise the importance of a genre that, if only in the sheer numbers of films and spectators, formed a significant part of how health and medicine were cinematically represented for our forebears before the Second World War.

Notes

1 My PhD thesis (Boon 1999), of which this chapter is a brief statement, is the first study of the whole range of interwar health education films. Readers seeking more detail on the matters discussed here should refer to this. Rachael Low's two works on 1930s non-fiction films are invaluable catalogues (Low 1979a; 1979b). Annette Kuhn's work on VD films is a useful analysis of part of this territory (Kuhn 1988).

2 Daley 1924: 311, 313. For discussion of costs of production see Boon 1999: 43, 177–8.

3 BSHC propaganda committee, 9 July 1929, CMAC SA/BSH/C, London: Wellcome Library.

4 The role of flies in public health campaigns is discussed in Rogers 1989.

5 Anstey interviewed in *On the March*, series on the history of the *March of Time* Newsreel, Flashbacks production, 1985.

6 For the nutrition debate, see Smith 1986.

7 BSHC Propaganda Committee meeting, 16 Oct 1922, CMAC SA/BSH/C, p.29.

8 BSHC Propaganda Committee meeting, 19 Mar 1923, CMAC SA/BSH/C, p.111.

9 Several authors have explored the implications of Nichols' distinction for various types of documentary film; see Pearson 1982, Kuhn 1988.

10 In H. B. Brackenbury's book, *Patient and Doctor* (1935), 'The patient is construed as a passive object, expecting from the doctor certain qualities – knowledge, skill, carefulness, judgement, sympathy, understanding, moral character and ethical conduct' (Armstrong 1982: 113).

References

Armstrong, D. (1982) 'The doctor-patient relationship: 1930–1980', in P. Wright and A. Treacher (eds) *The Problem of Medical Knowledge: Examining the Social Construction of Medicine*. Edinburgh: Edinburgh University Press, 109–22.

Bloor, D. (1991) *Knowledge and Social Imagery*. Chicago: University of Chicago Press.

Boon, T. M. (1993) 'The smoke menace: cinema, sponsorship, and the social relations of science in 1937', in M. Shortland (ed.) *Science and Nature. BSHS Monograph* 8. Oxford: BSHS, 57–88.

_____ (1997) 'Agreement and disagreement in the making of *World of Plenty*', in D. Smith (ed.) *Nutrition in Britain: Science, Scientists and Politics in the Twentieth Century*. London: Routledge, 166–89.

_____ (1999) *Films and the Contestation of Public Health in Interwar Britain*. Unpublished PhD dissertation, University of London.

_____ (2000) '"The shell of a prosperous age": history, landscape and the modern in Paul Rotha's *The Face of Britain* (1935)', in C. Lawrence and A. Mayer (eds) *Regenerating England: Science, Medicine and Culture in the Interwar Years. Clio Medica* 60. Amsterdam: Rodopi, 107–48.

_____ (2004) 'Industrialisation and catastrophe: the Victorian economy in British film documentary, 1930–50', in M. Wolff and M. Taylor (eds) *The Victorians Since 1901: Histories, Representations and Revisions*. Manchester: Manchester University Press.

British Commercial Gas Association. (1939) *Modern Films on Matters of Moment* (catalogue). London: BCGA.

Brackenbury, H. (1935) *Patient and Doctor*. London: Hodder and Stoughton.

CCHE (1939) *Health Education Year Book*. London: CCHE.

Corrigan, P. (1983) 'Film entertainment as ideology and pleasure: a preliminary approach to a history of audiences', in J. Curran and V. Porter (eds) *British Cinema History*. London: Wiedenfeld and Nicolson, 24–35.

Crew, T. (1935) *Health Propaganda, Ways and Means*. Leicester: Bell.

Daley, A. (1959) 'The Central Council for Health Education: the first twenty-five years', *Health Education Journal*, 17, 24–35.

Daley, W. A. (1924) 'The organisation of propaganda in the interests of public health', *Public Health*, (September), 305–13.

Kuhn, A. (1988) *Cinema, Censorship and Sexuality, 1909–1925*. London: Routledge.

Lebas, E. (1995) '"When every street became a cinema": the film work of the Bermondsey Borough Council's Public Health Department', *History Workshop Journal*, 39, 42–66.

Low, R. (1979a) *Documentary and Educational Films of the 1930s*. London: George Allen and Unwin.

_____ (1979b) *Films of Comment and Persuasion of the 1930s*. London: George Allen and Unwin.

Luckin, B. (1990) *Questions of Power: Electricity and Environment in Interwar Britain*. Manchester: Manchester University Press.

Newman, G. (1925) *Public Education in Health*. London: HMSO.

Nichols, B. (1976/77) 'Documentary theory and practice', *Screen*, 17, 4, 34–48.

Pearson, D. (1982) 'Speaking for the common man: multi-voice commentary in *World of Plenty* and *Land of Promise*', in P. Marris (ed.) *Paul Rotha*. London: BFI, 64–85.

Richards, J. (1984) *The Age of the Dream Palace*. London: Routledge and Kegan Paul.

Richards, J. and D. Sheridan (eds) (1987) *Mass-Observation at the Movies: Cinema and Society*. London: Routledge.

Rogers, N. (1989) 'Germs with legs: flies, disease and the New Public Health', *BHM*, 63, 599–617.

Rotha, P. (1936) *Documentary Film*. London: Faber.

_____ (1973) *Documentary Diary: An Informal History of the British Documentary Film, 1928–1939*. London: Secker and Warburg.

Rowson, S. (1936) 'A statistical survey of the cinema industry in Great Britain in 1934', *Journal of the Royal Statistical Society*, 99, 67–129.

Smith, D. F. (1986) *Nutrition in Britain in the Twentieth Century*. Unpublished PhD dissertation, Edinburgh University.

Swann, P. (1989) *The British Documentary Film Movement, 1926–1946*. Cambridge: Cambridge University Press.

Williams, R. (1983) 'British film history: new perspectives', in J. Curran and V. Porter (eds) *British Cinema History*. London: Wiedenfeld and Nicolson, 9–23.

Wood, S. H. (1935) *Intelligence and Public Relations*. London: Public Record Office, MH78/147.

57

05

Tom Shakespeare

Sex, death and stereotypes: disability in *Sick* and *Crash*

In *Crash* I'm saying that if some harsh reality envelops you, rather than be crushed, destroyed or diminished by it, embrace it fully. Develop it and take it even further than it wanted to go itself. See if that's not a creative endeavour. If that is not positive. (David Cronenberg, quoted in Rodley 1993: 202)

Introduction

Discussions of disability representation in cinema tend to focus on individual disabled characters, to explore the role they play in a film, and sometimes to analyse what wider social values such characters reflect or reinforce (see Klobas 1988; Norden 1994). Critics have shown, for example, how incidental impairment has typically been used to create atmosphere or heighten the melodrama in films. Disabled characters often operate as two-dimensional ciphers: tropes such as 'tragic but brave victim' or 'sinister and crippled' or 'super crip' dominate treatments of disability (Longmore 1986). Disability-studies film criticism often revolves around assessment of the extent to which individual films endorse or expand these limited understandings of what it means to be impaired: whether they present 'positive images' or stereotypes. It is commonly claimed that the best possible representation of a disabled person would either have the impairment as incidental and irrelevant, rather than character forming and over determining, or else would focus on the social barriers which exclude people with impairments and, conversely, disabled people's struggle for civil rights and social inclusion.

Paul Darke has succinctly criticised the positive images/disapproving disability imagery approach to disability film criticism (Darke 1998). In a similar vein, I have previously suggested that disability film criticism can sometimes be shallow and predictable (Shakespeare 1999). Disability discourse is often more complex and multi-faceted than it first appears. Lazy and stereotypical representations of disability undoubtedly abound, and should be exposed for their shortcomings. But the 'positive image toolkit' is less helpful when it comes to films at the margins, which are striving to explore the existential challenge of impairment, or to comment on cultural fascinations with transgression, pain and death. That is to say, disability is not just about disabled people: it is about being human (Shakespeare 1994). Some filmmakers go beyond the obvious associations of impairment to explore deeper questions about embodiment, mortality and sexuality. Even when the barriers have come down and disabled people have achieved equality with other citizens, our encounters with limitations of body and brain will continue to fascinate and challenge, because they raise questions about the human condition which are relevant to us all.

59

Western biomedicine, and much of the modern technological world, is built on the human triumph over our nature, and the nature that surrounds us. Diseases can be vanquished; body parts can be replaced; human limitations can be surpassed with assistive technologies. Life expectancy has increased, and our ability to deal with the inescapable reality of our own mortality has consequently declined. Most people in the contemporary West are unfamiliar with death, except through sanitised media representation. We do not expect to encounter disease. Unlike previous generations, injury and impairment are not a fact of life, and mortality is dispelled to the margins (Bauman 1992).

In this chapter I will explore two films which, in different ways, raise questions about our control over our bodies, and the possibilities of a radical choice to embrace and explore injury, mutilation and mortality – a Heideggerian 'freedom towards death'. Each develops unusual and uncomfortable representations of disability. Perhaps, each could be called a freak show: an antithesis of the positive representation of disability. Central to the challenge which these death-obsessed representations make to contemporary perceptions is the conjunction of sexuality with disability, and sexuality with mortality.

Sick and Crash

Sick: The Life and Death of Bob Flanagan Supermasochist (Kirby Dick, 1997) is a documentary about a man with the genetic disease cystic fibrosis (CF), and his life as a performance artist. It follows Bob Flanagan (1952–96), and his partner Sheree Rose as they create video and live art and as they discuss his life with CF and their sado-masochistic relationship. It includes footage of Flanagan performing at a summer camp for young people with CF, and his interactions with a young woman with CF who wants to emulate his body-piercings. Finally, the film covers Flanagan's last days in hospital. After his death – having effectively suffocated from the mucus which filled his lungs – Sheree Rose shows us the container of phlegm drained from his corpse.

Crash (David Cronenberg, 1996) is adapted from the novel by J. G. Ballard. It opens with scenes of James and Catherine Ballard (James Spader and Debora Kara Ungar) each having sex with anonymous partners. James is subsequently involved in a car crash with another couple's car. He is hospitalised, as is Dr Helen Remington (Holly Hunter); her husband is killed. This marks the characters' entry into the deviant subculture of Vaughan (Elias Koteas), who obsesses about car crashes. James, Helen, Catherine, Vaughan and the disabled Gabrielle have sex with each other in a series of brutal and loveless permutations. James and Catherine attend a recreation of James Dean's fatal accident. Ultimately Vaughan is killed; James Ballard buys his car from the police pound, and takes his place in the car crash cult. The film ends with James caressing the injured Catherine after he has forced her car off the motorway.

Disability and sexuality

Part of the challenge of *Crash* and *Sick* is the imagery of disability and sexuality: having sex in an invalid car; a diseased and dying man celebrating his sexuality; the fetishistic celebration of callipers and other disability paraphernalia; Ballard having sex with the vaginal-shaped wound on Gabrielle's thigh. These images resonate and disturb because they refute the safe assumption that disabled people are passive, child-like and asexual beings, objects of pity, not agents of desire.

Research which I and colleagues conducted with disabled people (Shakespeare *et al.* 1996) revealed that respondents were familiar with cultural messages which told them that impaired bodies could not be sexy, that disabled people did not have sexual desires or sexual rights, and that they were not welcome in places such as bars and clubs where sex and romance were on the agenda. For example, Beth, a professional woman with MS, said:

> I am sure that other people see a wheelchair first, me second, and a woman third, if at all. A close friend assumed that for me, sex was a thing of the past. I think that this is a view shared by the majority. It may have little reality, but influences my self-image.

A tradition of films such as *The Men* (Fred Zinnemann, 1950), *The Waterdance* (Neil Jiminez, 1991) or *Forrest Gump* (Robert Zemeckis, 1994) reinforces this asexuality, particularly in terms of disabled masculinity.

One response to this prohibition is to assert the normality of disabled sexuality, to campaign for the inclusion of disabled people in the world of love and sex, and to argue that the differences between disabled and non-disabled people are less significant than the commonalities. The problems of disabled sexuality are about lack of function or other failures of the body, but arise from the social exclusion, prejudice and the poverty in which much of the disabled community finds itself. Several recent films have endorsed this normalisation of disability and sexuality: for example, Pedro Almodovar's *Live Flesh* (1997). Here the disabled character is played by Spanish heart-throb Javier Bardem, and it is clear that he is able to satisfy his partner sexually. Another example is the woman wheelchair-user in *Notting Hill* (Roger Michell, 1999).

However, another response is to refuse normalisation and to celebrate the potential of disabled sexuality to be marginal and polymorphously perverse. For example, some respondents in our research suggested that their sexual identity was not conventional, but that disability interacted with gender to produce another alternative position. Jazz said to us: 'I think disability is a breed on its own, neither masculine nor feminine.' Juniper, a heterosexual man, suggested that the vulnerability of some disabled men had some similarities with that of women; another, Eddie, said 'I very much see myself as a disabled man, not a heterosexual man.' Others actively subverted expectation, or developed transgressive identities as gay, lesbian, bisexual or transsexual. This strategy is exciting and unpredictable but also risky, because as well as the asexual cultural messages about disability, there is also the negative stereotype that certain disabled people – for example dwarfs – are hypersexual. In our research, Kirsten felt that the image of disability was 'very unsexy, but also slightly monstrous and perverted'. There has always been a sexual frisson about disability, as well as a negativity and taboo.

The films of Lars von Trier exploit this theme of perversity, in particular *The Idiots* (1998), which plays on the shock value of adults expressing their sexuality by pretending to have learning difficulties. A real-life example is the phenomenon of so-called 'hobbyists' or 'devotees': men who are particularly attracted to disabled women, particularly amputees or women with scars or callipers. 'Wannabes' are non-disabled people who simulate impairment by dressing up in callipers, or who go as far as mutilating themselves or requesting surgical amputation to develop their preferred sense of self. An edition of the BBC2 disability magazine programme *From the Edge* (broadcast on 24 February 1998) notably featured two able-bodied men who fantasised about being disabled, and pretended to be amputees or calliper users. Within the disabled community there is often ambivalence, anxiety or open hostility to some of these marginal expressions of disabled sexuality, and scepticism about the motives of filmmakers such as von Trier or the devotee community. *Sick* was censured by Michael Turner, the film critic of *Disability Now* magazine, for making connections between disability and sado-masochism:

> Regardless of how you feel about Flanagan's sexuality, linking his enjoyment of pain to his experiences of pain as a person with CF is very worrying, especially when he meets a young woman with CF who, it is suggested, has similar interests to himself. (Turner 1997: 22)

Sex and death

'Eroticism, it may be said, is assenting to life up to the point of death' (Bataille 2001: 11). The central resonances of the body are sex and death. Michel Foucault observed the shift in perceptions of sex and death that occurred between the nineteenth and twentieth centuries: in the former, death was omnipresent, but sex was taboo; in the modern age, sex is inescapable, but death is banished. Both *Crash* and *Sick* underline the continuing link between the two: here, sex is extreme, and death is a fact of life. As Flanagan says, 'my life is about death'. *Sick* includes footage of the autopsy rituals that Flanagan and Sheree Rose performed as part of their sado-masochistic relationship, and presents concepts such as the video-coffin. This ultimate posthumous artwork was to consist of a video-cam mounted in a coffin, so that viewers could watch the corpse decay over real time.

The connection between sex and death, between the 'petit mort' of orgasm and final annihilation has been made by many philosophers. The Marquis de Sade was perhaps the most notorious writer on these themes. Sigmund Freud started his work in psychoanalysis by foregrounding the sexual drives, but subsequently supplemented his thoughts on sexuality with his paradigm of Thanatos, the death instinct, the second major element in the psyche. The writings of Georges Bataille (2001) develop the connection, and Bataillean themes are evidenced in the narrative and characters in *Crash* and the life and work of Bob Flanagan. Ian Sinclair argues both that '*Crash* is Georges Bataille serialised in *Autosport*', and that it 'is a movie de Sade would have adored' (Sinclair 1999: 69). It might be noted in passing that the bisexual James Dean, whose fatal crash is recreated by Vaughan, had his own secret life as a masochist. For Bataille, transgression is central to the cultural system: sex and death hover on the margins and rupture the coherence of identity. Bataille extends Freud's work on taboo, the marginalisation of repressed desires, as Tanya Krzywinska argues: 'To become a clean and proper person within a particular culture is to sublimate aspects of desire that do not conform to the dominant norms of gender and sexuality in that culture' (Krzywinska 1999: 189). For Bataille, erotic identities are born of shame, but that shame is bound up with titillation.

Both of the films under discussion also work through Julia Kristeva's notion of the abject (1982). For Kristeva, abjection involves material which disrupts bodily continuity – bodily fluids such as excrement, sexual fluids, scabs, dead skin cells, menstrual blood, mucus and pus. Typically, these materials evoke a combination of fascination and repulsion. CF involves a failure of the body's mucous membranes, and is associated with continual mucus and coughing. One montage sequence in *Sick* shows a protracted series of coughing fits, reminding the viewer that the interviews with Flanagan are artifices, edited to remove the constant coughing which was the soundtrack to his life. Making his *Visible Man* artwork, a plastic model which leaks bodily fluids from appropriate orifices, Flanagan remarks that 'cuming and coughing are the only things which I do on a consistent basis these days'. Parallel associations in *Crash* are the scars and wounds which every character displays, the sperm-stained interior of Vaughan's car, and the regular emissions of blood.

Both *Crash* and *Sick* are ethnographies of deviant sexual subcultures. Bob Flanagan and Sheree Rose, Vaughan and his confederates, reject the norms, values and securities of mainstream American culture and celebrate transgressive desires focusing on pain, rupture and domination. By doing so, they join a notorious history of work which insists on linking sex and death and raising uncomfortable questions about our secret desires.

Choice and accident

Another of the parallels between these films consists in the radical and counter-intuitive choices which the characters make. Autonomy is a key principle in modern politics and ethics, particularly in health care. People must be free to choose for themselves what is best. But there is also an assumption that individuals will choose on the basis of the shared values of society: health, security, safety and comfort. The utilitarianism dominating contemporary ethical debates is about choices that avoid harm and pain. The transgression of deliberately choosing that which is taboo is, therefore, utterly shocking.

When cars collide, except in the controlled environments of road safety research, it is unintended. A crash is paradigmatically an accident. The entire apparatus of road and car design and social control is directed towards avoiding the violent encounter of vehicles which should proceed separately, discretely and safely to their destinations. In *Crash*, Vaughan and his companions have made the choice to flout these expectations and regulations and deliberately to realise the potential that every car has to become a weapon of death and destruction. Their sexual thrill derives from viewing and participating in collisions freely chosen, which perhaps therefore cannot be called accidents at all. Gabrielle is crippled by her own choice, Vaughan has chosen his scars.

For Bob Flanagan, his cystic fibrosis was an accident. A Caucasian has a 1 in 25 chance of carrying a copy of the gene mutation associated with CF. If two such 'carriers' have children together, each of their children has a 1 in 4 chance of inheriting both copies of the gene and thus developing the disease. Therefore the occurrence of CF in the Caucasian population is 1 in 2,500. To be born with CF in the modern era is truly down to bad luck, a twist of fate.

In future this may change. In a world in which every parent knows his/her genetic characteristics and every embryo can be tested, births of people with CF or other genetic conditions could be avoided. In such a world, a deliberate choice would have to be made to avoid prenatal surveillance, or to choose to continue a pregnancy affected by disease. Even today, some cases of congenital impairment could be avoided, and parents are offered prenatal diagnosis in the belief that it is their right to know the characteristics of a foetus, and perhaps their moral obligation to terminate affected pregnancies. To choose disability is shockingly counter-intuitive, because of the dominant view of disability as something to be avoided at all costs. For Flanagan's generation, CF was truly an accident, which medical technology could not have prevented. However, while CF was unintentional for Flanagan, his sexuality seems a radical choice. Flanagan chose the most painful expression of sexuality available. *Sick* includes scenes of bondage, flagellation, humiliation and other tortures. Notoriously, it also includes footage of his genitalia being pierced with needles and nails. All of these were freely chosen, consensual acts.

Traditionally, the sociology of deviance has identified those forms of deviance over which an individual has no control (and for which they cannot be blamed). Illness and disability, which bring exemption from normal social requirements, are examples of blameless deviance, or what Talcott Parsons (1951) calls the 'sick role'. However, deviance which is freely chosen may be defined as crime, to be controlled and punished. The legal status of sado-masochism has been contested: in the notorious 'Spanner' case, 16 consenting sado-masochists who performed and documented consensual activities for their own gratification were prosecuted and punished by the British state (1987–90). Until 1967, private consensual acts between men were illegal in the UK. In some states of the USA, and in other countries worldwide, consenting homosexuality continues to be proscribed.

But do *Sick* and *Crash* celebrate the radical autonomy of those who chose the unimaginable? Questions can be raised as to what extent transgressive sexuality is a matter of free choice at all. Biologists might argue that the origins of sexual identity and predilection lie outside the realm of agency. For example, many gay men report feeling 'different' from an early age. A number of studies have claimed that genetic factors, womb environment, or other biological processes play a key role in the pathway which leads to homosexuality. If so, it is not far-fetched to imagine that biology may play a role in other transgressive sexualities, such as sado-masochism.

Alternatively, both Bob Flanagan and his parents link his extreme sexuality to his experience of having a body affected by CF, and the medical treatments which were consequently necessary for his health. Flanagan admits in the film:

> My mother said that when I was a baby and really sick in the hospital, they had to stick needles in my chest to draw fluid out. I was always thrashing around and fighting (I was in pain), so the doctors tied my hands and feet to the bed so I wouldn't hurt myself. And that's still one of my favorite positions to be in: flat on the bed, tied up.

Draining his chest via a needle gave relief from pain and distress, perhaps accounting for some of the attraction needles held for the adult Flanagan. He goes on to offer a psychological explanation of his desires:

I'm sure that while I was tied up as an infant in the hospital my parents felt really sorry for me and were overly (or justifiably) concerned, trying to comfort me as much as possible. While horrible things were happening to me, I was getting extra love and attention, so the two contradictory feelings probably fused together … the horrible things happening to me were made into something better; a sweetness was overlaid.

Psychological or biological explanations of transgressive sexuality challenge the idea that such behaviours are freely chosen, and suggest that ultimately everything may be determined, if we can only look back far enough. But agency remains central. Many people with CF experience similar symptoms to Flanagan, but the vast majority do not choose to participate in extreme sexual activity. This indicates why films featuring extremly disabled characters are distasteful to many in the disability community: there is a risk of implying that these behaviours are typical of disabled people, or are straightforward responses to impairment. Disabled critic Michael Turner writes that:

> It is obviously senseless to argue with Flanagan's own self-analysis, but the connection between CF and any other disability which causes pain is certainly not an automatic one – not everybody who experiences chronic pain becomes a masochist. While Flanagan's interest in masochism may have been prompted by his CF, the connection between the two is ultimately superficial. (Turner 1997: 22)

While non-disabled characters are not usually taken as being representative of majority experience, any disabled character or role model risks being viewed as typical of their kind. However, *Sick* makes no claims to generality, and the video-diary format and autobiographical emphasis further mark out Flanagan as a unique and distinctive individual – although the film includes at least one other person with CF who follows a similar path.

Control of the flesh

Choosing your fate, or your sexual fulfilment, is ultimately about control. Flanagan explains that his desire is not simply for pain, but for a particular type of relationship: 'I don't get turned on just by slamming my hand in a car door.' Sarah, the 17-year-old fellow CF survivor who comes to visit him and Sheree, explains her interest in body piercing in terms of 'being able to control your body for a change'. *Crash*, too, has control as a strong theme. Vaughan is the impresario who presents the meticulous recreation of famous accidents. He is dominant in his sexual encounters. All the couplings are about penetration and domination, all the driving is about controlling the road and driving other road users out of the way. And the ultimate expression of control is about choosing the time and manner of your own death. Here, the films diverge: Flanagan's death in *Sick* reveals the limitations of his mastery of body and sexuality. At the end, he is unable to play domination games because he is finding it impossible even to breathe. Sheree Rose goes on playing the roles, but he is too exhausted to take part: he longs for release from the torture of his disease, and wants to forget the contractual obligations of their sub-dom relationship. Death from CF is the last thing that Flanagan wants, a failure which he resists to the end – just as David Cronenberg has spoken of the characters in his film as artists doomed to create and doomed equally to fail (Grant 1998: 184). Perhaps the fact that Flanagan is the author as much of the subject of Kirby Dick's film gives him the final triumph of immortality through cinema.

Disability is rarely seen as compatible with agency: patients and invalids are people who are sick and feeble, objects of other people's attention, or victims of their failing bodies, rather than masters of their own destiny. The radical choice of pain or humiliation – even the sacrificing of control to a dominator/dominatrix or a body piercer – is about asserting control over your life and over your flesh. While a masochist might be perceived as a weak person, masochism is actually an expression of strength and self-mastery. Bob Flanagan may have been disabled, but he endured what many others could not.

Paul Sweetman (1999) reports his research from the piercing subculture. Some respondents found pain to be pleasurable. However, for others, piercing was as much about a sense of achievement and a feeling of confidence: having overcome fears or expressed individuality or confronted taboos. Interviewees saw the act of becoming tattooed or pierced as asserting control of the body, or as reclaiming the body or even as self-creation. Tattoos and piercings challenge the meaning and cultural evaluation of pain, subverting the dichotomy between it and pleasure. Piercing could be seen as 'reclaiming one's body from the experts – in an act of deliberative, creative and non-utilitarian (self-)penetration' (Sweetman 1999: 178).

These accounts connect very strongly with Bob Flanagan's and Sarah's own accounts in *Sick*. As survivors of CF, they experience others tendering to their bodies from an early age: parents, doctors, physiotherapists. This lack of control, coupled with the lack of control of the disease itself, is countered by their deliberate acts of self-mutilation. It would be too simplistic to say that piercing or sado-masochism asserted a rejection of, or revenge on, the failing body – which is the explanation provided by Flanagan's mother. Rather, matching pain with pain is an expression of mastery over the body, and control over one's own life. As Sarah says, 'Bondage. I can relate to that. Being able to control *something.*' Flanagan calls it 'fighting sickness with sickness'. Equally, to non-disabled people, the impaired body may be a source of disgust and revulsion, and this response is something else beyond the control of disabled individuals, and is a denial of their humanity. As Sweetman found, piercing and piercings evoke a visceral response of disgust from onlookers (1999: 180). By transferring this disgust from the impaired body to the pierced body, Sarah and Bob Flanagan are regaining some control over the way they are perceived by others.

As a survivor of CF, an artist and a public figure, Flanagan was obviously a role model for many young people with CF, who perhaps rarely encounter positive images of life with the disease. *Sick* shows him performing his darkly comic songs as a counsellor at summer camp for the CF community. Some of his audience clearly found his sexuality and attitude to his own body also worthy of emulation. A weblog by a fellow CF survivor shows how Bob Flanagan's example inspires some others who share his disease:

> I was so excited to learn of an artist with cf. Through the years I would read more about him, and read works by him, and found myself simultaneously consoled and excited to learn of someone else who struggled with similar pain and frustration by creating other pain and control for themselves. My body is decorated with colours and metal rings – each from a painful ritual act to make peace with this vessel that betrays me. <http://www.dragonflypond.com/rumination/bob.html>

Conclusion

Crash shows people at the sexual margins performing disability, flirting with danger, and ultimately embracing death. As Linda Ruth Williams argues, it is 'genuinely polymorphously perverse; as the character-pairings cross and counter-cross in multiple sexual engagements, masculinity and femininity become less defining categories and more performative possibilities' (Williams 1999: 43). *Sick* shows an individual with physical abnormalities performing deviant sexuality, embracing pain and exerting control over his body in a challenge to death and disease. One film is a fiction, adapted from another fiction, and serves as a metaphor for our modern preoccupation with cars, technology and control. The other is a documentary, constructed from a life, which challenges viewers both to imagine being a victim of inexorable disease and volunteering to (stomach-churning) masochistic acts of mutilation and torture. Yet both films, despite violence and perversion, are strangely romantic. As Ballard and his wife lie entwined on the verge of the road, he whispers 'maybe next time' in a final moment of intimacy. The relationship of Bob and Sheree Rose is genuine and touching as well as unconventional and extreme. As one reviewer concludes, 'At the end, as Bob fights for breath and Sheree weeps and cares for him, what we are seeing is a couple who had something, however bizarre, that gave them the roles they preferred, and mutual reassurance' (Ebert 1996).

While the concepts explored in *Crash* are confrontational, the film itself is strangely anodyne. It is filled with scenes of sex and arousal, but the images do not disturb in the same way as some of Cronenberg's other horror films. Yet it prompted a media campaign and calls for censorship and bans on public performance (Kuhn 1999; Barker *et al.* 2001). Film critic Alexander Walker wrote in the *Evening Standard* (6 June 1996) that *Crash* contained 'some of the most perverted acts and theories of sexual deviance I have ever seen propagated in main-line cinema'. A *Daily Mail* article was headlined 'Ban this car crash sex film' (9 September 1996) and Tory Heritage Secretary Virginia Bottomley called upon local authorities to ban the film in their area. Three aspects of *Crash* were challenging for conservative critics and regulators in Britain. First, the dominant role of sex scenes in the movie. As Cronenberg has said, 'in *Crash*, very often the sex scenes are absolutely the plot and the character development' (Rodley 1993: 199). Second, the theme of deliberately creating car crashes and using the road system for murderous and suicidal driving. Third, the juxtaposition of sex and disability. It is this last element which raised particular concerns for many at the time.

Barbara Creed linked the film's banning by Westminster Council to 'crutch and calliper sex' (Creed 1998: 175). Explicit or violent films are not new, although the 1980s saw particular moral panics about their effect. But the idea of disabled people having active sexuality, or being desirable, or being perverts, was challenging to non-disabled people, and was felt by some to be insulting or humiliating for disabled people. The furore is perhaps reminiscent of the negative reactions to Tod Browning's 1932 American film *Freaks* (see Whittington-Walsh 2002). James Ferman and the BBFC took this reaction very seriously, to the extent of convening a special group of disabled people to view the film and comment on its treatment of disability, as well as consulting a forensic pathologist and a QC (Kuhn 1999). Paul Darke, who recruited the disabled audience and convened the discussion, found the process tokenistic and disheartening, believing that Ferman was looking for a compliant group to give the nod to a film he seemingly desperately wanted to get through un-cut. We obliged ... I invited 'in-the-know' disabled people who would be able to comment intelligently on the film. It was in no way a cross section or representative of the mass of disabled people ... The viewing room was not wheelchair accessible so wheelchair users were out ... Bizarrely though, the BBFC were extraordinarily happy with the result of the whole thing ... It was a strange experience I wish I had never been involved in. (Paul Darke, personal communication, 2003)

The reality, of course, is that in the real world sex is very much part of the everyday life of many disabled people. Many disabled people do not want their sexuality to be airbrushed into conformity. The irony is that *Sick*, an obscure video self-portrait of a disabled man, is a far more realistic, more authentic, more disturbing, and more transgressive portrayal of sex and disability than *Crash*. The documentary presents a roll call of photographs showing Flanagan's body in scenes of mutilation and torture. The series of images are like the films and photographs which Vaughan's group show and share. Both the sado-masochistic acts and the car crashes are intentional – recreated or engineered for gratification, rather than the involuntary injuries or accidents normally encountered and documented in the Accident and Emergency department of a hospital. The major difference is that the viewer knows that the shocking images in Cronenberg's film are the result of stunt men, trick photography and theatrical make-up, whereas every photograph of Flanagan's pierced, cut and bruised body is very much 'for real'. Perhaps it is facile to comment that the documentary is more authentic than the fiction. But the realities of *Sick* make the imaginings of *Crash* seem more trite by comparison. Despite the media furore, I would argue that *Crash* is a rather dreary film: cool, un-engaging and superficial, a 'necrophile masque' (Sinclair 1999: 57), theatrical rather than dramatic. In contrast, *Sick* comes alive and is moving, partly because Flanagan approaches his life, sexuality and art with humour – telling comic anecdotes while nailing his penis to a plank – and partly because of the reality of Flanagan's CF predicament and the bravery with which he deals with it.

To what extent do these films explore issues which are central to our culture or lie deep in our psyche? Barbara Creed argues that 'the postmodern desiring subject yearns for an experience marked by crash culture – division, simulation, brutality, obscenity, perversion, death' (Creed 1998: 175). This generalisation verges on glib academic rhetoric. Away from the world of film studies, mainstream viewers often reject films like *Crash* or *Sick* (Barker *et al.* 2001). Audience members at the Sundance Film Festival, for example, walked out rather than watch Flanagan nailing his penis to a plank.

When we view *Crash* or *Sick*, is it possible for us to identity with any of the protagonists, or to long for the fulfilment they seek? Bataille or de Sade might argue that the attraction of both films is the presentation of repressed desires and forbidden pleasures. A Foucauldian would see the frenzy of prohibition surrounding *Crash* as evidence of the relevance and symbolic power of the images of sexuality and technology in the film. Perhaps all this abnegation of the flesh, sacrifice and martyrdom, is happening on our behalf: Cronenberg has suggested that his characters suffer for us, the audience (Rodley 1993), while Flanagan was partly inspired by his Catholic upbringing. So a comparison with the Crucifixion may not be too far-fetched.

Both films are limited by a male-centred vision of sexuality, in which women feature as accomplices or dominatrixes. Creed has argued that *Crash* is phallocentric, with its repeated scenes of heterosexual rear penetration and violent possession of women (Creed 1998: 179). Linda Ruth Williams (1999) claims that Cronenberg has an ongoing concern with masculinity in crisis: femininity is marginal, despite (or because of) the lingerie-clad female cast. However, males are certainly present as objects of desire in both films. There is an explicit homoerotic connection between Ballard and Vaughan. Both films present male bodies as objects for the gaze. Males are as often passive as they are active: by definition, Flanagan submits to domination, while James Spader's performance as Ballard is characteristically languid and passive. Both films foreground issues of voyeurism, as performances are staged for audiences in the film as much as for audiences of the film. We feel voyeuristic thrill and guilt at witnessing Flanagan's death, just like the spectators at Vaughan's recreations of famous car crashes, and just as, in real life, we slow down to rubberneck at the scene of a road traffic accident.

At a deeper level than their images of gender or disability or extreme sex, both films connect to the undercurrents of mortality and physicality which I earlier claimed were deeply repressed in contemporary culture, with its quest for bodily perfection, for youth, and for biomedical and technological fixes for the vulnerabilities and limitations of human embodiment. Both films celebrate refusal and resistance, and the agency of those counter-cultural outlaws who take their bodies to extremes, challenging the narcissism of consumption and the ideology of health. Their triumph may not be an experience to try at home, but it is something admirable, even heartening, nonetheless.

References

Balsalmo, A. (1995) 'Forms of technological embodiment: reading the body in contemporary culture', in M. Featherstone and R. Burrows (eds) *Cyberbodies/Cyberspace/Cyberpunk: Cultures of Technological Embodiment*. London: Sage, 215–37.

Barker, M., J. Arthurs and R. Harindranath (2001) *The Crash Controversy: Censorship Campaigns and Film Reception*. London: Wallflower Press.

Bataille, G. (2001) *Eroticism*. London: Penguin.

Bauman, Z. (1992) *Mortality, Immortality and Other Life Strategies*. Cambridge: Polity Press.

Creed, B. (1998) 'The *Crash* debate: anal wounds, metallic kisses', *Screen*, 39, 2, 175–9.

Darke, P. (1994) '*The Elephant Man* (David Lynch, EMI Films, 1980): an analysis from a disabled perspective', *Disability and Society*, 9, 3, 327–42.

____ (1998) 'Understanding cinematic representations of disability', in T. Shakespeare (ed.) *The Disability Reader*. London: Cassell, 181–97.

Ebert, R. (1996) Review of *Bob Flanagan Supermasochist*, originally published in *Chicago Sun Times*. Available at: http://www.suntimes.com/ebert/ebert_reviews/1997/12/12051.html

Grant, M. (1998) 'Crimes of the future', *Screen*, 39, 2, 180–5.

Klobas, L. (1988) *Disability Drama in Television and Film*. Jefferson, NC: McFarland & Co.

Kristeva, J. (1982) *Powers of Horror: An Essay on Abjection*, trans. Leon S. Roudiez. New York: Columbia University Press.

Krzywinska, T. (1999) 'Cicciolina and the dynamics of transgression and abjection in explicit sex films', in M. Aaron (ed.) *The Body's Perilous Pleasures: Dangerous Desires and Contemporary Culture*. Edinburgh: Edinburgh University Press, 188–209.

Kuhn, A. (1999) '*Crash* and film censorship in the UK', *Screen*, 40, 4, 448–50.

Longmore, P. (1986) 'Screening stereotypes: images of disabled people in television and motion pictures', in A. Gartner and T. Joe (eds) *Images of the Disabled/Disabling Images*. New York: Praeger, 65–78.

Norden, M. (1994) *The Cinema of Isolation*. New Brunswick, NJ: Rutgers University Press.

Oliver, M. (1998) 'Review of *The Sexual Politics of Disability*', *Disability and Society*, 13, 1, 150–2.

Parsons, T. (1951) *The Social System*. Glencoe, IL: Free Press.

Rodley, C. (ed.) (1993) *Cronenberg on Cronenberg*. London: Faber.

Sinclair, I. (1999) *Crash: David Cronenberg's Post-mortem on J. G. Ballard's 'Trajectory of Fate'*. London: British Film Institute.

Shakespeare, T. (1994) 'Cultural representation of disabled people: dustbins for disavowal?', *Disability and Society*, 9, 3, 283–300.

_____ (1999) 'Art and lies: representations of disability on film', in M. Corker and S. French (eds) *Disability Discourse*. Buckingham: Open University Press.

Shakespeare, T. K. Gillespie-Sells, D. Davies (1996) *The Sexual Politics of Disability: untold desires*. London: Cassell.

Sweetman, P. (1999) 'Only skin deep? tattooing, piercing and the transgressive body', in M. Aaron (ed.) *The Body's Perilous Pleasures: Dangerous Desires and Contemporary Culture*. Edinburgh: Edinburgh University Press, 165–87.

Turner, M. (1997) 'Sick: review', *Disability Now*, April, 22.

Whittington-Walsh, R. (2002) 'From freaks to savants: disability and hegemony from *The Hunchback of Notre Dame* (1939) to *Sling Blade* (1997)', *Disability and Society*, 17, 6, 695–708.

Williams, L. R. (1999) 'The inside-out of masculinity: David Cronenberg's visceral pleasures', in M. Aaron (ed.) *The Body's Perilous Pleasures: Dangerous Desires and Contemporary Culture*. Edinburgh: Edinburgh University Press, 30–48.

06

Andrew Moor

Past imperfect, future tense: the health services in British cinema of the mid-century

From the mid-1940s to 1952, a small line of British films – barely amounting to a cycle – tackled themes of health care provision or scientific progress. These films indicate something of Britain's ambivalence about modernity. By taking generic features of the medical film – innovation, utopian hopes, ethical issues and battles with, within and between establishments – and by peering anxiously back to a more primitive (pre-war) past – they have an acute cultural pertinence in mid-century Britain. They are motivated more or less openly by the post-war resettlement, by the re-charted boundaries between public and private spheres, and specifically, by the debate surrounding the new National Health Service.

The year 1946 saw the re-release of King Vidor's *The Citadel* (1938), based on A. J. Cronin's 1937 novel. Cronin was a doctor, with a doctor's professional point of view, and the film chronicles the early struggles of an ingénue doctor, although both film and novel chime with wider public health debates throughout the decade. In 1951, Alexander Mackendrick's *The Man in the White Suit* – not a medical film *per se* – satirically critiqued naïve scientific advancement as well as the industrial-social status quo which resists it. The same year saw Herbert Wilcox's stodgy biopic of Florence Nightingale, *The Lady with the Lamp*, as well as ex-documentarist Pat Jackson's contemporary hospital drama *White Corridors*. The following year found Alexander Mackendrick in non-comic mode with *Mandy* (1952), a moving drama about a child's deafness. Once diagnosed, little Mandy's deafness is a social and educational problem rather than a medical concern, but the way the film explores these issues allies it with medical films proper.

Faking the 1940s

There is a suggestive moment in David Lean's *Brief Encounter* (1945) when Alec (Trevor Howard), a general practitioner, tells Laura (Celia Johnson) what excites him about his job. His 'special pigeon', it transpires, is preventative medicine. She glazes over, winsomely parading a masquerade of well-trained, feminine docility. Alec drifts into a sociomedical reverie about industrial conditions and pneumoconiosis. Seduced by his polysyllabic mastery, she hears the soundtrack's Rachmaninov and they fall in love over a lecture on lung disease. This staggering incongruity characterises a film which repeatedly stages conflicts between Laura's romantic worldview and more regulated, 'masculine' structures. Alec's occupation is often overlooked, but is important, because it touches on the film's romantic ideals, and because it clues us into its slippery sense of time.

Alec's profession is proof of his idealism, for fictional 'good' doctors stereotypically hold to personal convictions, struggling against superstition and injustice to benefit humanity. Laura's willingness to listen fires him with zeal and makes him seem younger to her (in a film which charts its heroine's mid-life crisis). His vigorous optimism exceeds their little, conventional lives. The only solutions are escape or denial. For Alec, it is emigration to South Africa (how useful the 'Colonies' were for men with missions); but for Laura, a future of keeping her counsel and making do. The film's dream-like structure, emanating from her armchair-bound imagination, hints that Alec may be her own, idealised but non-existent 'fantasy' man. She avidly reads women's novels, and her daydreams of exotic romance suggest that Alec is the sort she would conjure into her life. The lay-person/doctor relationship is therefore part of what Richard Dyer calls the film's 'feminine angle' (Dyer 1993: 38). At their first meeting, Alec politely removes a speck of dust from Laura's eye, a diminutive chivalric rescue. She may be too 'ordinary' (her adjective) to grasp Alec's radical (masculine) social vision, but she quickly recognises it as a sign of his heroic status. The film draws and comments on popular fiction's recourse to gender-biased, romanticised visions of doctorhood while the style and *mise-en-scène* purport that we are within a sincerely realist register.

These suggestions – bedded in fantasy – counter the consensus that *Brief Encounter* is the 'locus classicus' of quality realism, the meld of understated maturity and documentary fidelity whose status in British cinema, by 1945, was assured. But it is a relic of the inter-war period, based on Noël Coward's 1936 play, *Tonight at 8:30* and set in the late 1930s. Its polished use of the 'quality realist' style, squarely planted in the 1940s, papers over this datedness, while the vague chronology adds to the unrealistic aura.[1] It is silent on significant topical issues, eliding re-settled post-war gender relations, the nationalisation of the coal mines and the inauguration of the NHS. Alec has his own practice, yet works a weekly hospital shift for his dapper friend Stephen Lynn (Valentine Dyall) – the sort of 'jack of all trades' arrangement which proponents of the NHS sought to eradicate. The NHS was in the air before the war, was much debated since the Beveridge Report (1942), presented in a Government White Paper in 1944, enshrined in legislation in 1946 and launched in July 1948.

Alec's passion for public health, with its implicit call for compensation for work-related diseases, is an echo of the 1930s. It loosely reflects the sympathies of the British documentary movement, which was committed to public discourse and the social fabric. Edgar Anstey's and Arthur Elton's *Housing Problems* (1935), for example, exposes slum living and applauds improvement projects.[2] Lean's film tokenistically appropriates this discourse and robs it of any leftist credentials (although admittedly, voices across the political spectrum railed against poor conditions on grounds of rationality, industrial efficiency and national gain). The temporal sleight of hand also makes Laura a creature of the 1930s and renders her unreconstructed romanticisation of Alec all the more plausible. The film puts the 'good doctor' cliché to private, romantic use, Alec's messianic fervour is alluded to but not acted upon (his connections secure him that hospital job abroad) and the Rachmaninov (= romance, = privacy, = sublimation) ensures that the off-screen coughing of marginalised industrial workers does not trouble us too much.

Anticipating the 1940s

If *Brief Encounter* trampolines a reactionary, reverse summersault back to the 1930s, King Vidor's *The Citadel* (a genuine 1930s artefact) looks forward to a better time, and its 1946 re-release capitalises on a new-found topicality. It soberly narrates Andrew Manson's (Robert Donat) arrival as a fresh assistant general practitioner in a Welsh pit village, following his career from a miners' medical aid society to smart Chelsea. Suspicion and systemic short-sightedness frustrate his early research into links between chronic chest complaints and silica inhalation in the mines. The film is animated by sociomedical rather than biomedical ideas, focusing on its doctor's dilemmas rather than his patients', and shying from any more radical socialist agenda. Despite an obsequious disclaimer (it 'is in no way intended as a reflection on the great medical profession which has done so much towards beating back those forces of nature that retard the physical progress of the human race'), its still indicts the irrationality and corruption of health provision in the 1930s, and calls for something better. On its post-war re-release, the NHS gave the film an acute new relevance, and retrospectively flagged up the prescience of Andrew's suggestion to the 'English Medical Union' in its closing scene: 'Gentlemen, it's high time we started putting our house in order.'

Many medical films are set in the nineteenth century onwards because that period saw more and better clinical treatments, the more extensive use of hi-tech equipment and the wider appreciation of public health. They express a sense of modernity and are haunted by the old 'ills' of Victoriana: tradition, ignorance and the structural inequalities which legislation sought to ameliorate: inadequate housing, bad sewerage and absolute poverty. Andrew diagnoses typhoid near his practice, and learns from his friend Denny (Ralph Richardson), a chemist and surgeon who has long fought the 'system' in the area, that an old sewer is to blame. This sewer solidly signifies the rotten past which endures into the present because of failures in the existing system (despite legislation as old as the 1848 Public Health Act and ongoing debates about infectious diseases like typhoid and cholera). A District Medical Officer will not even ask the council for a new sewer in case his wages are stopped to pay for it.

Denny and Andrew get recklessly drunk and dynamite the sewer. The film is ethically lax about this sabotage: its tone is wry and comic. Vidor views the direct action sympathetically, but his deadpan irony deviates from the film's realist project, deflecting any censure about his endorsement of illegal behaviour. It is a sign of the film's nervousness; proof of its conservatism. Despite its exposé of specific lapses in etiquette or ethics, it always nods to the way things 'should be'. Michael Shortland relates this ambivalence (and the forelock-tugging disclaimer) to the attention of the British Board of Film Censors, who took care to ensure that the film would not undermine public confidence in the medical services (Shortland 1989: 8).

Denny, a characteristically eccentric performance from Richardson, is a likeable rogue – Andrew's comic foil. His dog's name, Hawkins, suggests he identifies with Long John Silver. His heavy drinking, though, shows him to be a half-cousin of the dissolute doctors (and newspaper men) barely holding it together in John Ford's westerns, men whose struggles *within* ungovernable communities have beaten them down. The analogy holds good for Andrew too: a new sheriff, come to 'clean up' the town, a lone outsider trying to bring civilisation to the Welsh wilds, the remoteness of which is signalled by the train journey which instigates the film (and it is directed, after all, by a Texan). The differences, though, are important. Denny revels in his drink. He mixes comedy with homespun and clinical wisdom, and incites Andrew to shed his too-bookish, abstract sense of the profession and to 'become' a doctor. Andrew's problem is that he is not simply a stranger in the lawless West, but that he is the naïve agent of an illogically bureaucratised and failing institution. He is no existential hero yet.

Popular cinema is protagonist-driven, and demands that obstacles be overcome through personal conviction and effort. This form of motor energy may have to operate in tension with (or outside) the Law or the rigid dictates of the Establishment. Medical films which focus on sympathetic individuals and channel audience identification onto them typically figure ethical issues at a higher level where points of individual conscience run counter to prevailing norms. Tension may be created when a protagonist flouts established practice, but the culture needs utopian resolutions, and given the medical profession's emphasis on its own ethical procedure, transgressions – which are needed at a narrative level to prove the value of individualism – have to be justified by the outlaw-protagonist's foresight, his/her quasi-religious vocation, and the stark inadequacy of the status quo.

And starkly inadequate it is, as Andrew learns. After a spell as an assistant GP, he becomes one of four doctors contracted to the Aberalaw Medical Aid Society, the type of set-up instigated by Lloyd George's 1911 National Health Insurance Act to administer funds contributed by working men in the heavy industries for their primary health care. The committee secretary, Owen (Emlyn Williams), an articulate, visionary man not unlike Aneurin Bevan, endorses Andrew's laboratory experiments into silica inhalation, despite the miners' suspicions. Bevan, later credited as chief architect of the NHS, had early experience working with a medical aid society, and for this the BMA viewed him suspiciously. It always resented the societies' lay-interference into what they saw as their own jurisdiction.[3]

The Citadel dramatises various doctor/patient relationships, sometimes positively but usually to expose inadequacies or to show how easily they can be exploited. Andrew's role as a novice rather than as an exemplar of the profession makes him ambiguous, and in the early Welsh sequences Donat captures well his goodness but also his frustration, temper and self-doubt. 'Why do doctors always write prescriptions in Latin?' Christine (Rosalind Russell) asks Andrew. He parrots a well-schooled, lazy institutional response: 'So the patient won't know what he's getting. It's all – it's all part of the "good old system" you know. The patient wants his medicine and he gets it.' Andrew's Candide-like faith that this is an adequate account of the clinical encounter is offset only slightly by a hint of jest in his voice. He still falls short of a better answer for Christine.

Prescriptions and medicine are rejected as solutions. They neither stop the sewer spreading typhoid nor cure the miners' chest problems. Unfortunately, this is the consensual arrangement the miners are used to. Andrew asks his patients to forego palliative medicines and to take part in tests to check their lungs for coal dust. He refers one to a local hospital for more urgent tests for pneumonia. He embodies *social* progress, and fights to refigure the habitual, biomedically-driven relationship between doctor and patient. His microscope and laboratory signify commitment to scientific advancement, but with a socially beneficial impetus (point-of-view shots of plates seen through his microscope mark cinema's own technological allegiance with modern progress). By ignoring their more critical immediate needs, Andrew sparks an angry conflict. The miners get no compensation if they are off work at hospital (this was beyond the remit of the 1911 Act), and are asked to soldier on without medicine so that their symptoms can be charted more easily.

Andrew begins to win over intransigent villagers, but local resistance to modern science finally proves too strong and a delegation of miners ransacks his laboratory. This negative representation of the workforce sets the film apart from leftist visions of industry and mitigates its social conscience.[4] Facing committee opposition, Andrew resigns and heads to London. A year of struggle without patients ensues (12 months accelerated on screen by a clichéd montage sequence which indicates the quasi-biographical, American(ised) strand working through the film). A chance encounter with a fellow student, Lawford (Rex Harrison), leads him to the mercenary coterie of noted consultant Charles Every (Cecil Parker). Andrew rapidly acclimatises to this avaricious network of Chelsea specialists pandering to wealthy female patients. Only Denny's 'sacrificial' death, due to the negligent surgery of Every following a road accident, pulls Andrew back from Mammon to medicine's true cause.

The closing sequence resolves ongoing tensions about individualism, the social contract and the medical vocation. On a grief-stricken walk through London, Andrew observes its social ills – rear projection and intercut point-of-view shots etching out his isolation. Gazing into the Thames, he hears Denny's posthumous voice: 'Doctor Manson, this isn't *your* individual sorrow ... You're not one man fighting a battle *alone*. You're only one of a great profession ... continually fighting for the benefit of life, of health, of humanity.' (These metaphysical feelings echo religious elements earlier in the film, where the still-idealistic Andrew had miraculously seemed to bring a newborn baby back to life.)

The narrative sympathetically emphasises Andrew's flaws and virtues; and Donat, a fast-rising star in 1937 and a shining one by 1946, was trusted for his truthful performances (and his own chronic asthma brought him much public sympathy).[5] Denny's godlike proclamation imagines cohorts of doctors like Andrew, and rather too easily taps into utopian sentiments to reinvigorate him for a final conflict with the medical establishment. He assists Stillman (Percy Parsons), an unqualified American expert, to operate successfully on a friend's daughter, and is brought before the 'English Medical Union' for unprofessional conduct.

The film was produced with American money and directed by an American. Stillman is condemned as a 'quack' by the English Union, but is defended by Andrew, who compares him to Pasteur and Ehrlich: other men outside the profession who were belatedly canonised by it. Stillman's position beyond any recognised authority confers a type of nobility on him, and his New World background places him with the angels. There is a nuanced American aesthetic at work: Andrew's speech to the Union calls for a form of social contract which values individual effort, and is worthy of Capra, although the film's dispiriting view of the Old World has hitherto demonstrated how severely it constrains individualism. Stillman is the expert the text writes into history (Andrew is merely his advocate). Denny, had also looked to America for inspiration when planning a new health centre with a full range of specialists and modern equipment, all paid for locally by individual patients on an insurance principle ('a small fee – hang it all, we only want to live ... Works in the States!'). His excited plans anticipate a better system. His would be organised by medical professionals along American lines. Interventions like these contributed to the debate through which the NHS was formulated.

When Andrew leaves the tribunal after calling on his colleagues to look to their ethics, his own ethical violation is left unresolved and no reform has been tabled. It is unusual for so ploddingly traditional a film not contain a clear textual resolution, but *The Citadel*'s true closure is a synthesis of textual and extra-textual factors, in dialogue with historical movements for social reform. In the late 1930s, it is a call for change, the clearest endorsement of the future in an otherwise stolid work. By 1946, its re-release imported another meaning: the 1930s' utopian aspirations are now mutated into a righteous, proud recognition that change is already being effected.

Publicity material also sought to generate a social climate for the film. MGM emphasised the fastidious attention to detail, lavish scale and the quality (and stage credentials) of its stars, Donat, Richardson, Harrison and Williams, but also Rosalind Russell, its American 'love interest'. However, they also pitched the film as a romance. Exhibitors' were urged to place competitions in local newspapers, asking the public serious questions such as 'Should the State pay doctors?', an issue which would dog negotiations up to the launch of the NHS. Less publicly motivated questions might also be asked: 'Should a struggling young doctor marry?' Catch-lines might foreground the medical profession's humble public service. The British publicity material places the film within a public debate, but sweetens the medicine with a spoonful of sugar. In the USA the studio was less coy: 'Medical ethics will not attract movie patrons' they judged, 'Romance will!'

Celebrating the 1950s

Pat Jackson's *White Corridors* (1952) was released 13 years after *The Citadel*'s first appearance, and is starkly different – a sophisticated tapestry of narratives set in a hospital and shot in a muted, realist style, without musical soundtrack and with the tensely controlled but expressive scripting, editing and acting style which was perfected in the 1940s.[6] Publicity material, however, echoed *The Citadel*'s. Authenticity was boasted, and exhibitors were asked to provoke local debate regarding the film's issues. Rather than generating public letter-writing competitions, the studio suggested that groups of doctors and nurses should be invited to opening nights, and that their comments should be posted on boards outside the theatres. Curiosity about the trappings of the medical world was incited (the film is 'fearlessly spotlighting the private lives of a hospital staff'), pandering to melodramatic expectations, although the dominant thrust of the campaign underscored its ground-breaking realism. But the emphasis now was on the generality of the hospital staff, not the tribulations of a single young doctor.

This is not surprising, given Pat Jackson's career. He was central to the British documentary movement. He started work for the GPO Film Unit in 1934, assisted Harry Watt with *Nightmail* (1936), and directed *Western Approaches* (one of the high points of the Second World War's documentary-dramas) in 1944. *White Corridors'* focus on teamwork and its spotlight on a new recruit follows many pre-war and wartime documentaries in celebrating the effort of a branch of the services or of industry. Just as they had an educational purpose, *White Corridors* has comic scenes with guest star Basil Radford to explain access to NHS primary and hospital care.

Invited 'professional' audiences; the stress on the film's glimpse behind the scenes; its 'public' documentary-style format: what can be surmised is the new and more total institutionalisation of Britain's medical services by 1951. Hence, the film is set almost entirely within Yeoman's Hospital, and hence the structural associations of its title: clinical, futuristic, hygienic, perhaps celestially enlightened (or freshly painted), possibly labyrinthine, but also glacially unemotional, something which counters the melodramatic moments which lubricate its storylines. The lay-audience's access to this clinical world is channelled through the new recruit, nurse Joan Shepherd (Petula Clark) and also through the film's chief love-plot between two major characters, doctors Sophie Dean and Neil Marriner (Googie Withers and James Donald). There are no patient-centred scenarios.

Neil Marriner is a research pathologist conducting experiments into rare infections which are resistant to penicillin. Sophie is considering applying for promotion to a Resident Surgeon's position at Yeoman's, despite the lure of a job in London. Another doctor has applied for the post: Dick Groom (Jack Watling), a philandering house surgeon whose father is the Senior Surgeon, Mr Groom (Godfrey Tearle). Dick is engaged to marry into the family of the chair of the Hospital Management Committee, so feels confident about his application. Hurrying off shift, he fails to diagnose a cerebral abscess on a young woman and turns her out. Sophie finds the girl looking ill, and she and Mr Groom perform an emergency operation. Mr Groom learns of his son's negligence and throws his weight behind Sophie's application. Cross-cut into this storyline is another about a young boy, Tommy (Brand Inglis – one of the film's three non-professional actors, a form of casting derived from the documentary movement and used successfully by Jackson in *Western Approaches*). Tommy has blood poisoning and fails to respond to standard treatment. Neil uses Tommy's case to press the Committee for research funds (an ongoing battle). He is taking a blood sample from Tommy when the syringe accidentally punctures his own hand. Tommy dies and Neil gets sick. He has begun to develop a serum, but it has had no clinical testing. He asks Sophie to use the serum on him if all else fails: an unethical and potentially illegal act. She complies with his wishes, saves his life, and decides against the job in London. The subsidiary narratives of other patients are woven into these main storylines.

At times, *White Corridors* speaks the same language about health provision as *The Citadel*. One experienced doctor sees an older patient on his rounds: 'Drugs are no answer to bad housing and overwork', he tells a colleague. 'With rest and proper treatment that woman might have stood a chance, 20 years ago, but there were six kids to bring up and no health service to pay for her convalescent home.' The 1930s and its social ills are still remembered; the NHS – a citadel of modernity – has put those ghosts to rest. Andrew's struggle in Wales, partly political, was with ailments so common that they represented a catastrophe, and widespread suffering was caused by the injustices of the economic system. Pat Jackson's leftist politics chime with the welfare-ethos of the NHS, the mythology of which claimed that it was the answer to many social inequalities.

Hence, a clear optimism about the scope and efficacy of the NHS. The principle of free, universal health care accords with the post-war Labour government's egalitarianism, but some observers remarked early on that the NHS remit was too limited: its focus on clinical treatment and acute medical intervention – at the expense of 'Cinderella' services within and around health care such as the long-term treatment of chronic ailments,

Figure 3: *White Corridors* (Pat Jackson, 1952); courtesy of BFI Stills, Posters and Designs

mental nursing, social work and preventative medicine – suggested it should be called a National 'Sickness' Service, since it failed to embrace a more holistic vision of good health. Neither was it free for long: charges for prescriptions, eye tests and dental work were soon introduced. Despite the undoubted rationality of the new system, and its admitted cost-effectiveness, the Black Report (1980) and subsequently *The Health Divide* (1987) found that the NHS had had virtually no impact whatsoever on long-recognised links between poverty and ill-health (see Black *et al.* 1982). To lose faith in the NHS in 1951, though, would have been to regress to the Old World which the military and election victories of 1945 purported to have left behind. Hence the film's clinical, white-washed vision.

Neil's research is specialised: a shimmering pinnacle of scientific discovery about rare instances of resistance to medicine's 'Great Discovery': penicillin. James Donald's intense, intelligent performance quietly captures what Charles Barr sees as Neil's 'visionary quality … believably, strongly and sanely' (Barr 2001: 161). His work (however necessary) is strictly biomedical – the search for a serum has no socio-economic meaning – and is so rarefied that it is difficult for him to find patients (modernity, the film hints, has already cured more widespread ailments). Tommy's arrival at Yeoman's is a remarkable coincidence.

Neil's laboratory needs better equipment, and his own health suffers because of his research. Myths of scientific research often want to posit that breakthroughs are made through wisdom and commitment rather than funding. But Neil sees an advantage to his current set-up: Yeoman's, in its homely way, allows him more freedom to be 'his own master'. What is circulated here is a sense that quasi-amateurism in a small-scale unit away from the spotlight will best allow the scientific mind to produce results (Powell and Pressburger's *The Small Back Room* (1948) made similar claims). This sort of thinking expresses redundant ideas which connect science with irrationality and metaphysics. It is a lay-mystification of science, and feeds into images of 'back-room boys' (or girls) – the infantilisation renders them harmless – reclusively ploughing their furrows and selling their harvests in *The Lancet*.

New money is eventually diverted to Neil by the hospital committee, but it is too late for Tommy. Neil repeats Andrew Manson's deliberate violation of medical ethics and again, the breach of regulations is warranted because the consequences are beneficial. He uses his untested serum on himself, so only endangers his own life, but he delegates the injection to Sophie, whose career and liberty are jeopardised: her own motivation is as much love for Neil as it is faith in his cure. *White Corridors* has moments of quivering tension but they are all seen with a quiet, clinical (yet tastefully censored) gaze. Not so the brief sequence after Tommy's death where Sophie decides to use Neil's serum. She leaves Tommy's bed and runs to Neil's lab. The camera dollies back dramatically as she hurries to it. The pained groans of a male patient are heard. A clock starts to chime (midnight!) as she runs upstairs, with violent shadows cast on the walls and the closed grill of a lift shrieking fears of entrapment. High melodrama for the last great gasp of the British documentary-feature tradition, and a sign of the feature film's need to deal with medical, institutional questions at a personal level.

Dick Groom's unprofessionalism recalls the milieu of Lawford and Charles Every. *White Corridors'* exposure of Dick, and his father's unexpected rejection of him in favour of a capable professional woman, marks out its meritocratic, anti-feudal values. Googie Withers is good at playing tough-but-feminine, like a British Barbara Stanwyck: think of Jo de Vries, the Dutch resistance worker in Powell and Pressburger's '...*one of our aircraft is missing*' (1942); and Joan, the no-nonsense modern wife who smashes her husband's haunted Victorian mirror and drags him back to the twentieth century in Robert Hamer's contribution to *Dead of Night* (Alberto Cavalcanti, Charles Crichton, Basil Dearden and Robert Hamer, 1945). As Sophie, she is at least her best male colleagues' equal, and in the closing shot she walks into long-shot down a gleaming corridor and etherealises into distant whiteness. Charles Barr's careful consideration of the film suggests that this evaporation anticipates the fate of the 'strong female professional' in 1950s British film, a type which was set almost to disappear. While he notes the ambivalences of the final scene, he regrets Sophie's decision not to go to London and he sees, in her total 'absorption into the provincial hospital', shades of *Billy Liar!* (John Schlesinger, 1963) and signs that she is subordinating herself to her future husband's glittering career (Barr 2003: 69). While Barr's contextualisation is right in terms of Withers' career and the long view of cinema history (Sophie herself tempers her ambitions in a gesture of subservience to Neil), the film strongly implies (hopes?) that she is walking into a utopian future of duty and vocation. The London she has turned her back on could well still be the retrograde haunt of Lawfords and Everys. It is certainly not yet the swinging London which would tempt Julie Christie and terrify Tom Courtenay in *Billy Liar!*

Part of the final shot's meaning depends on how we read Yeoman's Hospital. Sophie talks about it being 'buried away in the country', but Yeoman's has no definite location. Its non-specific smalltown setting (seen in location footage behind the opening credits) may be anti-metropolitan to Sophie, but that means it can be 'localised' by audiences across the regions. Like the NHS, it seems to be decentred but is nationally specific. The name Yeoman's invokes an established discourse of 'village-Englishness' which retrogressively presents the nation in familiar, 'local', rusticated terms. The ideological connotations of 'yeomanry' hark anachronistically to a pre-capitalist, medieval era but still have an emotional pull. The white science inside the building contrasts with these ideas. Taken together, the institution represents the nation in 1951, part old-fashioned and conservative, part new and modernising, the dynamic 'contained' within the quant – a characteristically English, utopian compromise. It holds together the divisiveness between traditionalism and medical progress which hampered Andrew's TB research in *The Citadel*. Sophie is walking into modern England, not backwards or out.

Troubling the 1950s

A brief-ish coda on *Mandy*. Rather than situating itself entirely within one institutional discourse like *White Corridors*, it dramatises the ideological conflict when one set of institutions (Health/Education/Social Services) invades the territory of another (the family). This is not strictly a 'medical film' – a sign that 'the medical film' may be impossible to delineate – but its treatment of professionals is similar and it draws on feelings which are similarly animated by the past and the future.

Christine (Phyllis Calvert) and Harry (Terence Morgan), a married couple, discover their daughter Mandy (Mandy Miller) is deaf. They move from their modern home to live with Harry's parents where Mandy can be looked after privately. By the age of six, Mandy is insulated and isolated in a lonely world of silence. Christine visits Dick Searle (Jack Hawkins), head teacher at the Bishop David School in Manchester (based on a real school for deaf children in Trafford) and is impressed. Against her husband's wishes, she leaves him, moves north, and places the child in Searle's care. The film centres on Christine and Harry's marital dispute and Harry's fight for custody of the child, as Searle gradually displaces Harry's role as Mandy's male guardian (risking scandal when he is suspected of an affair with Christine). Mandy eventually utters her first word and timidly enters a world of healthy interaction with other children, while Searle retreats to allow Christine, Harry and their child to reconstitute themselves as a nuclear unit.

Pam Cook rightly emphasises *Mandy*'s 'transitional' nature and highlights 1951 as a 'cusp' year for Britain, looking backwards to celebrate the Labour government's achievements in a manner inflected by the community/documentary discourse of the war, while also shoring up the private concerns of the nuclear family and anticipating a consumerist future (Cook 1986). Establishing long-shots show Bishop David School to be a neo-gothic Victorian building. Harry decides they 'couldn't send Mandy to a place like that'. It gives him 'the shivers' and is like a 'barracks'. He shifts them to his parent's house, another Victorian edifice, but this time a private one with his old nursery and rocking horse, all signifying an unhealthy recidivism and contrasting with his wife's more modern open-mindedness. Phillip Kemp's observation that Harry's animosity to the school is a class-bound horror of public institutions – it is a free residential school – seems right (Kemp 1991: 77). It outwardly reeks of the Poor Law, although its apparent similarity to a barracks also hints at Harry's reaction against National Service too, another indiscriminate State intervention into private life. Inside the school, though, the atmosphere differs: it is engaged and caring, but troubled by the same difficult financing decisions and committee politicking as Yeoman's Hospital. Where the approachable facia of Yeoman's expresses *White Corridor*'s placatory mission to take audiences safely through its doors, *Mandy* centres on the family and admits that the girl's long-term care and education touches on deep-seated fears about parental control and institutionalisation.

As in *Brief Encounter*, a woman's voiceover (Christine's) anchors us to an 'ordinary' housewife's perspective, yet both films paradoxically deal with the silencing of women's voices. Kemp's argument that Mandy is used to comment on society's 'emotional blight – the habit of non-communication' is judicious, but perhaps underestimates the way that Christine, charged with the caring role, is also habitually ignored by her family (Kemp 1991: 77). The interaction between Christine and Searle, echoed more pressingly in that between Mandy and her teachers, contrasts with that between Harry and Christine. Discourse in the public sphere – which the film seems to endorse – is matched by frigidity in the male-ordered home. Is there a vision here of new English society's more caring 'feminine' public aspect? Few chests were ever more broadly masculine than Jack Hawkins', but he conveys, beneath Searle's curmudgeonly rudeness, an avuncular kindness at odds with Harry's brittle masculinity.

During an argument, Harry slaps Christine and tells her to shut up, and she counters that he *would* rather she remained dumb. But she later writes to Harry: 'I hate having made you hit me. It was my fault for saying those things.' *Post-hoc*, feminist sympathies probably and rightly bristle at this condoning of domestic violence, but the film's model of marriage works towards a modern one of partnership (albeit premised here on the wife's willingness to compromise) and Harry admires Christine for not being 'the sort of person that's easy to bully'. We know Phyllis Calvert, though, from her Gainsborough costume-dramas of the 1940s (*The Man in Grey* (1943), *Fanny by Gaslight* (1944), *Madonna of the Seven Moons* (1945), *They Were Sisters* (1945)) and her presence here is haunted by those more troubled, troubling and violent views of sexual relations. As Harry, Terence Morgan is likewise darkened by James Mason's penumbral presence. Surface realism is clouded again by retrograde melodrama. More than *The Citadel* or *White Corridors*, *Mandy* articulates an ideological clash of values around a family's turbulent encounter with 'public' welfare. These melodramatic signs are figured in some highly expressive visuals and occasional manipulations of the soundtrack which take us, briefly, inside Mandy's muted world. Annette Kuhn rightly remarks that such expressivity is unexpected from Ealing Studios, who produced the film (Kuhn 1995: 23). Mackendrick, though, was no mere 'studio-man', and is noted for a more highly-wrought, non-complacent style.

Ultimately, the film conservatively endorses old, patriarchal power in the shape of Harry's father (played by Godfrey Tearle, *White Corridors*' Senior Surgeon). When events become critical, the Grand Old Man eventually speaks, making his son see sense about Christine's suspected fidelity. This conservatism would seem to play up the values of private, domestic order, but the last scene is played out in public, on the open bombsight outside the 'Father's House'. Mandy is a child of conflict. Her first step towards interaction with the world is moving, not only because we invest in her difficult future, but because of its tentativeness regarding the parameters of social institutions, the awareness that the professional's relationship with patients or clients is fraught, and the fragile reconstitution of Harry and Christine's marriage. The tentativeness marks Britain's anxiety about social progress.

Notes

1   For a detailed account of the critical attitudes which define and underpin the idea of 'quality realism' in its specific British cinema context, see Ellis 1978, reworked in 1996.
2   In 1937 George Orwell published his attack on the slums of northern England in *The Road to Wigan Pier* (reprinted 1986). His initial awareness of the problem derived

from his reading of Friedrich Engels' 1845 report *The Condition of the Working Class in England in 1844* (reprinted 1993), which specifically contains a chapter on mines and miners' health.

3 For a sketch of the Tredegar Medical Aid Society, on whose Hospital Committee Bevan served, see Foot 1962: 63.

4 Raymond Durgnat (1973) links *The Citadel* to Warner Bros.' biopics on Pasteur and Ehrlich, and to Carol Reed's *The Stars Look Down* (1939) (which he mistakenly remembers as a Welsh-mining film, although it is set in West Cumbria and was partly filmed in Workington). Durgnat explores the right-wing politics at work in Vidor's film, and sees it as a case of American mores being hived off to the Old World.

5 King Vidor's autobiography (1952: 231) praises Donat's generous professionalism, and noted his winning ordinariness on their first meeting: 'He looked more like a shy bookkeeper or reticent bank clerk than the romantic star I had seen on the screen.'

6 For the director's account of the film, see Pat Jackson (1999).

References

Barr, C. (2001) 'Madness, madness!': the brief stardom of James Donald', in B. Babington (ed.) *British Stars and Stardom: From Alma Taylor to Sean Connery*. Manchester: Manchester University Press, 155–66.

_____ (2003) 'The national health: Pat Jackson's *White Corridors*', in I. MacKillop and N. Sinyard (eds) *British Cinema of the 1950s: A Celebration*. Manchester: Manchester University Press, 64–73.

Black, Sir D., J. N. Morris, C. Smith, P. Townsend (1982) *Inequalities in Health: The Black Report*. Harmondsworth: Penguin.

Cook, P. (1986) '*Mandy*: daughter of transition', in C. Barr (ed.) *All Our Yesterdays: 90 Years of British Cinema*. London: British Film Institute, 355–61.

Dyer, R. (1993) *Brief Encounter*. London: British Film Institute.

Ellis, J. (1978) 'Art, culture, quality: terms for a cinema in the forties and seventies', *Screen*, 19, 3, 9–49.

_____ (1996) 'The quality film adventure: British critics and the cinema, 1942–1948', in A. Higson (ed.) *Dissolving Views: Key Writings on British Cinema*. London: Cassell, 66–93.

Engels, F. (1993) *The Condition of the Working Class in England in 1844*. Oxford: Oxford University Press.

Foot, M. (1962) *Aneurin Bevan: A Biography, vol. one 1897–1945*. London: MacGibbon & Kee.

Jackson, P. (1999) *A Retake Please!: Nightmail to Western Approaches*. Liverpool: Liverpool University Press.

Kemp, P. (1991) *Lethal Innocence: The Cinema of Alexander Mackendrick*. London: Methuen.

Kuhn, A. (1995) *Family Secrets: Acts of Memory and Imagination*. London: Verso.

Orwell, G. (1986) *The Road to Wigan Pier*. London: Secker and Warburg.

Shortland, M. (1989) *Medicine and Film: A Checklist, Survey and Research Resource*. Oxford: Wellcome Institute for the History of Medicine.

Vidor, K. (1952) *A Tree is a Tree*. New York: Harcourt, Brace & Co.

07

M. Roy Jobson and
Donna Knapp van Bogaert

Just a story or a 'just story'? Ethical issues in a film with a medical theme

Introduction

Ethics is essentially concerned with the effects of and procedures involved in moral decision-making. In film, these decisions – in terms of the storyline and the processes involved in making the film – have of necessity been made by the time it is completed and released. Should the viewer wish to consider the correctness, wisdom or effectiveness of these decisions, it is up to him or her to do so. The viewer, of course, has the prerogative to simply 'enjoy' the product – the telling of the story – without any consideration of how or why the film was produced; or whether there is any underlying 'message' being conveyed through the film. If, however, the viewer does not have the insight or capacity to recognise those instances where fact has been made subservient to fiction, believes that the story represents reality, and acts on it, an argument could be made that an ethical line has been crossed.

Ethics is inextricably linked to 'moral' judgements, i.e. what would be considered 'right' or 'wrong' actions. In film the audience is presented with any number of contexts of which they may have had no personal experience, but through the story and the acting are given an opportunity to vicariously experience whatever the situation presents. In reflecting on the appropriateness of the decisions made in the film, the viewer may be confronted with the appropriateness of similar decisions she or he has made or may even face in his or her own life. Alternatively, the viewer may be confronted with the possibility of considering a decision that she or he would not expect to have to make in today's (Western) society. For example, in the film *Sophie's Choice*, a viewer who is a parent of more than one child may well be left wondering whether she or he could choose which of their children should live or die; in *The English Patient* or *Saving Private Ryan*, viewers may consider how circumstances may influence choice (benevolently overdosing with morphine).

When medical situations are portrayed in film, a number of specifically 'medical ethics' issues arise – not only in the portrayal and resolution (or not) of these issues, but in the decisions made in creating the final product. The discourse around medical ethics in the public domain often initially raises the issues of abortion, euthanasia and medical malpractice. These issues are also raised in film. Many medical-ethics issues are, however, not so obvious, and layer upon layer of subtlety can be explored.

The films most widely distributed and most likely to have been seen by the readers of this book (and indeed by the authors of this chapter) project predominantly Western images, and portray Western concepts and experiences of health, illness and disease. The health care system within which these experiences take place is usually efficient, technologically advanced and accessible. By default then, the ethical approaches considered in this chapter could perhaps be termed 'Westernised bioethics'. It should be borne in mind that generalisations to other cultures and non-Western contexts may not be appropriate.

In this chapter, we outline a few medical-ethics issues in relationship to film, using a simplified traditional bioethics approach, and then make use of one of these approaches in considering the film *Lorenzo's Oil* (George Miller, 1992).

Ethical aspects in films with medical themes

A particular ethical decision, action or question may form the crux or turning point of a medical story.

Ethical approaches in the everyday practice of medicine often cannot be pinned down by definitive statements. Individual contexts or situations create a vast number of options. Film depictions of health issues capitalise on this wide range of possibilities, and very few, if any, prohibited topics exist. Apart from the issues mentioned above, ethical issues in film may include birth, death, suicide, psychosis, miracles, 'alternative' therapies, public health problems (for example, glamorising smoking), graphic portrayals of injuries/surgical procedures/illness complications, and so forth.

Questions, as opposed to statements, are often more useful in exploring ethical issues and examples are provided below:

The story: Is the film primarily about an ethical issue? Does the film clarify the nuances of an ethical issue or does it merely exploit the issue for the sake of dramatic effect?

Health workers: Does the portrayal of the characteristics and qualities of health professionals in the film promote or detract from their overall role as helping professionals, or as trustworthy confidantes? Is their role undermined? Is the role of health workers sentimentalised? Are they portrayed heroically? Are they portrayed as having greater powers over life and death than is real; or more frequently than would normally be the case? How does the choice of actor affect the portrayal?

Patients: Are depictions of being a patient over-exaggerated or over-simplified in the film? Could the viewer surreptitiously desire to develop the same disease and overcome it in order to attain the accolades given to the character? What impact does the choice of actor (high profile or unknown?) in the role of a patient have?

Diseases or illnesses: Is the disease portrayed in the film one that is common and likely to be within the experience of the average viewer? Does the film contribute to an understanding of the illness or disease or does it remain a mysterious (or fearful?) condition?

Quacks and faith-healers caring for a patient : Is the portrayal of 'quacks', and/or 'faith-healers' in film alienating from standard therapies? Would it be justifiable to promote an unproven means of healing through film?

Treatment: Are particular treatments portrayed accurately in the film? Are adverse effects overemphasised? Is disproportionate significance ascribed to the benefits?

Miracles: Is portrayal in film of a seemingly miraculous outcome inappropriately sensationalised? Or is it appropriately contextualised to a particular situation? If it is able to be explained, does the film do so? Or does it leave the viewer under a misapprehension?

Death: Is death portrayed as the ultimate failure of the health care system – and if so, what are the implications of this? Is death portrayed as a normal part of life?

Historical interpretations: Are portrayals of significant medical discoveries (for example, antibiotics) presented with an understanding of how those very discoveries may now be taken for granted to such an extent that it is difficult for the viewers to conceive of a world without them? Do portrayals of medical malpractice or medical heroism in war situations contribute to, or detract from understandings of health care professionals' moral obligations and responsibilities in that context (and in general)?

Medical caricature/comedy: How does the setting of health issues within a comic context add to or detract from the potential gravity of medical experiences?

Production issues: Are there issues of confidentiality related to the screenplay? Do the actors themselves have an appreciation of any ethical issues being depicted? What is the impact of various settings? (for example 'live' surgery in operating theatres; post mortems; childbirth). Is the publicity and marketing of the film ethically justifiable?

Films with medical themes often contain information and educational elements of direct import to the viewer – although these may be neither intentional nor overt. Where these issues are taken into account, producers and directors find themselves walking a thin line between 'drama' and medical accuracy. For example: one of the authors (MRJ) was involved in the early stages of a dramatised health education series in South Africa known as *Soul City*. As a collaboration between professional scriptwriters, social science researchers and health care professionals, one of its objectives was to educate while entertaining. A frequent dilemma arose when the health professionals felt that the drama was so overwhelming and so enthralling that it was 'killing the health message'. In turn, the scriptwriters complained that the rather stilted imperatives of the health messages were 'killing the drama'. In this situation, however, the target audience had been clearly defined and research carried out into their specific needs. In a film which is released commercially, there is no knowing who will end up watching – and someone with a particular disease, or with a relative who has the condition portrayed in the film, may be taking medical messages home.

Do filmmakers have an obligation to ensure that medical messages embedded in their films are accurate – or do filmmakers assume that the average Western viewer has a sufficient degree of 'movie-literacy' to recognise when the medical messages are being made subservient to the 'story'? *Lorenzo's Oil* is one film that raises several bioethical issues. As Anne Hudson Jones states: '*Lorenzo's Oil* is an excellent example of a film that has both straightforward and subtle influential power. It provides a case worth examining not only for its own story but also for what it reveals about a movie's ability to work on many levels at once and thereby transcend its own particularities to illuminate wider aspects of medical and cultural realities' (Jones 2000).

At a superficial level, the film is a story about a young boy, Lorenzo Odone, tragically suffering from adrenoleukodystrophy – an incurable disease. The heroes of the story are the parents, Michaela and Augusto Odone, who refuse to give up on exploring every possibility to find a remedy for their son's illness – and in the process Augusto clarifies the biochemical pathogenesis of the disorder. With the administration first of oleic triglyceride and then erucic acid, Lorenzo's abnormal very long chain fatty acid blood levels return to normal, and there is slight improvement in his clinical condition. The film ends with a series of vignettes of several young boys who have apparently been 'cured' by the treatment.

A brief and broad overview of traditional bioethics

Udo Schüklenk provides what he calls a 'sketchy overview of the main concepts within bioethics' which guide the actions of health care practitioners (Schüklenk 2000: 7). The authors have selected three of these theoretical-based approaches (Principlism, Consequentialism and Deontology) as well as a non-theoretical approach to biomedical ethics (Postmodernism) as vehicles by which we consider cinematic portrayals of medicine and its concomitant ethical dimensions.

Principlism, or principle-based bioethics, consists of at least four commonly accepted ethical principles. These are: *autonomy*, which refers to a person's right to choose and the health care practitioners responsibility in respecting that choice; *beneficence*, which refers to the obligation of health care practitioners to 'help' (be good to) patients; *non-maleficence*, which refers to the obligation of health care practitioners not to harm patients; and *justice*, 'the requirement to act in a fair and equitable manner with regard to the dis-tribution of medical burdens and benefits' (Schüklenk 2000: 8).

Consequentialism is the philosophical label given to theories that hold that actions are right or wrong (good or bad) according to the balance of their good and bad consequences (Beauchamp & Childress 1994: 47). The most prominent consequence-based theory is utilitarianism. Utilitarians accept only one basic ethical principle: the principle of utility. The principle of utility states that we ought to always produce the maximal positive balance of value over disvalue (all things being equal). In other words, the rightness of an action lies on its ability to produce the greatest amount of happiness (pleasure) for the greatest number of people, all things being equal. There is something intuitively compelling in this theory – after all, who would deny that bad actions should be minimised and good maximised. Utilitarians are divided by the distinctions of 'act' and 'rule'. If one is an 'act utilitarian', one asks: 'What good or bad consequences will result from this action in these circumstances?' (Beauchamp & Childress 1994: 50). If a 'rule utilitarian', then it is the consequences of accepting moral rules that are emphasised; in other words, an act's conformity to a justified rule based on its utility, makes the act right. Moreover, such rules are not expendable in particular context, even, as Tom Beauchamp and James Childress write: 'if following the rule in that context does not maximise utility' (1994: 51).

Deontology objects to much of what consequentialism affirms. It is the ethical theory that focus on the idea that there are particular features of any actions which, in addition to consequences, make an action right or wrong. Increasingly this theory is referred to as 'Kantian', because such formulations are largely due to the works of Immanuel Kant (1724–1804). Kant's theory holds that morality is grounded on reason, and considers humans (at least the adult rational types) as having that capacity to overcome feelings, desires and impulses and act upon their rational will; humans have the desire and the capacity to act according to reason. For Kant, moral obligations are based on a human's moral maxim; an action has moral validity if it is performed by an agent who has a goodwill. A goodwill necessarily involves a morally justifiable maxim on which the action is grounded. Moral agents (humans), Kant says, should act not only in *accordance with* but for the *sake of* obligation or 'for duty sake'. From this perspective, those who practice ethical health care are supposedly solely motivated by their goodwill and reason. Because they involve rightful maxims, Kantianism stresses duty, obligation and responsibility.

Postmodern-based bioethics. Postmodernism is anti-theory, anti-'grand narratives', anti-modernism. Approaching ethics in a postmodernist perspective can best be unravelled beginning with recognition that for all those involved in any discursive practice to know the language games involved; that is, to recognise that they are local, as Lyotard says, 'limited in time and space' (1984: 66). So the player involved in the discourse, 'must assume responsibility for both the rules themselves and for the effects of the specific practice' (Cilliers 1998: 137). Because it was the hope of modernism to establish universal rules (such as Kant's maxims), and because the results of modernism have been overall so disastrous, it falls upon us to deconstruct and reconstruct our moral selves in relation with the Other. To take and accept our part as nodes in complex systems involves recognition of at least the following ethical components, as Paul Cilliers identifies (1998: 139–40):

(i) respecting otherness and differences as values in themselves
(ii) gathering as much information on the issue as possible, notwithstanding the fact that it is impossible to gather all the information
(iii) considering as many of the possible consequences of the judgement, notwithstanding the face that it is impossible to consider all the consequences
(iv) making sure that it is possible to revise the judgement as soon as it becomes clear that it has flaws, whether it be under specific circumstances, or in general.

A postmodern approach to ethics, as articulated by Zygmunt Bauman (1992; 1993) unshackles us from the constraints imposed by modernism. In doing so it sets us free – not to do whatever we want to do – but to behave ethically. This is because if we understand that we are bounded in complex systems we see ourselves as small nodes connected to and in and with larger systems; we and the Other are inexorably linked.

Consequence-based bioethics and *Lorenzo's Oil*

The major ethical issue to be addressed is whether this film is just a story – which legitimately allows for so-called 'artistic licence', or whether this film is a 'just story' – which represents the events as they occurred. 'Although the film did not proclaim itself "a factual documentary", it was presented (and generally accepted) as a true story' (Jones 2000). The ethical issues being focused on here, using the consequence-based model, are the consequences of its being a 'presentation as a true story'.

Lorenzo is the patient with the illness (the index patient); however, it is the parents who interact with the health care professions most of the time. The scene in which the diagnosis is first made known begins with Augusto Odone asking the doctor not to beat about the bush and to be perfectly truthful ('Please doctor … without equivocation'). The doctor – a fictitious Professor Nikolai (portraying Dr Hugo Moser, a leading researcher into the management of ALD) – is in fact brutal in his honesty: 'Its progress is relentless. The end is inevitable. All boys with ALD die, usually within two years of diagnosis.' This is followed by a long pause and Michaela's 'And there are no exceptions?' Nikolai confirms that there are no exceptions. Moments later, he says: 'You know, normally at this point we try to be constructive, we try to focus on what can be done, but in this case...' (he shakes his head).

From the sources consulted no clear conclusions can be derived as to the extent to which this brutal honesty was fiction, fact, a distorted memory or a deliberate misrepresentation of the doctor's apparent heartlessness. However, according to Christopher Snowbeck quoting a colleague of Dr Moser's: 'When the movie *Lorenzo's Oil* came out, it strained the relationship between the Odones and Moser, and it has taken years for that tension to ease ... That conflict in the movie between the community and the bad research physician is something that sells movies. It's unfortunate because it kind of broke his [Moser's] heart' (Snowbeck 2001). In the following scene, seated in a library, Augusto Odone has accessed a medical journal in which the outcomes of 17 cases of adrenoleukodystrophy have been documented. The camera lingers over the chronicle of increasingly grim effects, repeatedly focusing on and finally resting on 'death'.

The scenes reinforce the perception that ALD is a hopelessly and absolutely incurable condition always leading to death within a short time. At the time of Lorenzo Odone's diagnosis in 1984 this may well have been the extent of knowledge about the condition. Dr Moser has indicated that the condition is now known to have severe and mild forms – some boys with the mild form having lived a normal lifespan (Snowbeck 2001). However in the years since the release of the film, this differentiation has not become widely known and the more tragic and severe form of the disease is the only one that people are made aware of. This is a consequence of the dramatic portrayal of Lorenzo's deterioration in the film. It could be argued that a positive consequence is that more people, including more health care professionals, are now aware of the condition than previously.

In the next sequence, Augusto and Michaela Odone are informed of a clinical trial involving a dietary intervention that is being carried out on boys affected with ALD. After a brief explanation of the role of 'very long chain fatty acids' (VLCFAs) and how they damage the brain, Professor Nikolais explains that enrolling Lorenzo would not reverse any damage already done and may not help him at all – 'but if it's any consolation to you, you'll be helping us to understand the biochemistry of this heartless disease'. He then quite casually asks: 'So, can we enrol Lorenzo in our trial' and after a short pause, Michaela barely audibly replies, 'I suppose so'. Ironically, Augusto Odone does end up helping with the understanding of the biochemistry – but not as anticipated in this scene.

This portrayal of the process of being enrolled into a clinical trial is particularly misleading – and could lead to major misapprehensions about the seeming ease with which it is possible to participate in clinical research. It could be argued that this is an instance where an ethical line, such as referred to above, has been crossed.

The Odones then become involved with the United Leukodystrophies Foundation – a support group for parents and caregivers of boys with ALD and similar disorders. At a meeting Michaela raises the issue that Lorenzo's blood levels of the fatty acids had been rising on 'the diet', and voiced her doubts about the diet. Another mother had noticed a similar response and Augusto suggests finding out amongst all the parents on the trial how the children had been responding, simply by a show of hands. The convenor of the meeting states very bluntly: 'This is not the way we do things here.' He and the other presenters go on to explain that they are not scientists and it is the doctors' responsibility to keep track of, and statistically analyse, the outcomes. The interaction ends with a statement about how the strict adherence to the protocol is the way in which medical science works and is the only way in which the scientists can get the information they need. Michaela then makes the damning statement: 'So what you're saying is that our children are in the service of medical science – how very foolish of me, I always assumed that medical science was in the service of the sufferers.'

The rather rigid and controlling portrayal of the Foundation was however false. To quote Dr Moser again: '[The film] presents an inaccurate and malicious portrayal of a valued parents' organisation' (Jones 2000). The word 'malicious' would indicate how the real-life protagonists experienced the film portrayal. This hurtful consequence, in terms of a utilitarian model of bioethics, could be considered as unethical. It is surmised that there is a story behind the story which has not been made public.

The Odones manage to raise the funds for the First International ALD Symposium in November 1984 – within months of Lorenzo's diagnosis. At this point oleic acid – in its triglyceride form is mentioned. Olive oil contains oleic acid. Nikolais objects as olive oil is forbidden in diet. A major factual error, but one around which much of the film is constructed, is the clinical trial involving this 'diet'. The trial was actually concluded in 1982, whereas Lorenzo's condition was only diagnosed in early 1984.

One of the screenplay authors and a director of the film, George Miller, was also a medical doctor. Did he use this film to 'tilt at the windmills' of the medical establishment in Don Quixotic fashion? His training as a medical practitioner could account for the unusual clarity of the depictions of the medical aspects of the film. But it is also possible that Miller was never involved in clinical research, and he may well have been subject to popular perceptions about how this is carried out.

A telling scene takes place between Augusto Odone and Professor Nikolais when Odone informs 'Gus' (Nikolais) that Lorenzo will be given oleic acid. Nikolais states: 'I am a scientist and I am of absolutely no use to you whatever unless I can maintain my objectivity.' Odone retorts: 'And I am not a scientist. I am a father and nobody can tell me what dressing I put on my kid's salad.' Nikolais softens the confrontation: 'This science of medicine … you know it's not like physics – there's no mathematical certainty – and because we deal with human beings who suffer it can appear heartless.' Prof Nikolais then 'unofficially' collaborates and recommends a dose of oleic acid.

The consequence of this sequence is to provide a reasonably accurate indication of the tensions between clinical researchers and their subjects when the problem being researched is a terminal disease. As Anne Hudson Jones succinctly summarises: 'There is an inherent conflict between the goals of physician-researchers and those of terminally ill patients and their families. This conflict is unlikely ever to be resolved, and it cannot be argued away, no matter how much evidence researchers try to provide to the contrary' (Jones 2000).

Another example of this 'conflict' is portrayed in the film, when the Odones invite the leaders of the Foundation to a meal. They are hoping to persuade them to distribute the information about the positive effects of the oleic acid to the members. The wife of the President of the Foundation clearly states: 'We take our guidance from the medical doctors.' Augusto Odone states: 'Sometimes the interest of the scientist is not the same as the parent.' He requests that the news (of the effectiveness of the oleic acid) be spread to members of the foundation. The leader's wife objects: 'Our parents suffer enough without being made victims of false hopes.' The scene ends with Augusto's impassioned outburst 'The doctors are so powerful, they are so powerful … but they are not gods – this acquiescence is so disgusting.' As it turned out, oleic acid on its own is only partially effective in lowering the levels of VLCFAs – and may well have given the organisation's parents false hopes.

The simmering conflict is highlighted again when the Odones inform Nikolais that they are exploring the possibility of using erucic acid in combination with the oleic acid, and want his collaboration. He finds an article which shows that erucic acid caused cardiac problems in rats, and stated that it would not be possible to get a review board to accept such a study. Michaela somewhat naïvely states that the human studies had been accomplished by history as rapeseed oil, widely used in certain parts of the world, contains erucic acid. Nikolais responds that a protocol 'based on that kind of assertion' could not be developed. (Normally, a clinical trial protocol would detail laboratory and animal studies before starting with Phase I [mainly safety] studies in humans.)

Michaela responds: 'Well perhaps you should examine your protocol when children are dying and a find a way to research these … it's common sense.'

Nikolais asks: 'If something goes wrong, what then?'

Michaela: 'Then I suppose the risk-reward ratio is too unattractive for you … the life of one boy is not enough reward for you to risk the reputation of the institution and the esteem of your peers.'

Nikolais: 'Your responsibility is merely towards your own child, my responsibility is towards all the boys that suffer from this disease, now and in the future. Of course I anguish for the suffering of your boy and of course I applaud you for the efforts you make on his behalf. But I will having nothing to do with this oil.'

Michaela: 'We are not asking, *doctor*, for your anguish or your applause. We are asking merely for your courage.'

Nikolais' acknowledgement of his (and medical research's) broader responsibility is obscured by the insinuation that all that was required was the doctor's courage. This does not take into account the strict regulatory processes involved in carrying out clinical research, but the viewers would not know this and would mostly be left with the impression that it is merely a matter of the doctor's 'courage' or lack thereof. These issues are raised again at another meeting of the Foundation but are expanded on in terms of not being able to apply for funds or obtaining insurance cover if approval for a protocol is not correctly obtained. This meeting is shown to end in a riot.

In September 1993 the *New England Journal of Medicine* published the results of a two-year study of Lorenzo's Oil on another version of adrenoleukodystrophy called adrenomyeloneuropathy. The conclusion states: 'In this open trial we found no evidence of a clinically relevant benefit from dietary treatment with oleic and erucic acids … in patients with adrenomyeloneuropathy' (Aubourg *et al*. 1993). In June of the following year, a letter from Augusto and Michaela Odone was published in the same journal. In contrast to the portrayal of their statements in the film, their letter uses scientific language and logic in questioning the above conclusion (Odone & Odone 1994). Indeed their arguments echo those of Professor Nikolais in the film. In 1999 Dr Moser himself stated:

> The introduction of Lorenzo's oil therapy 10 years ago raised high expectations, heightened by the motion picture of the same name … The oil normalises the concentrations of very long chain fatty acids (VLCFA) in plasma … there is evidence that excess of VLCFA contributes to pathogenesis … These considerations, coupled with the tragic course of untreated childhood cerebral X-ALD, led myself and others to conduct non-randomised rather than placebo controlled therapeutic

trials. Information obtained since that time highlights drawbacks of this decision and provides a lesson for the future. The drawback is that more than a decade after the first use of Lorenzo's oil, we still do not know if it is of clinical value. Even though most symptomatic oil treated patients continue to progress, our incomplete knowledge of natural history and the lack of a control group may have masked a moderate benefit. (Moser 1999)

Further studies have been carried out using 'Lorenzo's Oil', but as described in the evidence-based health care publication *Bandolier Extra*: 'Lorenzo's oil has no value in patients with established symptoms. It may be of value of asymptomatic patients, and may delay onset of symptoms, but the extent of any effect is unclear. This is a story of high hopes that a cure for an awful disease was at hand in Lorenzo's oil. It even spun off into a film of the same name. A side-effect was to make randomised trials impossible, so that a decade and more on we're still guessing whether this treatment has any benefit for anyone with this condition. It is not possible to say that it does. It is possible to say that it does not, at least for patients with established neurological symptoms' (*Bandolier Extra* 2002). This surely is the main ethical consequence of the film – and the question must be raised as to the extent to which the film has interfered with medical science.

Michaela Odone (who died in June 2000 of lung cancer) in an interview about the film said that: 'Our message to parents is: realise that your interests and the doctors' interests are not parallel. You may have a motivation and a time limit that these people do not have' (Jones 2000). Augusto Odone's view of the film is stated as follows: 'The real value of the movie has been to show people that in cases where you have a disease in the family or yourself, you have to be proactive – don't wait for doctors to tell you what the remedies are. It might be there is a doctor in Australia or France who has the answer, but you never know if you don't get in touch with them. I think the movie contributed to the changing relationship between doctors and patients' (Snowbeck 2001).

This may be true of Americans – but is not necessarily true of people who are still in awe of, or who find doctors and other health care professionals intimidating. Without detracting from the extraordinary work that Odone and his wife did, it must be acknowledged that they were each highly intelligent, confident, well-educated people with certain resources, connections with powerful people, and the ability to raise funds.

Other positive consequences of the film have been the establishment of *The Myelin Project* by the Odones and the various research projects funded by it. Future benefits of this research may be to patients with other forms of demyelinating disease, such as multiple sclerosis. In the organisation's December 2003 newsletter Augusto Odone releases information related to 'new, stronger data from the follow-up of the international study of Lorenzo's Oil as a proven preventive treatment for asymptomatic ALD boys' (Odone 2003). These results were initially presented at the 14th Annual Meeting of The Myelin Project Work Group in September 2003 by Dr Moser.

Conclusion

From a utilitarian standpoint, *Lorenzo's Oil* has had both 'good' and 'bad' consequences – as so often happens with ethical questions. The question ends up being whether the 'good' outweighed the 'bad' or vice versa. The opinion of Dr Moser himself is helpful in this regard. As Christopher Snowbeck states: 'Moser doesn't dwell on his past conflicts with the Odones when talking about the history of Lorenzo's Oil. "It's a very complicated situation, but on the whole the movie has been a benefit," he said' (Snowbeck 2001).

However, in an interview the year before, Moser was more explicit (as already partially quoted above): 'As a work of fiction, *Lorenzo's Oil* is an excellent film. However, as a factual documentary it has three main flaws: it overstates the success that can be achieved with the oil, it invents conflicts between the parents and the medical establishment, and it presents an inaccurate and malicious portrayal of a valued parents' organisation' [the United Leukodystrophy Foundation] (Jones 2000).

Clearly then, *Lorenzo's Oil* was 'just a story' and not a 'just story'. The film's close association with actual events and real people meant that it was generally seen as a true film. The misrepresentations of dates of the clinical trial, the relationships with the health care professionals and the parents' organisation could all be considered unethical. Furthermore the hopes raised that the oil would 'cure' the disease could also be considered unethical.

References

Aubourg, P., C. Adamsbaum, M.-C. Lavallard-Rousseau, F. Rocchiccioli, N. Cartier, I. Jambaque, C. Jakobezak, A. Lemaitre, F. Boureau, C. Wolf and P.-F. Bougneres (1993) 'A two-year trial of oleic and erucic acids ("Lorenzo's oil") as treatment for adrenomyeloneuropathy', *New England Journal of Medicine*, 329, 11, 745–52. Available at: http://content.nejm.org/cgi/content/full/329/11/745 (18 January 2004).

Bandolier Extra (2002) *Lorenzo's Oil for Adrenoleukodystrophy and Adrenomyeloneuropathy* Available at: http://www.jr2.ox.ac.uk/bandolier/booth/neurol/lorenz.html (18 October 2003).

Bauman, Z. (1992) *Imitations of Postmodernity*. London: Routledge.

_____ (1993) *Postmodern Ethics*. London: Blackwell.

Beauchamp, T. A. and J. F. Childress (1994) *Principles of Biomedical Ethics*. New York: Oxford University Press.

Cilliers, P. (1998) *Complexity and Postmodernism*. London: Routledge.

Jones, A. H. (2000) 'Medicine and the movies: *Lorenzo's Oil* at century's end', *Annals of Internal Medicine*, 133, 7, 567–71. Available at: http://www.annals.org/cgi/content/full/133/7/567 (4 February 2004).

Lyotard, J.-F. (1984) *The Postmodern Condition*. Manchester: Manchester University Press.

Moser, H. W. (1999) 'Treatment of X-linked adrenoleukodystrophy with Lorenzo's oil' [Editorial], *Journal of Neurology, Neurosurgery and Psychiatry*, 67, 279–80. Available at: http://jnnp.bmjjournals.com/cgi/content/full/67/3/279 (4 February 2004).

Odone A. (2003) *The Myelin Project Progress Report, December 8 2003*. Available at: http://www.myelin.org/12082003.htm (9 March 2004).

Odone, A. and M. Odone (1994) 'More on Lorenzo's Oil' [Letter]. *New England Journal of Medicine*, 330, 26, 1904–5. Available at: http://content.nejm.org/cgi/content/short/330/26/1904 (3 February 2004).

Schüklenk, U. (2000) 'An Introduction to bioethics', in C. Ernest (ed.) *Principled Choices: Medical Ethics in South Africa*. Johannesburg: The Center for the Study of Violence and Reconciliation, 7–13.

Snowbeck, C. (2001) 'The mixed legacy of *Lorenzo's Oil*', *Pittsburgh Post-Gazette*. Available at: http://www.post-gazette.com/healthscience/20010508hlorenzo1.asp (18 October 2003).

08

Graeme Harper

'Either he's dead or my watch has stopped': medical notes in 1930s film comedy

Comedy – personal or public?

Speaking personally, I first considered the relationship between medicine and film when re-reading Henri Bergson's book *Creative Evolution*, back in 1997. Originally published in English in 1911, this book had a considerable impact on me during my years of doctoral study; however, I had read it almost entirely in tatty, folded photocopies obtained on a tight student budget, so the idea of re-reading it in a new soft-cover version was a treat.

Creative Evolution, probably Bergson's most famous book and a major contributor to his Nobel Prize for Literature (1927), discusses, quite literally, the meaning of life – more specifically, intelligence and the intellect, and the order or disorder of nature. Perhaps predictably, the book has had as much impact on historians of science (including, of course, those of medical science) as on those working in the arts because it explores a range of ideas around creation and evolution, instinct, consciousness and illusion in a way that probes the formal dimensions of all knowledge.

Creative Evolution concludes with the chapter 'The Cinematographical Mechanism of Thought and the Mechanistic Illusion – A Glance at the History of Systems – Real Becoming and False Evolutionism'. This book should not, therefore, be insignificant to film scholars, though we might well consider how many ever refer to it.

Bergson writes:

It is because the film of the cinematograph unrolls, bringing in turn the different photograph of the scene to continue each other, that each actor of the scene recovers his mobility; he strings all his successive attitudes on the invisible movement of the film. (1911a: 305)

Bergson made the case for such a cinematographical method, arguing that it was ridiculous to suggest that 'movement is made up of immobilities' (Bergson 1911a: 308). Intelligence likewise was mobile, not static as the activities of 'the intellect' could be, fixing in time and space what in fact was constantly evolving.

Bergson's many other books include a famous work, *Laughter: An Essay on the Meaning of the Comic* (1911), looking at the nature of comedy.

Why begin a discussion of the relationship between medicine and film comedy so personally?

Simply, because laughter relies heavily on the melding of the personal and the public in a way that is distinctively connected with the nature of what might be called 'being human'. It was nineteenth-century writer and journalist William Hazlitt who said 'man is the only animal that laughs and weeps; for he is the only animal that is struck with the difference between what things are, and what they ought to be' (Hazlitt 1855: 1). And writer and parapsychology devotee, Arthur Koestler, who wrote 'laughter is a reflex, but unique in that it serves no biological purpose; one might call it a luxury reflex. Its only utilitarian function, as far as one can see, is to provide relief from utilitarian pressures' (Koestler 1964: 31). Laughter, as the principal aim or result of comedy appears, at least to some commentators, to be both specific to humankind and without much real weight.

Mass comedy, or what is generally agreed to be humorous or even funny, is even more confined to a specific human condition, defined by notions of 'release from everyday pressures' or 'pure entertainment' or even, in colloquial terms, 'cutting loose' from the bounds of tedious life – and, of course, the relatively new area of mass media comedy is the defining comedic mode of the late twentieth and early twenty-first centuries, as opposed to literary or dramatic comedy, the comedy of the public house or the laughter and frivolity of the carnival which were paramount in centuries past.

Comedy in its mass form aims to provide, for as many people as possible, that 'relief from utilitarian pressures' that Koestler pinpoints – thus, in some senses the formulaic or generic naturally becomes heightened. A mass consumer product, film comedy is definition and brand, packaging and discourse, pre-packed relief in a form not that dissimilar to mild paracetamol or low-dosage aspirin – though not to push a medical analogy too far. Popular film magazines, needless to say, are overflowing with new film releases listed as 'comedy' (romantic, teen and otherwise). The genre is one of film's most successful and, unfortunately, one of its least well analysed. So, for example, commentators as skilled as Frank Krutnik and Steve Neale can write in *Popular Film and Television Comedy* (1990) that 'comedy ... plays on deviations both from socio-cultural norms, and from the rules that govern other genres and aesthetic regimes' (Krutnik and Neale 1990: 3) while simultaneously defining those rules, but not theoretically. Comedy, being intimately connected, both physiologically and psychologically, with what it is to be human, provides an ideal platform for the exploration of medical science, and film comedy has actively pursued this exploration.

The case of screwball comedy

In the MGM screwball comedy *Love Crazy* (Jack Conway, 1941), a husband acts insane in order to prevent his wife divorcing him – the wife believing the husband is having an affair and him believing the only way to prevent divorce is to plead insanity. This act results in an interesting, medically-validated, reversal of fortune. William Powell plays husband, Stephen Ireland; innocent, in fact, of any infidelity. Myrna Loy is his potential ex-wife, Susan. Powell and Loy, who had worked together through ten or so previous films, films such as *The Great Ziegfeld* (Robert Z. Leonard, 1936) and *Double Wedding* (Richard Thorpe, 1937), use their off-screen familiarity to give their rocky on-screen marriage a believable underpinning and the action follows neatly from there.

Like all great screwballs, the comedy in *Love Crazy* is built around a series of errors, lies and barely-possible plot twists, with the eventual outcome – the recognition by the key players that their hold on fidelity, marriage and love is as solid as always – confirming the comedy's temporary but natural spirit of release. What is notable about *Love Crazy*, however, is that while the eventual outcome is in keeping with the lightness of the screwball comedy genre, or sub-genre more accurately, it is also an exemplar of the kinds of issues raised by medical film comedy.

In *Love Crazy*, the psychological, or psychiatric, is never anything less (or more!) than a particular kind of informed empirical science and when Powell's act – including the pitching of his meddling mother-in-law, played in delightfully matronly fashion by Florence Bates, fully-clothed into a swimming pool – results in him being *actually* confirmed as insane the question is not raised merely about the accuracy of the psychiatric evaluation but, rather, of the accuracy and intention of medical science generally.

Not that the clash between the medical science of psychiatry and the machinations of human relationships was anything unique to this particular screwball comedy. In *The Moon's Our Home* (William A. Seiter, 1936), a screwball starring Henry Fonda and Margaret Sullavan, Sullavan is carted away to an asylum by men in white coats, Fonda effectively assisting. While in *Bluebeard's Eighth Wife* (1938), directed by already distinguished comic actor/director Ernst Lubitsch, Claudette Colbert takes away Gary Cooper. *Bluebeard's Eight Wife* is the first of Lubitsch's two screwballs.

In the second of Lubtisch's screwballs, *That Uncertain Feeling* (1941), Merle Oberon plays Mrs Jill Baker, married for six years to Lawrence, this feat considered fairly miraculous by her social set. In fact, it is viewed as so miraculous that the society magazine *Town and Country* publishes a picture of Jill and Lawrence along with its suitably atrocious caption: 'The Happy Bakers'. All mostly well, then. However, Jill Baker is suffering from persistent hiccups and, somewhat against her better judgment, is convinced to seek psychoanalytic help to alleviate the problem. There, in the waiting room of psychoanalyst Dr Vengard (Alan Mowbray), she meets eccentric pianist Alexander Sebastian (Burgess Meredith), and this meeting sets in motion the temporary destabilisation of the Baker's relationship. It is on this underscoring of the frailty of human relationships, and the inadequacy of medical science to deal with them, that Lubitsch and screenwriter Walter Reisch hang this recognisably Lubitsch touch comedy.

Plainly put, informed by the famous Lubitsch talent for innuendo and visual spice, *That Uncertain Feeling* places the simple medical responses of psychoanalysis against the complicated relationship story of Lawrence and Jill Baker, suggesting that Lawrence's failure to give adequate attention to wife Jill is both reason for her psychosomatic hiccups and an open invitation to the intrusion of somewhat mad, at least in a colloquial sense, Burgess Meredith. The place of medical science in all this is quickly set up:

'Doctor, I'm going to be frank with you,' Jill Baker tells Dr Vengard, 'I'm absolutely certain there's nothing wrong with me.'
'I'm sure you'll feel differently when you leave this office,' replies Vengard.

Medical science here is presented as certain, fixed, easily read, superior. Human relationships, however, are uncertain, changeable, almost impossible to read, and therefore, by inference, inferior. If the Bakers are ideal they are ideal not *only* in a cultural or social sense, but ideal in terms of what seems to be their compatibility with a scientised version of the world. Scientism, meaning a version of science in which it might be believed that aspects of the human will eventually be understood if a sufficient number of events are closely examined (Lloyd 1986: 125) – a very different thing to science, in which aspects of the unpredictable, the creative, the human are accepted, and explanations not simply dependent on vulgar empiricism. So, for example, it is suggested that if Dr Vengard is given enough event-based evidence relating to Jill and Lawrence Baker there is no reason why their relationship cannot be pinned down like any other scientific problem.

But, of course, this is a key point of both *That Uncertain Feeling* and of *Love Crazy* and, indeed, of a number of other screwball comedies. Medical science, in these cases psychiatry or psychoanalysis, is presented as detached from reality, a kind of naïve, overly-confident sense of things in which the world can be reduced to a physical mathematics. While Tina Olsin Lent, in her comments on screwball comedy (in Brunovska Karnick and Jenkins 1995: 316), suggests a concentration on gender issues is not to dismiss other possible readings of screwball, there is no doubt that such a concentration fails to engage fully with the issue of the investigation of medical science – particularly psychiatry and psychoanalysis – in this specific strand of film comedy.

The screwball sub-genre made its mark in the 1930s, between the Great Depression and the Second World War, hung on what has most often been labelled as a 'battle between the sexes'. Screwballs are equally psychological and physical in force, weaving their often wild plots around a sense in which no matter how mad the world might get the relationship between a woman and a man would somehow survive – if, indeed, true love determines that it should survive.

It would be easy to suggest that such a 'love focus' means that screwballs are simply proto-typical versions of the romantic comedy, fuelled by the blackness of the Depression years, and preceding the need for Hollywood to engage with austerity of the Second World War period. Lightweight relief, in other words, in which hefty matters of heterosexual love are played out in music-hall style, the entrances and exits of the key players often resembling the pratfalls of vaudevillian range. Ed Sikov is certainly correct to say, likewise, that screwball comedy owed a great deal to the arrival of the Production Code (1934), which brought to bear on the plots, characters and themes of Hollywood the moral and, indeed, overtly religious concerns about the nature of 1930s American cinema (Sikov 1989: 20).[1] If screwball comedies addressed the issue of producing 'sex comedies' without the sex, then their penchant for melding the physically combative and the psycho-babbling popular was founded well enough on the restrictions the moral right would seek to impose on Hollywood's affect on the popular imagination.

But the question must be asked: why psychology and/or psychiatry? Why doctors presented as official gauges of good and bad, right and wrong? Why the character of Dr Lehmann in *Bringing Up Baby* (Howard Hawks, 1936)? And 'The Psychiatrist' in *Mr Deeds Goes to Town* (Frank Capra, 1936). Or, for that matter, why Dr Kohlar in *My Favourite Wife* (Garson Kanin, 1940), Drs Downer and Eggelhofer in *Nothing Sacred* (William A. Wellman, 1937), Dr Kessler in *Fifth Avenue Girl* (Gregory La Cava, 1939), Drs Betz and Shultz in *The Good Fairy* (William Wyler, 1935) and Dr Kammer in *After the Thin Man* (W. S. Van Dyke, 1936). Why medical science as both plot point *and* character?

Perhaps, in fact, medical science is also one of screwball comedy's primary themes.

Certainty and superiority

As popular history confirms, the word 'screwball' entered the American vernacular in the 1930s and, by mid-decade, was sighted in such primary cultural denominators as *The New Yorker*, the *Saturday Evening Post* and *Time* (Chapman 1987: 374). The word, while also associated with a particular kind of baseball pitch, quickly came to relate to eccentricity, extending as far as a colloquial definition of insanity. The label 'screwball comedy', of course, draws directly from this. Like the baseball pitch, one of its primary propulsive mechanisms is its unpredictability. This scatological approach is certainly meant to represent, both literally and metaphorically, the mystery surrounding the relationship between men and women – or, more accurately, between a man and a woman. That is, it would be wrong to suggest that screwball comedies deal mostly in archetypes: the key players, most often one man and one woman, are presented as individualistic, driven by often quite idiosyncratic reasoning, personally confused or, at least, on the borderline of confusion, and motivated by quite complex personal history. However, there is one archetype that many screwball comedies do present, and that is one connected with medical science.

The psychiatrist or psychoanalyst in the screwball comedy is associated with certainty, and in their belief in the right and power of their science they present a picture of superiority. A picture of superiority, of course, that is ultimately the subject of scorn because, as the plot unfolds, it becomes the strength of the 'uncertain' relationship between the male and female leads that defines what is truth in these films, not the strength of the medical definitions or diagnosis offered.

It is worth considering that, in the period following the First World War, medical science was at a key evolutionary moment. As Roy Porter points out:

> For centuries medicine was impotent and thus unproblematic. From the Greeks to the First World War, its tasks were simple: to grapple with lethal diseases and gross disabilities, to ensure live births and manage pain. It performed these with meagre success. (Porter 1997: 718)

Beyond the First World War, medical successes were greater; but, likewise, as Porter notes, they became connected with 'inflated expectations' (ibid.). In other words, as medicine achieved more so more was naturally expected of it – and, eventually, the public's expectations would become unfulfillable. Porter's analysis is ironically echoed in the words of Charles Greene Cumston, writing in 1926 in his book *An Introduction to the History of Medicine: From the Time of the Pharaohs to the End of the XVIIIth Century*:

We believe that it is not possible precisely to distinguish what belongs to art and what belongs to science, for the reason that everything begins as an art which in turn becomes a science. (Cumston 1926: 14)

A confidence finely honed on success. Not that medicine in the 1930s was unique in being a successful and yet increasingly problematic 'art-come-science', as Cumston saw it. Economic theory, of course, as one branch of the social sciences, was called considerably into question in this period. Even preceding the impact of the Great Depression, economics in the inter-war period was haunted by pressing questions about the relationship between its ideas and doctrines and the problems occurring in the world around. Reality seemed somewhat different to the suggestions being made by economists and the affect of the First World War on social, political and cultural integrity only managed to make surety an even more dubious concept.

Science, in the broader sense, continued to provide evidence of its success, despite a sense that it might not have absolutely *certain* answers to the problems humanity faced. In this period, E. D. Adrian and C. Sherrington were awarded the Nobel Prize for Medicine (1931) for the discovery of the functions of neurons and Thomas Hunt Morgan was awarded the Nobel Prize for Chemistry (1934) for the hereditary transmission functions of chromosomes, vitamin C was synthesised (1933), E and B6 identified (1938) and A and K crystallised, insulin was used for the control of diabetes (1937), and the first artificial heart was developed (1936). At the end of the period, Sigmund Freud died (1939), though not before having established one of the more pervasive of psychology-based medical fields ever founded and, in 1940, Howard Florey developed penicillin as a practical antibiotic.

In the fields of science generally, there were advances in radio astronomy, quantum mechanics, refrigeration technologies, the fields of radiation and nuclear research, jet-engine development – with flight now properly challenging sea travel – and a great deal more. And yet, both the atrocities of the First World War and the instability of the Depression brought into question the role of all kinds of science in providing key points for human development. Confidence gave way to insecurity and what might be called a sense of needing to 'scrape the surface' of many established discourses in order to find what really held them together became tantamount to being an informed, modern individual.

In avant-garde art, for example, perhaps most poignant of all was the development of the Surrealist movement out of the immediate influences of Dada, and the longer-established tenets of Metaphysical art. Of course, Hollywood film, that popular, mostly narrative form that produced the screwball comedy, could hardly be said to draw its lessons directly from Surrealism. However, what was in the air of its history was not so dissimilar. A bolder analyst might even be tempted to suggest that the scatological narratives of screwball comedy owed a little something to the involuntary psychic connections made in Surrealist self-expression. A less provocative one can at least find in the work of Salvador Dalí, Joan Miró, Max Ernst and René Magritte evidence of the same determination to scrape the surface that Hollywood's populist art was attempting.

Dalí's work, aided by his own longevity, continued these explorations well into the late twentieth century. From 1929 onwards, he gave artistic form to the foundations laid down by Freud and to the machinations of the movement between the psychological and physical worlds. If in Dalí's work we see the high art manifestations of uncertainty we also see a kind of black comedy – the same black comedy that screwball portrays in its incessant warring sexes and convoluted plots. We likewise see a combination of physical and psychological dissolution. The famous Dalí painting *The Persistence of Memory* (1931) consists of clock faces hung rag-style over corners and stark bare branches, the melding of memory with fantastic landscape a direct reference to Freud's ideas of displacement and dream distortion. The effect is disturbing, but also strangely humorous. Comedy, for Dalí, is located in the mismatch of psychology with the machinations of reality. Likewise, in *Illuminated Pleasures* (1929) Dalí portrays the results of what he often referred to as his 'paranoid critical' mode, letting himself enter a dreamlike state and producing a work in which the physical (for example, a bloody hand carrying a knife, a set of boxes, men on bicycles) and the dreamlike (for example, a stark desert atmosphere, the emergence of figures from the crest of a wave) occupy the same space. Dalí was not the only member of the Surrealists to be working in this vein. In René Magritte's *The Human Condition I* (1933) we look at a 'window' that is also a canvas on an artist's easel. Again, comic result and the questioning of physical and psychological reality go hand-in-hand. Screwball comedy, emerging in the same period, references a similar manifestation of the nervousness felt by the general population about the separation of representation from actuality.

Incongruity and medical cinema

Theories of comedy can be grouped into three broad areas: superiority, incongruity and psychic release. The first, discussed in part already, talks of comedy as the result of mismatch between individual or social expectation and obvious, contingent result. So, for example, the pompous 'upper crust' socialite being fooled by the marriage of his daughter to a working-class 'stiff', the self-loving detective being foiled by the clever, happy-go-lucky crook and, of course, the over-confident medical practitioner being beaten by the actual workings of the human body or mind. Critics as distinguished as Aristotle, Plato and Thomas Hobbes are associated with the Superiority Theory of comedy.

The second theory of comedy, the Incongruity Theory, holds that comedy results from a clash between thoughts and perceptions and a particular set of circumstances. This theory, which has been explored over time by such critics as Henri Bergson, Søren Kirkegaard, Immanuel Kant and Arthur Schopenhauer, focuses not on positioning within an individual or social frame but, rather, on a particular set of events, a particular portrayal. While the Superiority Theory might be said to result from the observation that there is more than one set of realities, the Incongruity Theory results from the idea that even reality itself is a set of dramatic ironies, paradoxes and ironic twists of fate.

As would be imagined, in film the Incongruity Theory of comedy can be supported by a vast array of examples. Film, after all, is most often an event-based art form. Its historical range owes a considerable debt to the vaudevillian and to the popularly theatrical. It is a combination of sensory experiences of which the plot-driven shifting of colour and sound and shape play a fundamental part. So congruity, generated by event or circumstance, is often a formal and structural expectation in film. Filmmakers consider it, not only in traditional narrative and technical ways through such things as continuity editing and maintaining the line, but also by often fitting broadly into a range of market-friendly genre categories. And film audiences expect to be confronted with it. Incongruity, or the mismatch of thought and perception and circumstance or event, *most* often occurs in film in the form of visual spectacle, aural affront or narrative twist; and *least* often in technical or genre-busting ways.

Medical science, of course, must be anything but incongruous. In the popular imagination medicine depends both on a confident superiority and a congruous relationship with the world around it. 'Medicine', Charles Cumston wrote, 'is a kind of machine that furnishes remedies for human suffering' (Cumston 1926: 9). Medicine is, in other words, in tune with the thoughts and perceptions of the population and, in its every action, it confirms this congruity. This position is further enhanced by the cultural establishment relating to medicine so that we can still talk about, despite vast advances in communication between various regions of the world, 'Western' medicine and 'Eastern' medicine. Though Western medicine, due at least in part to economic hegemony, has made significant inroads into 'Eastern' regions, 'Eastern' medicine remains culturally marginalised in the West, to the point at which its practices might be said to be incongruous with the trajectory of Western culture.

Any situation in film in which medical science, or a representative of the medical profession, acts in a way not in keeping with public perceptions and thoughts regarding medicine has the potential to result in comedy. These public perceptions certainly include the following: seriousness, or a condition of import attached to the practice of medicine; logic, or the operation of an enquiring but not overly speculative mind; a regard for the integrity of the human mind or body. Already, listing these, there is a sense in which not film comedy but a horror film might result. The murderous doctor, the frivolous, self-aggrandising risk-taker, and so forth. Equally, violence and certain kinds of comedy – slapstick, situation – travel similar roads. Laughter itself, sometimes physically disruptive to the point of disablement, can have the appearance of violent physical act. But the physical closeness of the manifestations of laughter must not confuse the analysis. Rather, a dissolution of the relationship between incongruity and amorality might well be the clue to medical film comedy – the doctor out of place or out of kilter with expectations; the institution of medicine or medical practice out of place with the perception or thoughts of the public.

Michel Foucault notes in *Discipline and Punish* (1977) that one of the most important parts of establishing institutions and their disciplinary practices is in relation to the control of individualism (Foucault 1977: 167). For Foucault, through institutionalised control of space, time, the coding of activities and the composition of forces, real individualism is turned into institutionalised individualism. Though the individual might appear to be free-thinking and relatively free-acting, movement is prescribed, expectations tabulated and tactics arranged so that control is maintained. Foucault's *Discipline and Punish* was preceded by his *The Birth of the Clinic: An Archaeology of Medical Perception* (1973) in which, through a method of treating the history of medicine in a relatively non-linear and spatialised fashion, he is able to make a case for seeing the shift from classical medicine to modern, clinical medicine as being essentially a shift away from 'health' as the aim of medical practice to 'normality' as its aim. This, of course, is quite a paraphrasing of Foucault's ideas; however, considering that shift even as generally as this offers a considerable insight into the relationship between medicine and film comedy.

There is little doubt that the common perception of the clinically aware, morally correct and medically competent doctor is one in which 'quirks' of personality are subdued and a 'normality' (Foucault 1973: 35) linked to the clinical gaze is confirmed. However, in Anglophone film circles we must be wary of interpreting Foucault's translated discussion of the clinical 'gaze' too literally as a primary version of the filmic gaze. The French word Foucault uses is 'regard' which can mean a gaze or a look or an expression or a glance. It is the English translator of *The Birth of the Clinic* who chooses the word 'gaze' to cover these meanings, but there is a strong indication that Foucault's original meaning was far more multi-layered.

That said, and broadly following Foucault, the common perception of the medical practitioner is one in which they are individually recognisable, but not out of step with the majority – thus declarations of gender, race and/or sexual orientation are often subdued, if not completely suppressed. A medical practitioner must appear engaged with the world around them, but not be overly contemporary, capitalistic or perhaps even politically active (for example). 'Younger' doctors, by and large, are less trustworthy than 'older' doctors – so popular myth goes. For many years, female doctors were considered less trustworthy than male. Flamboyant dress, overt enjoyment of leisure time, even visible evidence of another life with a family, spouse or, worse still, undefined partner of opposite or same sex: each of these seems somehow slightly out of sync with the general public perception of the Western medical practitioner. The medical profession is not so much a bastion of conservatism as the home of a highly tempered version of individualism. Anecdotal evidence suggests the expression 'he (or she) is good', when referring to a medical practitioner, usually attaches itself to something along the lines of 'he (or she) seemed suitably engaged with my problem' and 'he (or she) seemed to be suitably concerned about my ailment' and 'he (or she) seemed not vastly different in attitude to myself'. Similarly, as noted, while it seems reasonable for the Western practitioner to display evidence of their success (for example, expensive home and car; children at a private school; suitable, perhaps culturally invigorating, vacations) there are limits to the public toleration of this display of wealth. What might be considered ostentatious for the medical profession seems to begin at quite a frugal level. And this attaches itself to a general belief in the congruity of a certain kind of seriousness with the act of 'being a doctor'.

Medical film comedy according to Marx

Dr Hugo Z. Hackenbush, or Quackenbush as the character began life (French 1993: 4), or Hackinapuss, as Chico Marx calls him, is the not-so-legitimate doctor of the Marx Brothers film *A Day at the Races* (1937) and a primary example of the work of comedic incongruity. Dr Hackenbush craves success, wealth and the opposite sex, and is very far from serious.

The word *quack* is short for *quacksalver*, combining *quack* (meaning to prattle) with a derivation from the verb *salve* (meaning: heal or remedy). The word was used from about the seventeenth century onward. *Quack* also has links to the word *croak*, with its colloquial meaning of 'to die'; and *salve* has links, by the nineteenth century, with the definition: 'to clear up or explain'. No surprise, then, that Hackenbush (Groucho Marx) began as Quackenbush in this second Marx film for MGM, directed by Sam Wood, with a screenplay by Robert Pirosh, George Seaton and Robert Oppenheimer.

Dr Hugo Z. Hackenbush is not really a doctor but rather a 'horse doctor' (Marx Brothers 1993: 174), a veterinarian. Entangled in a plot in which a wealthy woman (Mrs Upjohn), who is in love with him, is prepared to support a struggling sanitarium if he is made Chief of Staff, Hackenbush arrives on the back of equally difficult financial circumstances and proceeds to entangle in Marx Brothers mayhem the sanitarium's entire medical staff. If wealth in the medical profession is easily associated with ostentation then Hackenbush's desperate poverty is equally unacceptable. Doctors should not need money, it seems; in having it, they should not have too much of it. But Groucho Marx's Hackenbush has more problems than his credit rating:

MRS UPJOHN: Now, Doctor, I'd like you to meet your new associates. (*Long shot of everyone.* The FIRST DOCTOR *steps forward*)

FIRST DOCTOR: Johnson, Bellevue Hospital, nineteen-eighteen. (*He steps back*)

SECOND DOCTOR: (*Steps forward*) Franko, Johns Hopkins, twenty-two. (*He steps back*)

THIRD DOCTOR: (*Steps forward*) Wilderming, Mayo Brothers, twenty-four (*He steps back*)

HACKENBUSH: (*Steps forward, clicks his heels*) Dodge Brothers, late twenty-nine. (*He steps back*) (Marx Brothers 1993: 177–8)

Dodge Brothers being automobile makers, of course, not the location of esteemed medical education. Later in the same scene, when Hackenbush gives Mrs Upjohn a horse pill and one of the other doctors asks if he has made a mistake, Hackenbush comments 'You have nothing to worry about. The last patient I gave one of those won the Kentucky Derby' (Marx Brothers 1993: 179).

Wonderful comic stuff. And yet, Groucho Marx's Hackenbush provides a more interesting angle on quackery than perhaps even this suggests. While we can laugh at the incongruity of the depiction we are also drawn, more subliminally perhaps, to consider the foundation of medical integrity. In Foucaultian terms, Hackenbush is outside the system and, in being outside the system he is potentially a challenge to it. If we laugh at Hackenbush because he is incongruous, we also learn from him that what might be labelled 'quackery' can sometimes provide solutions that legitimate, 'serious' medical practice cannot. Decidedly, the 'legitimate' doctors in *A Day at the Races* are of marginal use to anyone at all – they might as well be marble busts labelled 'The Famous Men of Medical Science', and often appear in the film to be exactly that.

Lesley Hall and Roy Porter, in their book on the creation of sexual knowledge in Britain, *The Facts of Life* (1995), deal with quackery in the nineteenth century this way:

The quacks, living by them, perhaps knew better than the average medical practitioner what sexual anxieties bothered the man in the street; aware of what would sell, they advertised their wares … Doubting that sexual problems could be sympathetically dealt with by a regular doctor, patients continued to turn to quacks. (Hall & Porter 1995: 138)

What Hall and Porter miss is that the binary 'quackery versus non-quackery' is indeed a structure functioning to maintain a centralised discourse of medical practice, both bio-medical and psychological. The gap in Hall and Porter's analysis is that the quacks dealing with sexual anxieties are quite obviously providing an important service that legitimate medicine cannot provide. Comic incongruity in *A Day at the Races*, in an analogous way to a metaphoric shift of plain of reference, or an ironic overturning of viewpoint, results in us seeing the world of medicine anew. Dr Hackenbush/Quackenbush thus provides his own service, a medical service, but one that challenges our notions of what medicine actually is.

If, however, this appears at first too portentous a reading for a film as populist and as fun as *A Day at the Races*, then it might be recalled that there are other narrative and thematic structures that identify the film as complex. The film's title, for example, refers to an outing at the horse track, it also relates to the race to save the sanitarium, a race to save lives – when Stuffy (Harpo) is brought by Tony (Chico) to see Dr Hackenbush, Hackenbush comments 'Sit down here while I snatch you from the jaws of death' (Marx Brothers 1993: 198) – the romance between Gil and Judy, which revolves around Gil's horse winning a race and him getting his big break as a singer, and the race to get the sanitarium back on its feet *before* Mrs Upjohn realises the scam. Similarly, while the Marx Brothers' act might well be 'extra-cinematic' (Krutnik and Neale 1990: 104), it is actually complicit with film's sense of the physiological, not against it, as Krutnik and Neale seem to intimate. That is, whether metonymic or metaphoric, film deals almost exclusively in movement and shape and colour, and, in these ways and more, thus emphasises the physically vital. Everything in *A Day at the Races* supports this.

If medicine here revolves around a kind of incongruity, it is an incongruity of the system with truth, not of medicine and the individual *per se*. The doctors of the Standish Sanitarium hide from the truth in pomposity; hypochondriac Mrs Upjohn hides from the truth by supporting Dr Hackenbush, the only doctor who will tell her she is not well; when Dr Hackenbush examines Stuffy he hides from the truth in pseudo-medical jargon:

> He's got about 15 per cent metabolism with an overactive thyroid and a glandular affectation of about 3 per cent ... With a 1 per cent mentality. He's what we designate as the Crummy Moronic type. (Marx Brothers 1993: 200)

This is all much more than light relief.

Comedy unearths what humorist Luigi Pirandello once called 'the perception of the opposite' (Pirandello 1960: 119). That is, in this case, the perception of the truth in medical science.

Concluding on medicine

The final theoretical approach to comedy, the Psychic Release Theory – favoured by Sigmund Freud and Herbert Spencer, to name just two of its proponents – considers that laughter is a venting of excess psychic or nervous energy, energy that would otherwise be channelled into potentially more harmful activities, into 'suffering' as Freud puts it (Freud 1966: 111). Comedy therefore provides a tool for personal as well as social interaction, promoting social harmony and stability – a physiological function with social results, akin to other such functions in other animal species, but specific in this instance to humankind.

In *Love Crazy* or *A Day at the Races*, in *That Uncertain Feeling* and *Mr Deeds Goes to Town*, among other films, the empirical evidence in support of the Psychic Release Theory seems strong. Equally, the themes of these films (*Love Crazy* with its revelation that true love is not crazy at all; *That Uncertain Feeling* with its focus on what might be called 'the certainty that strong human relationships can ride out uncertainty' and *A Day at the Races* with its emphasis on the winning qualities of goodness, no matter how scatterbrained it might seem) surely match the general nervousness of the 1930s Western populous in relation to issues of science generally, and of medical science more specifically.

One note of caution – while these films are a useful exemplar of the kinds of issues raised in medical film comedy, the issues themselves are not exclusive to 1930s cinema, nor to Hollywood. The period perhaps provided a heightened opportunity for exploration, egged on by the effects of the First World War and the Great Depression, but it would not be unreasonable to jump forward 20 or 30 years, and from Hollywood to Britain, and wonder what elements of similar questioning exist in films such as Ralph Thomas' *Doctor in the House* (1954), *Doctor at Sea* (1955) or *Doctor at Large* (1957) or his brother Gerald Thomas's *Carry on Doctor* (1968) or *Carry On Again Doctor* (1969).

The medical discourses of these films too are revelling in the same mode, or position, as Hall and Porter's quacks: not legitimate in terms of the structures and functions that surround them (and certainly the medical practitioners in these films raise as many questions as they answer), but not presenting one pole of a fixed oppositional binary either. Henri Bergson's statement in 'The Cinematographical Mechanism of Thought and the Mechanistic Illusion' that 'matter has appeared to us as perpetual becoming. It makes itself or it unmakes itself, but it is never something made' (Bergson 1911a: 272) is well-founded. What is at stake here is the making and unmaking of the cultures and conception of medicine.

The lessons that come from considering medical film comedy are twofold. Firstly, that theories of comedy identify the multiple ways in which comedy's discourses constantly reassess the structures and functions of the world. 'The comic spirit has a logic of its own, even in its wildest eccentricities. It has a method in its madness' Bergson notes elsewhere (1911b: 66). This, however, is a general point.

Secondly then, and more specifically, medical film comedy travels through difficult terrain – terrain that spreads out around the foundations of medical truth, the role of the medical establishment in maintaining certain kinds of practices and institutions, the ability of individual doctors and other medical personnel to effect the discourse of medicine itself, the role of cultural perception in medical attitudes, outlooks and diagnoses. In this, medical film comedy makes a significant contribution to our understanding of the role of medicine in our cultural histories. If this were all, it would be significant enough. However, as medicine places itself at a particularly 'human' point in the interaction between institutions and individuals, between the personal and the public, it stands to reason that comedy, which situates itself similarly, should have considerable force when linked to it. Add to this medicine's role in generating questions about the relationship between science and everyday life, as well as the narratives of superiority, incongruity and psychic release which spring up around comedy, and the complex popular art form that is film seems the ideal vehicle in which to unite these two discourses in order to negotiate this terrain. These film comedies of the 1930s certainly prove this to be the case.

Note

1   The discussion of Screwball Comedy in this chapter owes a debt of gratitude to Ed Sikov's *Screwball: Hollywood's Madcap Romantic Comedies*, which is a lively examination of the genre. While I do not entire follow Sikov's analysis, naturally concentrating more on the medical references, the excellent film choices made by Sikov are noted, and his book sincerely recommended.

References

Bergson, H. (1911a) *Creative Evolution*. New York: Henry Holt.

_____ (1911b) *Laughter: An Essay on the Meaning of the Comic*. London: Macmillan.

Brunovska Karnick, K. and H. Jenkins (1995) *Classical Hollywood Comedy*. New York: Routledge.

Chapman, R. L. (1987) *New Dictionary of American Slang*. London: Macmillan.

Cumston, C. G. (1926) *An Introduction to the History of Medicine: From the Time of the Pharaohs to the End of the XVIIIth Century*. London: Kegan Paul, Trench and Trübner.

Foucault, M. (1973) *The Birth of the Clinic: An Archaeology of Medical Perception*. New York: Vintage.

_____ (1977) *Discipline and Punish*. London: Allen Lane.

French, K. (1993) 'Introduction', in *The Marx Brothers: Monkey Business, Duck Soup and A Day at the Races*. London: Faber.

Freud, S. (1966) *Complete Psychoanalytical Works*. London: Cassell.

Hall, L. and R. Porter (1995) *Facts of Life: The Creation of Sexual Knowledge in Britain, 1650–1950*. New Haven: Yale University Press.

Hazlitt, W. (1855) *Essays on English Comic Writers*. London: George Bell.

King, G. (2002) *Film Comedy*. London: Wallflower Press.

Koestler, A. (1964) *The Act of Creation*. London: Hutchinson.

Krutnik, F. and S. Neale (1990) *Popular Film and Television Comedy*. London: Routledge.

Lloyd, C. (1986) *Explanation in Social History*. Oxford: Blackwell.

Marx Brothers (1993) *The Marx Brother: Monkey Business, Duck Soup and A Day at the Races*. London: Faber.

Pirandello, A. (1960) *On Humour*, trans. A Iliano and D. Testa. University of North Carolina Press: Chapel Hill.

Porter, R. (1997) *The Greatest Benefit to Mankind: A Medical History of Humanity from Antiquity to the Present*. London: HarperCollins.

Sikov, E. (1989) *Screwball: Hollywood's Madcap Romantic Comedies*. New York: Crown.

09

Julia Hallam

Angels, battleaxes and good-time girls: cinema's images of nurses

Working women are often depicted as nurses in classical Hollywood films; usually based in hospitals, films focused on nurses project a 'feminine ideal' of vocational zeal and self-sacrifice that celebrates caring and service as woman's mission in life. In these films 'woman' as a socially and historically constituted subject is constantly elided with the image of 'woman' as a melodramatic signifier negotiating nascent desires for spiritual fulfilment through dedication to a higher ideal. During the fifty years in which nursing's traditional image of dedication and service held considerable cultural currency, notions of service in nursing films changed from abstract concepts of self-abnegation and martyrdom to more material concerns of obtaining and enjoying middle-class husbands and lifestyles. In the 1920s nursing often figures as a redemptive identity; 'bad' girls can 'save' themselves by becoming nurses; by the 1950s 'good' girls who become nurses are rewarded with handsome doctor husbands. Between the two World Wars images of nurses as ministering angels dominated all forms of popular representation of the profession, an image centred on the traditional nurses' uniform with its connotations of religious sisterhoods and the 'closed orders' of nursing life.[1]

In this chapter, the focus is on British films about hospital nursing in the aftermath of the Second World War, a period when the image of nursing on the big screen underwent rapid transformation, in part a reflection of changes in the organisation of health care services in Britain, in part due to the development of antibiotics and the rapid growth of biomedical science accompanied by mounting public faith in medicine. The period is of particular interest because it reveals the nursing profession's struggle to maintain control of its public image, a control it was able to exert quite forcefully until the late 1950s when comedy films such as *Carry on Nurse* (Gerald Thomas, 1959) began to mock the small-minded authoritarianism and petit-bourgeois values of the profession. Before the Second World War, there were few differences between the depiction of nurses in British and Hollywood films. In the 1920s nurses were either icons of sacrificial womanhood or beacons of sexual fantasy and desire; nursing frequently functioned as a transformative identity for wayward characters, one of the ways in which a 'bad' girl could hope to redeem her character and become 'good' (other than becoming a nun!). Although all kinds of 1920s female characters were nurses, careers were out of keeping with the only socially sanctioned destiny for women at the time, marriage; in consequence there are no images of career-orientated nurses on the big screen apart from biopics of famous nurses such as Florence Nightingale and Edith Cavell.

Nursing scholars Beatrice and Philip Kalisch (1982) have traced changes in the narrative trajectories of nursing films between the mid-1920s when nurses 'sacrifice' their careers for money and marriage and the late 1930s when nurses abandon their matrimonial chances and 'sacrifice' themselves to nursing. They claim that the period between 1930 and 1945 was the heyday of positive images of nursing and nurses on North American screens; during these years nursing is portrayed as a worthy and important profession that enabled women to earn a living without compromising the idealised 'feminine' values attributed to white middle-class women of respectability, self-sacrifice and caring for others.[2] The rigid moral values enforced by the Motion Picture Production Code in 1934 effectively banned the development of a sexually titillating erotic 'naughty nurse' image found in earlier films in favour of the new models for working women emerging in the context of the collapse of the American economy. Richard Maltby has argued that the administrators of the Production Code regarded narrative structure as a strategy for controlling oppositional identifications, beliefs and ideas at a time when the depression was straining popular belief in the American dream (Maltby 1983). One of the adverse ideas that needed to be contained was the blatant display of consumerism through woman-centred spectacle as this was incompatible with the crisis of capital during the depression; instead, there was a turn towards films where women sacrifice material wealth to be broke but happy. The only feature-length films to focus entirely on contemporary nursing life were released during these years: *Night Nurse* (William Wellman, 1931), *Once to Every Woman* (Lambert Hillyer, 1934), *The White Parade* (Irving Cummings, 1934), *Registered Nurse* (Robert Florey, 1934), *Wife, Doctor and Nurse* (Walter Lang, 1937), *Four Girls in White* (S. Sylvan Simon, 1939) and *Vigil in the Night* (George Stevens, 1940), the latter adapted from the British writer A. J. Cronin's novel about nursing life.[3]

Nursing in these films is depicted as hard and demanding work that offers enormous personal satisfaction but little monetary reward; not all women can be nurses because, similarly to a religious vocation, nursing demands self-sacrifice and dedication to duty. To answer the question of what kind of women can become nurses, principal characters are polarised into 'good' and 'bad' types to play out the rigid moral values enforced by the Production Code. In *Vigil in the Night* the bad nurse makes negative and critical comments about the demands of nursing work; the good nurse altruistically ignores her own needs in the interests of those in her care. 'Badness' amounts to neglecting a patient to satisfy one's own needs, in this case leaving the bedside of a child with smallpox to make a cup of tea for herself. While she is absent the child dies; she is punished for this neglect of her duty by contracting the disease herself and dying. The good nurse is given the final lines of the film: 'We're here to serve, and if we do it well, we find pleasure, freedom, perfect freedom.'

Figure 4: *Vigil in the Night* (George Stevens, 1940)

The moral message is clear; it is a woman's duty to serve others, both in the literal sense of performing services, and in the abstract sense of serving particular ideas, beliefs and values. Self-sacrifice and dedication to duty is rewarded by romance with a handsome male doctor, setting the scene for the wave of medical romances that gain rapidly in popularity in the post-war world.[4] Only through willing and obedient self-sacrifice and service to nursing (and, by implication, the patriarchal institution of medicine) can women who become nurses hope to find true happiness and fulfilment.

Somewhat surprisingly perhaps, the largest group of Hollywood films to feature nurses in the 1930s were detective and crime stories. The Mary Roberts Rinehart character Miss Pinkerton and Mignon Eberhart's Sarah Keate were popular nurse sleuths who worked as private duty nurses for wealthy patients in their own homes and became embroiled in the mysterious goings-on of the mansions' other occupants. The nurses in these films display wit, mental acuity and courage; they are worldly wise, not easily taken in by outward appearances yet are portrayed as sympathetic and kindly women. Little attention is paid to actual nursing care in these stories – nursing work is depicted as administering medications, taking temperatures and delivering meals. The narratives usually end with the nurse in the arms of a police detective boyfriend, but they were not primarily romantic stories and did not end in marriage. By focusing on nurses as sleuths, a tactic used in the popular American 'Cherry Ames' nursing career books for girls,[5] nurses are depicted as intelligent, rational women with logical powers of deduction who are capable of bravery, determination and forbearance, an image much favoured by the Kalischs, who regard these images as highly positive representations of the profession.

With the entry of America into the Second World War, nurses on the screen assumed a patriotic, activist character which, in the Kalischs' opinion, has never before or since been bettered (1982: 608). Here, with the need for nurses at its most acute, Hollywood produced a tribute to the nursing profession focused on the activities of the American Red Cross. *So Proudly We Hail* (Mark Sandrich, 1943) was one of the top box-office films of 1943 and was Academy Award-nominated; three attractive young nurses (Claudette Colbert, Veronica Lake and Paulette Goddard) display self-sacrifice, heroism and stamina as they battle against overwhelming odds that culminate in the largest military surrender of troops in American history. Described by critic James Agee as, 'Probably the most deadly accurate picture ever made of what war looks like through the lenses of a housewives' magazine romance' (in Halliwell 1989: 934), the film emphasises their professional work and the *esprit d'corps* that characterises their relationships with each other.

Few British films with nurses as central characters were produced in the 1920s and 1930s although it is probable that British film audiences were thoroughly familiar with Hollywood's images of nurses. Comedy vehicles such as the 'Old Mother Riley' series and *Jack's the Boy* (Walter Forde, 1932) treated nurses as pantomime dames, drawing on their roots in variety theatre (Richards 1984: 255). The only films to treat the profession seriously were biopics of national nursing heroines who had sacrificed their lives in the First World War such as Herbert Wilcox's biography of Edith Cavell *Dawn* (1928) starring Sybil Thorndike and the Michael Balcon and Victor Saville production *I Was a Spy* (1933) starring Madeleine Carroll as the Belgian nurse Marthe Cnockhaert. The idea of the nurse as a heroic, patriotic figure is heavily promoted in the home front films of the early 1940s with the aim of recruiting women to help the war effort. Christine Gledhill argues that these films combine melodrama and realism in their attempt to negotiate the role of women as both a stabiliser of patriarchal society and her newly mobile status (Gledhill 1996: 219). There is a clear disjunction between these British films and their Hollywood counterparts; developed by the Ministry of Information (MoI), they lack the binary oppositional structure that polarises characters into 'good' and 'bad' nurses typical of earlier films. From the 1940s until the mid-1950s British films featuring nurses are pre-occupied with delivering education and information in an attempt to recruit young women to work as nurses first of all to serve the war effort and, from the mid-1940s, to work in the newly nationalised health service. In an analysis of leading female characters on British screens during this period, Janet Thumim points out that nursing figures as one of the few diegetically significant occupations for women only outstripped by the numbers of maids and performers of various kinds (Thumim 1992). Even so, nurses feature in only four popular films of the mid-1940s, ten in the mid-1950s, with this number falling to zero by the mid-1960s.

Realism, melodrama and recruitment

Throughout the war, documentary realism worked hand in hand with melodrama in the service of official propaganda to recruit women to help the war effort; the MoI Films division supported the production of films such as *The Gentle Sex* (ATS Training, Leslie Howard, 1943), *Millions Like Us* (munitions factory work, Sidney Gilliat and Frank Launder, 1943) and *The Lamp Still Burns* (nursing, Maurice Elvey, 1943). The elite group of senior nurses who ran the nursing profession during the 1930s, primarily the matrons of the powerful London voluntary hospitals, were active in promoting their image of nursing through articles in magazines such as *The Lady*, aimed at a middle-class female readership. It is no surprise to find that members of this self-selected group also acted as advisors to British filmmakers wanting to depict nursing in wartime and its immediate aftermath. A combination of advice from those who sought every opportunity to project their reified ideal of nursing as a vocation with filmmakers using stylistic strategies associated with the British documentary film movement produced several unexciting, didactic films made with the specific intention of boosting morale and raising levels of recruitment.

Monica Dickens was the most influential chronicler of nursing life at this time.[6] Her best-selling novel *One Pair of Feet* (1942), based on her experience as a first-year nursing trainee, led to a screen adaptation *The Lamp Still Burns* and a co-written recruitment documentary commissioned by the MoI, *Life in Her Hands* (Philip Leacock, 1951). In her novel Dickens claims she chose nursing not only because: 'it's one of those adolescent phases like wanting to be a nun', but because she saw *Vigil in the Night* at the cinema: 'I was going to be a nurse in a pure white halo cap, and glide swiftly about with oxygen cylinders and, if necessary, give my life for a patient' (1957: 9). Although she acknowledges the powerful emotions generated by working in life and death situations, emotions which melodramatic forms can aptly convey, as a 'middlebrow' writer Dickens uses irony to emphasise her awareness of the sentimentality of popular forms such as melodrama and her own critical distance from them. This resistance to popular expression was characteristic of the attitudes and tastes of her class at this time; establishment values promoted realist aesthetics, typified in the first two films Dickens scripted.[7] Her work was popular and found a wide and appreciative audience perhaps because, as *The Listener* commented in a quote published on the cover of a later edition (1957) of her novel, 'Miss Dickens succeeds, almost in spite of herself, in conveying the essential nobility of the profession and the supreme satisfaction of a life saved'.

Given the shortage of nursing labour in wartime, what is surprising about *The Lamp Still Burns* is that nursing is depicted as work for middle-class women; in spite of evidence that nursing's main labour pool consisted of shop girls and low-grade clerks there are no depictions of working-class women as nurses on the big screen in the 1940s.[8] Hilary (Rosalind Johns) is a middle-class architect who gives up her profession to train as a nurse at a time when women were gaining entry to male-dominated professions in increasing numbers. It is difficult to envisage how she offers an image of aspiration or inspirational allegiance for the majority of women in the cinema audience; she spends more time in the sluice scrubbing dirty bedpans than caring for patients. Senior nurses are depicted as petty disciplinarians, trainees' lives are ruled by mundane tasks and constant drudgery; by foregrounding this aspect of nursing life, the use of realism seems to undercut the film's ostensible purpose, that of persuading educated middle-class women to undertake training in a traditional woman's profession.

Stylistically *The Lamp Still Burns* has many of the features of British realism that distinguishes films of this period from their Hollywood counterparts; Hilary's decision to become a nurse hinges on a rational recognition of the value of nursing work following the injury of her office boy in a car accident, rather than the moment of sentimental identification with a Hollywood star described by Dickens in her autobiographical novel. While designing a waiting room for her surgeon uncle, Hilary tells him how she wants to be more useful in her life; a flashback of the nurses' air of calm efficiency and competence as they perform their duties and care for the injured boy accompanies her voiceover commentary. Gledhill notes how this documentary moment is fused with personal desire as the tracking camera 'merges Hilary's gaze with the return look of the patients, marking her emotional response to a social demand', welding the film's melodramatic address with its documentary purpose (Gledhill 1996: 225). The unrequited romance in the film between Hilary and the wealthy factory owner (Stewart Granger) who falls in love with her emphasises Hilary's determination to put social duty before personal desire in the uncertain wartime environment. Following the threat of dismissal for a petty infringement of hospital rules Hilary mounts an impassioned defence of why she should continue to nurse before the hospital's governing board. Commitment to nursing is combined with an intention to change the out-dated training system that forbids entry to married women, an indication of changing professional attitudes towards vocationalism and a rehearsal of the negotiations that will nationalise nursing services as part of a programme of wider health service reform after the war.

Life in Her Hands, produced eight years later by the MoI with the specific aim of recruiting women to nursing in the newly nationalised health service, was also co-scripted by Dickens; dubbed by publicity 'a documentary of nursing life' the film was distributed on all the major cinema circuits. Like Hilary, the leading character Anne is from a middle-class background and is older than the usual age of entry to nurse training, arriving at her decision only after her husband's death in a car crash. Warned by family and friends of the long and difficult training she will have to undertake, Anne is deemed a 'born' nurse by the Sister Tutor. Given the changes in nursing following nationalisation such as the introduction of a two-tier system of training and cadet nursing schemes aimed at young working-class women in secondary modern schools, the film's emphasis on the vocational aspect of nursing, visually signified by the nurses' flowing, veil-like caps, seems outmoded even for its time. The film was made with the sole intention of informing viewers about nursing work and has no romantic or other narrative interest but the visual depiction of nursing work lacks detail. Only one sequence stands out, a montage that cuts between Anne's hands and her facial expressions as she performs a number of routine nursing tasks, emphasising hand/eye co-ordination and concentration, creating an impression of skill and dexterity in the nursing process. Apart from this, nursing characters veer towards caricature; one sister is obsessed with weighing tea to check if the night nurses are using too much; another, a stereotypical large-chested 'battleaxe', warns her patients, 'You'll be dead before Christmas if you don't do what I tell you.'

The considered opinion of many in the profession was that films like these did little to encourage girls into nursing; films featuring famous nursing heroines such as Edith Cavell and Florence Nightingale were deemed far more influential.[9] By the mid-1950s, Anna Neagle epitomised the heroic commitment to the vocational ideal that many nurses sought to promote. Neagle played Florence Nightingale in the only British biopic of her life, *Lady with the Lamp* (1951) directed by her husband Herbert Wilcox. By this time the actress and director duo were well established makers of popular melodrama about the lives and loves of the aristocracy. Experts in patriotic nostalgia, in the 1930s they made *Victoria the Great* (1937) and *Sixty Glorious Years* (1938) with Neagle playing Queen Victoria in the starring roles. In 1939, they made their first nursing biopic, *Nurse Edith Cavell*, remaking Wilcox's earlier version of the same story (*Dawn*, 1928); by the early 1940s Neagle was well established as one of the top British stars at the box office alongside Margaret Lockwood, Phyllis Calvert, Celia Johnson and Ann Todd. By the time she came to play Nightingale, she had accrued the star persona of an upper-class English lady, a role she played in her 'private' life as well as on the screen. In an article published in the *Nursing Mirror* shortly after playing the Matron in *No Time for Tears* (Cyril Frankel, 1957) Neagle claimed that 'the portrayal of nurses has given me great personal happiness, and I am indeed gratified if the nursing profession has found my portrayals satisfying' (Neagle 1958).

Considerable pains were taken to construct a historically accurate biography of Florence Nightingale in *Lady with the Lamp*, in part a response to the romanticised image projected in Hollywood's earlier version of her life *The White Angel* (William Dieterle, 1936) with the result that the film has all the hallmarks of an expensive quality production but is made in black and white. Emphasis is placed on Nightingale's dealings with the 'drunkards and prostitutes' who are the tenders of the sick until her programme of reform, substantiating middle-class views of working-class women as irresponsible and vulgar and nursing as a career for well bred middle- and upper-class women. In essence *Lady with the Lamp* conveys Nightingale's life as worthy but uninspiring, in part the result of a narrative that focuses on funding, foregrounding contemporary preoccupations with the financial cost of the newly created National Health Service. In contrast, as the title suggests, Hollywood's version of the Nightingale story *The White Angel* presents Florence Nightingale (Kay Francis) as an iconic figure tailored to prevailing notions of feminine self-sacrifice and desire in 1930s films for women.[10] Nightingale's decision to become a nurse is presented as sudden and forceful, like a religious conversion. Visually situated as a queen on a throne, dressed in long white robes and a veil, with her face brilliantly illuminated, Francis projects a radiant image of female power that is both bridal and religious in its connotations.[11] Beauty and virginity merge with her whiteness to create associations of purity and goodness at a level of universal abstraction far removed from any racially-specific national or historical context.[12]

In *Lady with the Lamp*, the scenes where Nightingale walks at night with her lamp amidst the sick achieve a similarly iconic effect through the cluster of popular associations that circulated around images of Nightingale's life and work such as self-sacrifice, humanity and endurance. The explicit moral and aesthetic superiority implied in these images masks the socio-historical conditions on which such claims to superiority lie and the implicit power relations on which they were built; nursing's roots in the British imperialist project are naturalised as female service in aid of the common good and need no further explanation.[13]

In post-war films about nurses and nursing the image on offer is one of eagerness to undertake a life of duty, counting it as a privilege to serve a great and noble profession; the ministering 'angel' is juxtaposed with older, more experienced nurses who present imposing images of matriarchal authority. It is hard to avoid the conclusion that becoming a nurse heralds the possibility of displacing thwarted sexual desire with vocational zeal in a personal transition from 'angel' to 'battleaxe'. In the immediate aftermath of war, this image had undoubtedly had resonance; Anne, for example, in *Life in Her Hands* is narratively positioned as a widow searching for a substitution for her loss.

Romantic melodramas and irreverent romps

The reification of traditional Nightingale values encapsulated in these films was followed by a rapid shift in style in favour of romance and melodrama. Between the mid-1950s and the mid-1960s, an unusually high number of films were produced which used a hospital environment as their background most of which featured doctors in leading roles but a number profiled nurses and nursing. During the 1950s the medical establishment rose to a pinnacle of popular belief in its power to cure and heal, with the result that doctors became folk heroes in popular stories, replacing sons of the gentry and other minor aristocrats as symbols of masculine power and virility. Medicine and nursing began to feature heavily in popular genres, in medical melodramas on television and in the romantic fictions of Mills & Boon, publishers specialising in the production of cheap, mass-produced paperbacks for a primarily female readership. In the late 1950s the 'medical approach' to sickness and disease was unchallenged by other health discourses such as the consumerist lobby that developed during the 1960s alongside other powerful social resistance and liberation movements (Karpf 1988: 52–3). A change in address is apparent in nursing films by the mid-1950s, in part a result of a shift in address to the younger audience that typified the cinema-going public by this time (Geraghty 2000: 9). The 1950s marked the beginning of what Karpf refers to as an infatuation with the London teaching hospitals – an infatuation that is clearly apparent in nursing films such as Ealing's *The Feminine Touch* (Pat Jackson, 1956) and much of the doctor/nurse popular romantic literature of the time. *The Feminine Touch* depicts a Technicolor fantasy of nursing life centred on 'new look' fashion and kitchen-centred caring filmed with soft-focus lenses that emphasise female vulnerability: accentuated by close-ups of trembling-lipped femininity and the shrill tones of eager girlish voices. The high production values present a nursing workforce at the peak of its glamour; the traditional nursing uniform, with its tightly-belted waist, billowing white apron and starched cap, was ideally suited for subtle adaptation towards the 'new look' that became fashionable during the 1950s. Attributed to designs by Christian Dior, the 'new look' heralded a return of constricting fashion after the more relaxed styles of wartime, creating

Figure 5: *The Feminine Touch* (Pat Jackson, 1956)

Figure 6: *The Feminine Touch* (Pat Jackson, 1956)

clothes that were difficult to move about in. Cone-shaped breasts, corseted abdomens and waspish waists exaggerated the female form of a body draped in long full skirts accompanied by pointed-toe shoes with slim heels. Read by some cultural critics as a sign of post-war nostalgia for the values of Edwardian femininity, 'new look' fashion eschewed the 'masculine' tailored suits and slimline dresses that had marked female fashion throughout the 1940s in favour of an abundance of soft flowing fabrics and dainty accessories.[14]

Although ostensibly about becoming a working woman, the articulations between fashion and femininity in *The Feminine Touch* signify a contradictory attitude to women that places female nurses securely at the altar beside their male medical colleagues rather than at the bedsides of their patients.[15] Here, and in *No Time for Tears* which followed it a year later, nurses are seen less on the wards attending to their patients or in sluices scrubbing the bedpans, and more in the ward kitchens where they prepare food, often for doctors. Consorting with the doctors and squabbling with other nurses over who should be privileged enough to feed them the food that should be given to the patients is a major activity in these films rather than interactions with the patients or demonstrations of nursing skill.

Doctors are depicted doing many of the minor tasks for patients that, in earlier films, were the province of nurses; their role is diminished, confined to the kitchen. *The Feminine Touch* exemplifies how 'new look' fashion is part of a wider discourse on femininity that re-situates women in the domestic sphere, even though women (and, in particular, married women) were recruited into the workforce in increasing numbers (Wilson 1980; Geraghty

2000). Nursing is projected as a suitable training for a woman's 'real' work in life, looking after her (doctor) husband and children.

The Feminine Touch and *No Time for Tears* were the last nursing films to employ the matron elite from the London teaching hospitals as their advisors; thereafter, films depict nurses as figures of fun or objects of voyeuristic fantasy. The only film that treats nursing work with the kind of matter-of-factness with which doctoring is treated during the 1960s is a low-budget black-and-white comedy and minor 'B-movie' screen filler, *Twice Round the Daffodils* (Gerald Thomas, 1962). This story of life in a tuberculosis sanatorium focuses on a men's ward in the care of Catty, a nurse who is shown to be more than capable of coping with her difficult patients, in both physical and psychological terms. Although tending towards the 'ministering angel' stereotype, Catty is neither a sexually sublimated vocationalist nor a doctor's handmaiden; no doctors are depicted in the film, although there are veiled references to their presence. As well as coping with routine nursing tasks, Catty and her team have to deal with the psychological problems of their patients created by long-term illness and institutional confinement, including anger, depression and sexual frustration. In contrast to this positive image of professional competence a nurse 'unwittingly' loses her skirt, revealing beneath her uniform a typically voyeuristic fantasy of frilly knickers, suspenders and black stockings to the male patients hiding in the cupboard – and, of course, to the film audience.

By the early 1960s, the film industry was faced with increasing competition from television leading to demands for relaxation in censorship; in 1962, the Hays Production Code, regulator of Hollywood's moral conduct, was defeated by an action in the Supreme Court, ending a system of censorship which had remained virtually unchanged since 1934 (Randall 1979). Following the general drift towards misogynistic images of women that commentators and critics have noted during the decade, nurses are depicted as devious criminals (*The Burning Court*, Julien Duvivier, 1963), murderers (*The Honeymoon Killers*, Leonard Kastle, 1970), prostitutes (*Women of Desire*, Vincent Sinclair, 1968) and nymphomaniacs (*I, A Woman*, Mac Ahlberg, 1966), or they are subjected to violence: they get murdered (*Night of Bloody Horror*, Joy N. Houck Jr, 1969; *The Strangler*, Burt Topper, 1964)), raped (*Day-Dream*, Tetsuji Takechi, 1964) and generally abused. In British films nurses become the butt of smutty jokes, their petty authoritarianism ridiculed and sexuality mocked in a string of successful comedy films. The popular 'Doctor' series followed the life and loves of a newly-qualified medic in a light-hearted look at the British medical institution,[16] while the 'Carry On' series found in hospital life an ideal vehicle for lampooning the British establishment and its paternalistic values. For the first time, working-class nurses are depicted on the screen appearing as busty sex objects (Barbara Windsor in *Carry On Doctor*, Gerald Thomas, 1968) and targets of derision (Hattie Jacques in *Carry On Matron*, Gerald Thomas, 1973). Nurses are easy targets for 'toilet' humour as well as generative sources of it; peering under the bedclothes on the pretext of preparing a male patient for theatre, Joan Sims' character comments, 'What's all this fuss about such a little thing then?' exemplifying the irreverent approach of these films. Nurses are no longer asexual middle-class 'nice' girls coolly detached from the bodily functions of their patients, but pneumatic busty blondes, working-class women who talk in saucy sexual innuendoes and delight in causing out-of-control physical responses in incumbent male patients.

The image of nursing authority encapsulated in the 'battleaxe' is perhaps the cruellest of these stereotypes, with Hattie Jacques playing the frustrated matron or sister who is

Figure 7: *Carry On Doctor*
(Gerald Thomas, 1968)

Figure 8: *Carry On Doctor*
(Gerald Thomas, 1968)

Figure 9: *Carry On Matron*
(Gerald Thomas, 1973)

too old, too plain and too fat to be sexually attractive. While younger nurses demonstrate hearty sexual appetites and a knowing cheeky intelligence, for older women sexual desire is depicted as grotesque and laughable. Ineffective in their ability to attract men, senior nurses are depicted as institutional puppets, petty tyrants who play out their frustrations on powerless junior nurses and patients.

The hospital was a popular venue for 'Carry On' films because of its suitability for creating comic scenarios based around socially taboo topics such as bodily functions and sexuality. Much of the humour is generated from the institution's inability to control the physical actions and reactions of its inmates through its timetables, regimes and regimentations. Male working-class patients wreak havoc by refusing to obey orders, pointing out in the process how the regulated sterile environment creates impotency amongst male doctors and sexual frustration leading to petty authoritarianism in the female nursing staff. Amidst the ensemble-playing of the regular cast, Kenneth Williams invariably plays an effeminate consultant, his camp performances a knowing play with the taboo topic of his personal homosexuality, while working-class male patients (particularly those played by Sid James) are always depicted as worldly wise and (hetero)sexually voracious. Marion Jordan argues that the characters and the humour are those of the most demotic types of fiction – the comic postcard and the bar-room joke – providing a safety valve for our more anti-social impulses. The jokes are not only sexually obscene but express a masculine worldview where the castrating mother-in-law is always the wife's mother, sexual desirability (however much parodied) is most commonly female, sexual desire and potency most commonly male (Jordan 1983: 318).

These filmic images stand in stark opposition to earlier ones and are certainly derogatory of professional nursing's preferred image of middle-class respectability; situated in a film genre that aims to poke fun at middle-class prudery and restraint, they follow in a tradition of music-hall humour where the working man mocks those who seek to order and control his life. Created to entertain the young male audience who formed the bedrock of cinema's declining clientele by the late 1950s,[17] their critique is class-based, aimed at mocking middle-class propriety and working-class mores. They ridicule not only the prudery of white middle-class femininity but the ineffectiveness of the state's patriarchal institutions and those who run them. An early symptom of public unease with health care's medical autocracy, they question the automatic relegation of patients to infantile status and the powerlessness of individuals confronted by the system.

One British film, more than any other, seems to sum up fictional representations of nursing and hospitals by the early 1970s. Released hot on the heels of *Carry on Matron*, *The National Health or Nurse Norton's Affair* (Jack Gold, 1973) mixes tragedy and farce in a satirical comedy that mocks Britain's ailing NHS. The film opens with a shot of a pillared portico hospital entrance and the sound of a public address system exhorting hospital staff to use less hot water because of a failing boiler; the countryhouse architecture may be reminiscent of Britain's past glories but the soundtrack curbs any such romanticised notion of the present. Cutting to an internal shot, a black nurse in the traditional nursing uniform escorts a white male patient down a corridor where a woman wearing a sari is on her knees scrubbing the floor. Entering the ward, a general air of anarchy prevails; a male patient tears around in a wheelchair while the others cat-call abuse at the nurses who try to smile cheerfully through the chaos. In the kitchen, the porters sit smoking and drinking tea while the PA calls in vain for Dr Singh; in the patient's sitting room an American medical melodrama, 'Nurse Norton's Affair', is just beginning on the television. The opening shots emphasise the spacious corridors, comfortable patient rooms and high-tech medical support systems of the privatised American health care system; as the actors' faces appear in the opening credits it becomes apparent that the tired, frazzled hospital staff we have just seen are the glamorous good-looking stars of this glossy American drama. Social realism and primetime melodrama ironically juxtapose two medical fictions, one informed by commentary on economic recession and industrial conflict within an ailing NHS, the other by a melodramatic narrative of heroic medical progress; the contrast between the two modes of address could not be more apparent.

The National Health was one of the last British feature films to foreground the activities of nurses. Between the 1950s and the 1970s, public perceptions of medicine and nursing changed markedly, a process mediated by the increasing presence on television of dramas and documentaries about medicine and hospital life. Within this context, depictions of nurses and nursing underwent a significant shift; at the beginning of the 1950s, nursing is represented as a noble profession; to become a nurse is to serve the sick, the nation and the common good of the NHS. Images of nurses in British films reiterate the ideology of the nursing elite in the teaching hospitals attached to university schools of medicine; nursing is depicted as a profession for young, white middle-class women and there are no images of black or working-class women (and certainly no men) as nurses in popular films. By the mid-1950s, the female cinema audience desired romantic melodramas of hospital life; doctors become the nation's new heroes and nurses are depicted as handmaidens in service to the high priests of the medical order, the doctors. The development of independent television and the international market in television programmes made images of handsome American medics such as Doctor Kildare (Richard Chamberlain) and Ben Casey (Vince Edwards) increasingly available to British viewers.[18] By the early 1960s, nurses are depicted in television melodramas serving medical ideologies of cure rather than nursing ideologies of care; they become silent background presences on the small screen, while in films they are satirised as petty authoritarians and sexually frustrated 'battleaxes' or depicted as prostitutes and sexual playthings. Although nurses continued to appear as characters in numerous films, by the 1970s the iconic relationship between notions of female servitude, self-sacrifice and white femininity was fractured and socially obsolete; the traditional image of the nurse in her starched white uniform and flowing cap had faded into history, its trace found only in pornographic fantasies where it continues to be fashioned to suit (male) sexual desires.

Notes

1   Most nursing was undertaken by religious sisterhoods or untrained working-class women until the Nightingale reforms of the 1850s and 1860s secularised nursing and fought to establish it as a profession for women; see, for example, Smith 1982; Dingwall, Rafferty & Webster 1988.

2   Their conclusions are based on content analysis of the nurse's role and function in over 200 feature films produced between 1930 and 1979; see Kalisch & Kalisch 1982, 1987.

3   Cronin also wrote the novel on which *The Citadel* (King Vidor, 1938) was based, an Academy Award-nominated film about British medical practice made by MGM's British studio.

4   Doctor/nurse romances became a mass-market commodity in the 1950s when Mills & Boon, publishers of romantic novels, decided to cash in on the popularity of medical melodramas on television; see Hallam 2000: 68–73.

5   The Cherry Ames career books, written by Helen Wells and Julie Tatham, were first published in the early 1940s and widely read in Britain as well as in North America throughout the 1940s, 1950s and 1960s; see Hallam 1996.

6   Granddaughter of novelist Charles Dickens, Monica was privately educated and presented at court in 1935. A writer of distinctively 'middlebrow' taste, she considered herself a commentator on the 'condition of England' sharing some similarities with her contemporary George Orwell (but not his politics!).

7   For a more detailed account of the relationship between realist aesthetics and liberal

humanist politics in the 1940s see Ellis 1978, 1996. For a more nuanced account of the relationship between melodrama and female viewers see, for example, the collection of essays edited by Gledhill 1987.

8 The Athlone Committee (1939).

9 Interviews were conducted with a small number of Sister Tutors who recruited young women for training throughout this period; see Hallam 2000: 41–2.

10 See, for example, Haskell (1974) on women in US films and Harper (2000) on women in British films.

11 Marian McMahon (1991) deconstructs this imagery in her experimental film *Nursing History* (1989), an analysis of home-movie footage of family weddings and her nursing graduation.

12 Photographic lighting technology and film stock developed around lighting the white face created a culture of photographic practice and assumptions about 'beauty', 'glamour' and 'truthfulness' that were adopted and adapted by the movie industry; see Dyer 1997, 'The Light of the World', 82–144.

13 The use of character-centred biography to depict historical events in popular cinema perpetuates common sense ideologies that individuals are the motor force of history rather than underlying structural formations. For a more detailed critique see Hallam with Marshment 2000: 145–83.

14 On the 1950s, see Lewis 1992; on the New Look, see Hopkins 1963. For a detailed account of the relationship between fashion, film and femininity in British cinema see Cook 1996.

15 Geraghty argues that the 'new woman' was found most readily in what came to be called 'the companionate marriage', a marriage in which the wife, because of her expertise, was accorded a balanced and equal status with her husband even though the nature of their responsibilities differed (2000: 34). Companionate marriage is a marked feature of some medical romances; see Hallam 2000: 62–73.

16 The first of these films, starring Dirk Bogarde, was *Doctor in the House* (Ralph Thomas, 1954); sequels followed at regular intervals throughout the 1960s.

17 Between the post-war period and 1961 audiences declined from around 900–1,000 million visits a year to 515 million; for a discussion of these changes see Docherty, Morrison and Tracey 1987: 16–29.

18 *Dr Kildare*, BBC 1962–66, *Ben Casey*, ITV 1961–67. The first British medical soap was *Emergency Ward 10*, ITV 1957–67.

References

Aspinall, S. (1983) 'Women, realism and reality in British films 1943–53', in J. Curran and V. Porter (eds) *British Cinema History*. London: Weidenfield and Nicolson, 272–93.

Cook, P. (1996) *Fashioning the Nation: Fashion and Identity in British Cinema*. London: British Film Institute.

Dingwall, R., A. M. Rafferty and C. Webster (1988) *An Introduction to the Social History of Nursing*. London: Routledge.

Docherty, D., D. Morrison and M. Tracey (1987) *The Last Picture Show? Britain's Changing Film Audiences*. London: British Film Institute.

Dyer, R. (1997) *White*. London: Routledge.

Ellis, J. (1978) 'Art, culture, quality: terms for a cinema in the forties and seventies', *Screen*

19, 3, 9–49.

_____ (1996) 'The Quality Film Adventure: British critics and the cinema 1942–1948', in A. Higson (ed.) *Dissolving Views: Key Writings on British Cinema*. London: Cassell, 66–93.

Geraghty, C. (2000) *British Cinema in the 1950s: Gender, Genre and the New Look*. London: Routledge.

Gledhill, C. (ed.) (1987) *Home is Where the Heart Is: Studies in Melodrama and the Woman's Film*. London: British Film Institute.

_____ (1996) 'An abundance of understatement': documentary, melodrama and romance', in C. Gledhill and G. Swanson (eds) *Nationalising Femininity: Culture, Sexuality and British Cinema in the Second World War*. Manchester and New York: Manchester University Press, 213–29.

Hallam, J. (1996) 'Nursing an image: the Sue Barton stories', in S. Sceats and G. Cunningham (eds) *Image and Power: Women in Twentieth Century Fiction*. London: Longmans, 91–102.

_____ (2000) *Nursing the Image: Media, Culture and Professional identity*. London: Routledge.

Hallam, J. with M. Marshment (2000) *Realism and Popular Cinema*. Manchester and New York: Manchester University Press.

Halliwell, L. (1989) *Halliwell's Film Guide*. 7th Edition, London and New York: Paladin Grafton.

Harper S. (2000) *Women in British Cinema: Mad, Bad and Dangerous to Know*. London, Continuum.

Haskell, M. (1974) *From Reverence to Rape: The Treatment of Women in the Movies*. Middlesex and Baltimore: Penguin.

Hopkins, H. (1963) *The New Look*. London: Secker and Warberg.

Jordan, M. (1983) 'Carry On: follow that stereotype', in J. Curran and V. Porter (eds) *British Cinema History*. London: Weidenfeld and Nicolson, 312–27.

Kalisch, B. and P. Kalisch (1982) 'The image of the nurse in motion pictures', *American Journal of Nursing*, 82, 4, 605–12.

_____ (1987) *The Changing Image of the Nurse*. California: Addison-Wesley.

Karpf, A. (1988) *Doctoring the Media*. London and New York: Routledge.

Lewis J. (1992) *Women in Britain since 1945*. Oxford: Blackwell.

Maltby, R. (1983) *Harmless Entertainment: Hollywood and the Ideology of Consensus*. Metuchen, NJ: Scarecrow Press.

McMahon, M. (1991) 'Nursing histories: reviving life in abandoned selves', *Feminist Review*, 37, 22–37.

Neagle, A. (1958) 'Portraying Edith Cavell and other nurses', *Nursing Mirror*, 10, 1–11.

Randall, R. S. (1979) 'Censorship: from *The Miracle* to *Deep Throat*', in T. Balio (ed.) *The American Film Industry*. Madison: University of Wisconsin Press, 432–57.

Richards, J. (1984) *The Age of the Dream Palace*. London: Routledge and Kegan Paul.

Smith, F. B. (1982) *Florence Nightingale: Reputation and Power*. London: Croom Helm.

Thumim, J. (1992) *Celluloid Sisters: Women and Popular Cinema*. London: Macmillan.

Wilson, E. (1980) *Only Halfway to Paradise: Women in Post-war Britain 1945–68*. London and New York: Tavistock.

10

Bruce Babington

'To catch a star on your fingertips': diagnosing the medical biopic from *The Story of Louis Pasteur* to *Freud*

Sameness/difference

At the beginning of *Madame Curie* (Mervyn LeRoy, 1943), young Maria Sklodowska (Greer Garson) – later Marie Curie, the discoverer of radium – attends a lecture at the Sorbonne. Beautiful, poor, half-starving (shortly to collapse in her seat from a combination of hunger and intellectual rapture), 'haunted by dreams, invincibly eager' as James Hilton's distinguished voiceover puts it, she listens intently to the Professor (Albert Basserman). Though he tells his students that, unlike Galileo and Newton, they will probably never 'catch a star on your fingertips' – a phrase so resonant that he repeats it soulfully – he promises them the wonder of scientific knowledge. However, it is the image of the star that grips Marie/Greer Garson in luminous close-up and is reminisced throughout the narrative. Returning home after having been fed by the kindly Professor, she looks at the night sky, repeating his words, 'To catch a star on your fingertips'. Then, years later, at the paralysing crisis caused by her husband Pierre's (Walter Pidgeon) death, the Professor reminds her of his words. Finally, old and frail, renowned and revered, she addresses the University of Paris, on the twenty-fifth anniversary of the discovery of radium, in variations on the image which transfixed her: 'Yet each of us perhaps can catch a glimpse of knowledge which modest and insufficient in itself may add to men's dream of truth. It is by these small candles in our darkness that we see before us little by little the dim outline of that great plan that shapes our universe.' Despite its differences – *Madame Curie* is a 'great woman' rather than a 'great man' biopic; an eccentric love story in a sub-genre which typically marginalises the erotic; produced at MGM with its tradition of glamorous and aristocratic biopics (*Queen Christina*, Rouben Mamoulian, 1933; *Marie Antoinette*, W. S. Van Dyke, 1938) and softer, more romantic modes than Warner Bros. or RKO – the moment encapsulates something of the ethos of the medical version of the great man/woman biopic, its aura of idealistic sacrifice, its secularisation of religious impulses into a 'religion of humanity'. This last, while true to the secularism of its subjects – Curie, for instance, as her daughter relates, lost her religious faith early (Eve Curie 1938: 52, 280) and no trace of religious belief occurs in of any of the medical biopics investigated here (though Ehrlich's and Freud's Jewishness has other importances) – is nebulous enough to be inoffensive, even inspiring, to its primary American, predominantly religious original audience. Garson/Curie speaks of 'the dim outline of that great plan that shapes the universe', the 'beauty' of science 'with its great spiritual strength', ambiguously enough to appeal to both believers and unbelievers, and ends by seeing no possible exhaustion of what might be broadly called a religious (or at least 'oceanic') impulse: 'Even when man's sight is keener far than now, divine wonder will never fail'.

This chapter asserts a real if limited specificity to the Hollywood medical biopic, or rather, more accurately, 'the medical researcher biopic', since its heroes are, broadly speaking, researchers (in the cases of Elizabeth Kenny in *Sister Kenny* (Dudley Nichols, 1946) and William Morton in *The Great Moment* (Preston Sturges, 1944), pragmatic experimenters, one a nurse, the other a dentist) rather than the medics or surgeons who are the staple heroes of soap operas but not of biopics. In asserting this limited specificity one should remember that the classical Hollywood biopic is largely seen as a homogenised phenomenon, a view persuasively formulated in George Custen's *Bio/Pics* (1992) which argues that whether its subject is Alexander Graham Bell, Al Jolson or Dr Paul Ehrlich, a repetitive narrative obeys the same semi-immutable laws. These can be summarised as Darryl F. Zanuck's famous 'rooting interest' for a progressive individual fighting for innovation against an outmoded establishment; a narrative formed around a 'trial' scene vindicating the protagonist; an extraordinary degree of research devoted to 'authentic' replication which, however, is contradicted by the unashamed invention of imaginary, and the suppression of real, incidents. The biopic life, then, is seen as more derived from intertextual relations with previous biopics than from more analytical extrinsic biographical, scientific and historical discourses, and in part powerfully derived from the worldview of the Hollywood studio bosses, imposed on the public genre (Custen 1992).

I have no intention of denying these perceptions' overarching correctness. Yet they are subject to two immediate critiques. First, the biopic (as Custen is sometimes aware) changes over time, rendering it a less monolithic genre in which films such as *Patton* (Franklin J. Shaffner, 1970), *Raging Bull* (Martin Scorsese, 1980) or *Freud* (John Huston, 1962), involve substantial anti-classical movements. More extraordinarily, Sturges's *The Great Moment* performed comparable subversions during, rather than after, the classical model's hegemony. The second critique is that even if the classical biopic's different types are all governed at the deepest level by identical laws, their surface differences are hardly unimportant experientially. A montage charting the Curies' extraction of radium from pitch-blende in *Madame Curie* and a montage of Jolson's accelerating career expressed by speeding trains and visited towns as he sings in *The Jolson Story* (Alfred E. Green, 1946) may both at the level of narrative function compress time and events, but their emotional, connotative meanings are distinct, one imbued with minute calculation and dogged reiteration, the other with glamourful eupeptic thrust, and while both embody the 'teleology of fame' (Custen 1992: 186), to wholly dissolve into an undifferentiated light both the ghostly glow of the researchers' radium and the lights of Broadway is to lose too much. My approach also differs from Thomas Elsaesser's discussion of Warner Bros.' Wilhelm Dieterle biopic cycle started in 1936 by *The Story of Louis Pasteur*, which bypasses the 'pro-filmic' reality of the texts to analyse them both more particularly and more generally – that is, both as the refraction of events at Warner Bros. (Dieterle's struggles against the system, Paul Muni's ambitions as actor, the studio's simultaneous preempting of censorship and gaining of prestige through a more culturally-acclaimed genre than gangster films and musicals), and as dramatising the larger contradictions of capitalist American ideology (Elsaesser 1986: 21–4). The substantial insights achieved here are gained, however, through ignoring any specificity the medical biopic has.

What follows defines the medical researcher biopic in its limited specificity against these views. Whereas Custen generalised over all classical biopics, and Elsaesser over a hybrid cycle including medical biopics (unified by their origin at Warner Bros., by Dieterle as director and Muni as star), this chapter investigates five Hollywood biopics (1936–48) which constitute the subgenre of the medical or medical researcher biopic. These are the 'lives' or 'stories' of Pasteur, whose germ theory was possibly the most influential of all medical revolutions; of Paul Ehrlich, the pioneer of chemotherapy, and discoverer of salvarsan, the pre-penicillin cure for syphilis, *Dr Ehrlich's Magic Bullet* (William Dieterle, 1940); of W. G. T. Morton, if not the inventor or first user of ether anaesthesia, its most significant populariser, in *The Great Moment*; of Marie Curie, the discoverer of radium, with its potential for treating cancers; and of the Australian nurse Elizabeth Kenny, who developed methods of treating the child victims of infantile paralysis, in *Sister Kenny* (Dudley Nichols, 1946). Additionally as a point of comparison reference is made to a late entry into the subgenre, *Freud*, technically a British production, but post-studio Hollywood in all other respects. (Had *The White Angel* (Henry Blanke, 1936), a biography of Florence Nightingale, been available for viewing it might have been included in the section below.)

The classical medical biopic

In *On the Fourfold Root of the Principle of Sufficient Reason* Arthur Schopenhauer argues that knowledge depends on the two laws of homogeneity and specification summarised in the rules 'Entities should not be multiplied unnecessarily' and (Kant's dictum) 'The number and variety of entities is not to be limited without good reason.' 'The former bids us, by attention to the points of resemblance and agreement in things, get at their kinds, and combine them into species, and these species again into genera, until we have arrived at the highest concept of all, that which embraces everything', while the latter's command is that 'we must carefully distinguish the species which are united into a genus, and the lower kinds which in turn are united under these species; taking care not to make a leap and subsume the lower kinds and individuals under the concept of genus, since this is always capable of division, but never descends to the object of pure perception' (Schopenhauer 1995). What follows admits the former's claims but looks to the latter in characterising a significant subspecies of the biopic. To investigate such specificities is not to deny the films' shared formulaic nature. All have simple linear narratives, focusing on the subject's best-known achievements, omitting the subject's youth – as in many biopics, a characteristic persuasively explained as supporting an ideology of atomistic self-creation (Custen 1992: 152–6) – and, though they are all seen in old age, this is only as a brief, impressive, coda. So

Madame Curie, though announcing her daughter's biography as source, omits the early life (a quarter of the book) and almost all the last 24 years (over a quarter) even though these included Curie's war work with mobile x-rays, visits to America, and President Harding's presenting to her of the gramme of radium purchased for her by American subscription (Curie 1938: 301–20, 335–50, 343–4).[1] All idealise their subjects, with that combination of surface authenticity and unashamed invention characteristic of the genre, omitting such unideal material as Kenny's lack of nursing qualifications (Kohn 1993: 26) and Pasteur's penchant for self-publicity (Porter 1997: 435). All, more or less, embody major strategies outlined by Custen: 'signifiers of facticity', the 'trial' scene vindicating the protagonist, and an underlying narrative of which one formulation is 'resistance, the struggle between innovation and tradition, and the importance of the big break' (Custen 1992: 52–60, 186–92, 206–8).

Such shared elements extend to the films' nineteenth-centuryness (only Kenny, who died in 1952, after the film's release, was a basically twentieth-century figure, though Ehrlich (1854–1915) straddled the centuries). This temporal setting typifies many biopics, because the nineteenth century obviously underpins the audience's modern world, not least its most fundamental medical developments, structural – for example, the research laboratory, the clinical trial, and so on – and curative – for example, Pasteur's microbiology, Ehrlich's chemotherapy, the development of anaesthetics, so that the audience witness the creation of their own ameliorated conditions. As in other biopics the nineteenth century appears a vanished period of heroic individualism, with all but lone researchers in all but unsponsored primitive laboratories. Typically, these nineteenth-century protagonists move from an individualist, artisan's world into a proto-modern one where the individual may appear only the sum of structural forces, with even Elizabeth Kenny semi-industrialised into her multiplying clinics, thus dictating the need for myths of individuality. By the end of *Magic Bullet*, Ehrlich is part of a fully institutionalised, industrialised medicine (the montage of the 'Fordist' drug factory producing serums for the world). To a viewpoint stressing homogeneity this ending is identical with *The Story of Alexander Graham Bell*'s (Irving Cummings, 1939), where Bell's telephone is bought into by Western Union; from specification's perspective, it has an irreducibility of subject and visualisation (the industrialisation of medicine) and tone (serious, idealistic, whereas *The Story of Alexander Graham Bell* ends with comic insouciance). An instance, though, of both surface and subterranean difference lies in the near non-existence of 'the big break' in the medical biopic, something replicated only in the minority of biopics of the highest seriousness. True, in *Magic Bullet*, Heide's (Ruth Gordon) accidental heating of the slides solves a major problem for Ehrlich, and Pasteur's wife (Josephine Hutchinson) importantly reminds him that viruses decline with age. However, Ehrlich would surely have tried heat at some stage himself, and Marie is remembering something Pasteur has forgotten he told her. Fortune here acts, if at all, in very diminished modes, which is proper since an emphasis on luck would tend to undermine the protagonist's intellectual force and determination.

In moving to areas where specification outweighs homogeneity, the rest of this section concentrates on four clusters of meaning, formulated here as (i) 'Idols of (Mental) Production', (ii) Spectacle, (iii) The Law of Rules, and (iv) 'The Religion of Humanity'.

'Idols of (mental) production'

Stylistically 'old fashioned' in their tableauesque properties, these films are also backward-looking in resisting the shift from celebration of 'conventional elites' ('idols of production') to 'idols of [the society of] consumption' increasingly common by the 1940s (Custen 1992 [via Leo Lowenthal 1944]: 206–8). Democratic not aristocratic, this elite is not symbolic but productive in the most elevated sense of the mental production of ideas – ideas too that are not simply aids to convenience and ease (cf. biopics celebrating heroes of transport and communication), but of literally vital consequence. The choice of the charming Don Ameche as Alexander Graham Bell recognises this, whereas Muni's Pasteur, the paradigm of medical biopic protagonists, is all austerity, intellectual ardour and self-sacrifice. Accordingly these films eschew the comic, with only *Madame Curie*'s comedy of the hyper-intellectual couple surprised by love a substantial exception. In *Louis Pasteur*, there is Louis' occasional didactic wit, Marie Pasteur pretending to read out a letter denouncing Louis' tyranny, the sheep at Arbois baa-ing at Radisse; but such instances are few, and little wonder, for these protagonists tend literally to die from over-exertion and other consequences of their work. Ehrlich contracts tuberculosis in his laboratory; later collapses from this, then is felled by a stroke which, like Pasteur's near the end of his story, is the product of relentless schedules. Marie Curie suffers radioactive burns, and though Kenny's illness is only vaguely referred to (as noted, she was still alive in 1946) even Rosalind Russell has at the film's end the others' lineaments of exhausted body barely containing a relentless ardour of spirit.

Spectacle

With the musical biopic's obvious exception, the genre is not known for stylistic exuberance: indeed Elsaesser notes criticisms of Dieterle's biopics' 'slow and ponderous direction', before attempting more analytic definitions: 'different types of spatial construction' – a determined frontality of staging, and 'a different sense of continuity' – 'a sparing use of the point of view' structure, making 'lives appear as if already set in the picture frame of history' (Elsaesser 1986: 28). Montage sequences – obvious sites of spectacle – have a major function in the biopic, displaying 'a teleology of fame' as well as the more obvious role of concentrating chronology. The medical biopic's montages display a specific *mise-en-scène* and iconography – hospital wards, early kymographs, primitive laboratories (often recreated minutely from contemporary photographs), minatorialy oversized hypodermics, newspaper headlines listing epidemic death counts, and so on and on. Related recurrent spectacles emphasise pathos, vulnerability, life's tenuousness, showing the body (above all the child's) in the grip of disease, torqued by pain. *Louis Pasteur* and *Magic Bullet* share a major trope in the microscope's view of an invisible world otherwise indicated only in bodily symptoms. As synecdoche for the new medicine the instrument's centrality is dramatised by both films' credits taking place over its silhouette. Both films have multiple moments where the audience share the researcher's view of the hidden microscopic dimension in a recurrent shot of the brightly-lit circle with its teeming miniature world against the darkened rectangle of the screen, these light values dramatically reversed where we see in *Magic Bullet*, against a black background, the dreaded, ghostly-pale syphilis spirochetes. A further, intimate spectacle, if not absolutely restricted to these films, again is only shared by the most heightenedly serious biopics. When a committee man inspecting Ehrlich's laboratory questions Hato, his Japanese assistant, with 'You associates seem to do all the work here. What does the Professor do?', Hato's reply is 'He thinks', underlining the constant drama of the exteriorisation of thought in these films – with Muni the cogitational paradigm, hairline slightly retracted as if thinned by mental effort, spare face weighed down with tiredness, but eyes blazing with indefatigable ardour as he touches his

Figure 10: *The Story of Louis Pasteur* (Wilhelm Dieterle, 1936); courtesy of BFI Stills, Posters and Designs

lip with walking-stick handle or, removing pince-nez from blinking, refocusing eyes, taps them on his fingers, or wags one of the latter in donnish emphasis. Robinson, Garson and Russell follow him, but with characteristic differences – Garson's semiotics of mystically-inflected materialism, Russell's of a still vivacious obduracy and determination, Robinson's – his gangster's gash mouth hidden by moustache and beard – quieter, more retracted than Muni, but still flaring with sudden energy.

The law of rules

This can be seen as a sub-species of the genre's larger innovation versus conservatism dualism in which the protagonist bypasses conventional practices, as Sister Kenny does when she accuses the polio specialist Dr Brack (Philip Merrivale) of being unable to see the truth because his perception is too affected by the books he has read. Though spread across the genre, its presence is especially intense in the medical biopic and also, arguably, more ambivalent. Two of the films (*Louis Pasteur*, *Magic Bullet*), and indeed Huston's *Freud*, almost immediately bring their protagonists into conflict with institutional rules. Ehrlich, for instance, is criticised by Dr Wolfert (Sig Ruman) for spending too much time with patients, then reprimanded for researching in hospital time, then warned by his superior to conform. It is hard to see audiences not on his side against such pusillanimity (and, indeed, proto-Nazi racism with Wolfert), but later, during the diphtheria epidemic, things become more complicated. Moved by the plight of the children not injected with his serum, he dismantles the controlled experiment, that touchstone of modern medical research, which will give proof of the serum's viability, and injects them. Here, though the stakes are higher, the audience presumably agrees that humanity takes precedence over experimental protocol, however important that may be. The final instance is, though, more complicated still. After the discovery of the effectiveness of '606' against syphilis, Ehrlich refuses to release the inadequately tested 'specific'. Appealed to 'in the name of humanity', he eventually agrees, an action paralleled in *Louis Pasteur* when Pasteur injects Joseph and the rabies-infected Russians with his serum, even though he imagines being guillotined if they die. Since Pasteur's risk is 100 per cent successful, the moral question of using an untested preparation recedes. However, in *Magic Bullet*, though salvarsan is enormously successful, 38 people die of side effects, leading to the libel action Ehrlich brings against his persecutor Wolfert. After von Behring's (Otto Kruger) testimony, focusing on the trope that 38 should be 39, the extra death being that of syphilis itself, the court accepts the deaths as 'sacrifices' to 'the public good' – a more complex position than in *Louis Pasteur* where the issue is settled without moral questioning.[2]

Innovation versus tradition may in many biopics feel like rather a formal contest against straw men. In the medical biopic, however, it poses the hero(ine) against a pillar of society, the medical profession, that is both reactionary and formidably powerful, but also ultimately needed, both in its healing capacities and as a guardian against quackery. While the protagonists attack nineteenth-century blindness, reactionary figures like Charbonnet (Fritz Leiber) in *Louis Pasteur* are understood to have their twentieth-century equivalents, actualised in the more modern figures: Wolfert (whose prejudice marches into the twentieth century) in *Magic Bullet* and Dr Brack in *Sister Kenny*. This doubleness, enacting the audience's fear and resentment of the wealth and unassailability of the American medical profession and its highly conservative, indeed reactionary, mouthpiece, the AMA, alongside its dependence on them, is reflected in the films' careful balancing of a Dr Brack, Kenny's persecutor, with a Dr MacDonald (Alexander Knox), her supporter, and their equivalents in other texts. This explains the *volte-face* in *Sister Kenny*, where, interrupting his lecture, Kenny tells him and his medical audience that 'sincerity doesn't excuse a shut mind or the cruelty to which stubbornness subjects thousands of people', yet years on, again addressing an audience of doctors, she celebrates them for the sincerity of their opposition to her: 'the very fact that they fought so bitterly for what they believed has made me respect them'. In *The Great Moment*, that most surprising of biopics of the time, Morton's supporter, Dr Warren, a figure of complex sympathy, pragmatism and uprightness, eventually agrees with the medical establishment's position against using Morton's anaesthetic unless he discloses its makeup. Though aware of the flawed motives behind resistance to Morton, he eventually accepts the letter of the law: 'the ethics of our profession have done much more good than harm. They don't happen to fit this case. That is regrettable.' Compare this with a minor instance in *Louis Pasteur* where the young Martel (Donald Woods) introduces himself to Pasteur, expressing his disdain for his boss, Charbonnet, and Pasteur upbraids him for disrespecting his superior. Perhaps rather than being the product of Pasteur's authoritarian or other psychology, his action's logic lies in the films' characteristic balance between critique and support of the establishment, with whom in all the classic versions the protagonist is eventually reconciled.

'The religion of humanity'

As we have seen, a certain 'oceanic' or displaced religious sense is part of these narratives. This despite a surprising absence of both the religious personnel, whom one would expect to be present in epidemics and hospitals in nineteenth-century France and Germany, and of references to religion. The nearest is Pasteur's exchange with the midwife at a childbirth deathbed: 'Providence', she asserts. 'Not Providence: Ignorance!' he replies – a characteristically ambivalent exchange since Pasteur's words could mean that Providence ruling the world is to be wholly rejected: or that, since Ignorance rather than Providence is responsible for the death, the idea of Providence (whether religious or humanist-optimistic) still stands. Such ambivalence tends to soften the films' secularity, making it possible to read the absence of religious personnel (a prohibition only broken in *The Great Moment*) doubly – either as a mark of their irrelevance, or as ensuring they are not questioned by narrative events. On the other hand, another mark of these films' seriousness is that one invention they refrain from is to claim the protagonist as ultimately a believer. Nevertheless, religious allusions proliferate – Pasteur's saved (inoculated) and damned (untreated) sheep; the hospital head's words to Ehrlich apropos the diphtheria cure: 'In the last days my hospital has become a place of miracles'; Kenny's cripples walking; Ehrlich's healing of the blind syphilitic, where the realistically lengthy processes of medicine are preceded by his faith-healer-like touching of the patient's body and eyes. Here the audience may adopt any of several outlooks: (i) the moments reconcile religion and science, moderating a conflict that does not appear in other biopics; (ii) they use religious metaphors because they are familiar to the audience, but we know that what we watch is purely scientific; (iii) the latter, but the medic is the heir to Christianity in at least its healing dimension, and his/her spiritualised materialism suggests the healing of soul/psyche alongside the body. This kind of trope can appear in other films with protagonists of the highest moral seriousness – as in another Dieterle/Muni collaboration, *The Life of Emile Zola* (William Dieterle, 1937) where, apropos the Dreyfus trial's injustice, Zola's lawyer declares, 'Once before the centuries reversed the judgement. That too was a closed case', at which there is a point-of-view shot involving both lawyer and Zola looking at a painting of Christ on the cross – but it is most consistently developed in the medical biopic.

As noted, the protagonists are all seen in old age, in Ehrlich's case actually on his deathbed, so that their final statements have the aura of the religious leader leaving his disciples. If the road pointed to is a materialist one, it is a spiritualised materialism, deep in oceanic feeling, spurred by humanitarianism. Addressing the Academy, Pasteur's speech is similar to, if slightly less oceanic than, Curie's: 'Live in the serene peace of libraries and laboratories … until the time comes when you may have the immense happiness of thinking you may have contributed to the welfare and progress of mankind.' The dying Ehrlich is surrounded by his international cohort of assistants (with an Indian, in addition to Hato, the Japanese – whose real-life eminence the film may downgrade, but whom it does not expel even in the eve-of-war Japanese-American tension of the film's making). Before dying, Ehrlich speaks of the tasks of fighting disease in the future but, clearly alluding to Nazi anti-Semitism in words that bring together the moment of his death (actually 1915 though there is no sense in the narrative of that war, as distinct from that of 1939) and the moment of the film's making, refers not only to 'diseases of the body' but to 'diseases of the soul' and moral 'epidemics', concrete political allusions that intertwine with the unmistakably religious-alluding epigraph, 'And the temples to his memory are human bodies purified and made whole.'

Unclassical variations

Sturges' *The Great Moment* was a personal project pursued despite Paramount's eventual hostility, which resulted in a release version disapproved by the director. Such circumstances were very different from Dieterle's whose ambition to direct 'quality' features uncontentiously intersected with Warner Bros.' drive to secure prestige through the biopic (Elsaesser 1986: 21–3). Radical though it is, *The Great Moment* retains recognisable features of the classic model. Unlike its source, René Fulop-Muller's book *Triumph Over Pain*, which explores much other material than Morton's vicissitudes, it centres on the single individual. Yet, inflected by Sturges' comic-satiric drives, it is distinct from the other films. Again the contrast with Dieterle is notable, with the latter's biopic interests in no way in tension with the classical model, which to a large degree he defined, whereas Sturges subjected it to ironic scrutiny. The characteristic intersection of Sturges' comic-satiric drives with the subgenre can be seen in the striking parallel between the narrative debacles of his comedy *The Great McGinty* (1940) and *The Great Moment*, where both protagonists fall, with a sardonic logic appropriate to the capitalist contradictions whose comic satiric potential the director exploits, from the heights they have attained, through committing not immoral, but *moral*, acts.

The *fabula* of *The Great Moment* follows Morton's growing interest in anaesthesia, prompted by his experiences in the crude world of nineteenth-century dentistry, his early experiments, his relations with his old teacher, Professor Jackson, and another dentist Horace Wells, who after Morton's success, claim his achievements as their own. When 'Letheon' is used in a painless major operation, Morton's success seems assured, as he applies for the patent that will secure him against rival dentists, while allowing hospitals free use of his method. However, disaster strikes through regulations forbidding doctors to use preparations with undeclared ingredients. Morton refuses to declare the content of his patent, but, facing the servant girl about to undergo unanaesthetised surgery, he enables the operation by giving away his secret. His business destroyed by rivals appropriating his method, he retires to farm and bring up his family. Twenty years later, informed of Congress' plan to grant him $100,000, Morton raises money to go to Washington. But President Pierce will not sign the bill without Morton bringing a suit against a naval surgeon who has used his method. In doing this, Morton puts himself in a bad light and, vilified in the press, loses the case. Soon after, he dies.

The original's *syuzhet* (only recoverable through the screenplay) profoundly disorders this chronology, most strikingly by recounting Morton's life after his fall near the narrative's beginning. The studio's opposition to the original was clearly driven by dislike of such a complicatedly anticlimactic mode of telling. But though as much as possible the release version was recut into a conventional chronology, this was impossible to do comprehensively without rendering the narrative opaque. Thus the released film still begins with Morton's short-lived moment of triumph, then clusters layers of flash-forward and flashback in its first few minutes, before settling into an uninterrupted chronological progression which nevertheless still ends at a point before the ironies of Morton's decline which narratively precede it. Though formally less radical than the lost film Sturges shot, the release version of *The Great Moment* is still a highly creative and subversive version of the biopic, more so than Brian Henderson's view, perhaps fixed on narrative structure to the exclusion of other elements, allows.

Various of these other elements play significantly against generic expectations. For instance, casting Joel McCrea as Morton foregrounds an actor of handsomely rugged limitations – stoical, wilful, but with neither the intellectual energy of Muni and Robinson, nor Greer Garson's visionariness nor Rosalind Russell's relentless drive. These lacks might suggest aberrant casting but, as in Sturges' *The Palm Beach Story* (1941) where McCrea's virile stolidity contrasts with the usual expectations of romantic comedy heroes, it marks an ordinariness and mundane contingency that the film insists on as it locates the hero's great discovery in a mixture of pragmatism, commercialism, self-seeking, altruism and chaos. Though *The Great Moment* takes place in a primitive enclave of nineteenth-century medicine in some ways closer to the barbershop or medicine show than to the high research ethos of Pasteur, Curie and Ehrlich, in spite of, or perhaps partly because of, this it suggests perspectives on the world of modern medicine not found in the other biopics – a sceptical interrogation of the idealised researcher, an emphasis on medicine as an entrepreneurial undertaking, an inclusion of self-advancement among the motives for research, and a refusal to leave alone the largely uncontaminated ideal lines of the traditional treatment. The sub-genre's eschewing of comedy has already been noted, but *The Great Moment* employs the mode extensively – for instance in Eben Frost's (William Demarest) fainting in the surgical auditorium; his constant inopportune repetition of his rote statement of his role (as patient) in 'Letheon''s discovery; the grotesque physical comedy of the early bungled experiments; the callously festive atmosphere in the surgical amphitheatre; Morton's drugged condition after an anaesthesic experiment being mistaken by his wife for drunkenness; his farcically unsuccessful stalking of the family dog as experimental subject. All these, while they may not exhibit systematic thematic linkages, function as deconstructors of the high-toned idealism of the prototype, insisting on a messier, more accidental world than usually depicted. At the same time, though, it would be misleading to separate out the comic strain in a film which is notable for cultivating instabilities of tone. Both *The Great Moment*'s beginning and end illustrate this well. Although Sturges' original prologue was slangier, angrier and less constrained (Sturges 1995: 316–20), what Sturges replaced it with, under studio pressure, has a distanced philosophic resonance in its awareness of the complexities of deconstructive processes that is, if anything, more interesting in its insistence on differing perspectives, angles of view, and complexity of tone. (The epigraph shifts from the original's 'One of the most charming characteristics of Homo Sapiens, the talking gorilla on your right' to 'Of all things in nature great men alone reverse the laws of perspective and grow smaller as one approaches them'.) The film's ending is notable for its unalloyed extremity of tone: its imagery of religious light and salvation (commented on by Henderson in Sturges 1995: 314–15), the pathos of the servant girl attended by the priest and lit by a shaft of seemingly celestial light, accompanied by the music of 'Ave Maria' – all Sturges' rather than a studio imposition. More extreme than the secular-religious resonances of the endings of the other films, it however unmodulatedly clashes with the tones of the rest of the narrative, creating instabilities rather than unsullied resolution, and, as Henderson aptly notes, thus 'directly challenges the hundreds of homogenised biopics that Hollywood turned out in the 1930s, 1940s and 1950s' (Sturges 1995: 316).

A note on Huston's *Freud*

Is *Freud* to be classed as a medical (researcher) biopic? Or does its difference, constituted around the exteriorisation of the interior world of dream and fantasy (the psychic equivalent of the spectacle revealed by the microscope?) over and above the spectacle of the neurotic's symptom-shaken body, demand a further sub-generic differentiation into the psychoanalytic biopic (candidates: *Freud*, *The Three Faces of Eve*)? However defined, this film, emerging from a complex renegotiation of the traditional biopic: a script by Charles Kaufman, never filmed; Sartre's enormous screenplay, abandoned, but then palimpsested onto Kaufman's original in Huston and Wolfgang Reinhardt's final reworking (Hayman

1986; Cohen-Solal 1987; Kaminsky 1978), extends the biopic's possibilities in ways noteworthy both in themselves and for the retrospective light they shed on the earlier films. *Freud* is still in touch with the traditional biopic – organised around a single paramount individual, its temporal restriction to the years of Freud's (Montgomery Clift) first major theorising comparable to the *Young Mr Lincoln* (John Ford, 1939) and *Young Tom Edison* (Norman Taurog, 1940) pattern of some classical biopics, and part-structured around 'trial scenes' where Freud scandalously publicises his researches in lectures. The contractions of its sophisticated narrative – the presence of Charcot and Breuer, but the absence of Fliess; the condensing of the material of several of Freud's and Breuer's (Larry Parks) cases, as well as the inventions of screenwriters versed in Freud, on to two patients, Carl von Schlosser (David McCallum) and Cecily Koertner (Susannah York), especially the latter – show that equivalent processes, irrespective of such banalities as Zola meeting Nana's sympathetic prototype in *The Life of Emile Zola* are not the errors of crude prototypes but essential to the genre's economy, like the equally necessary simplifications of medico-scientific material for audiences (like myself, alas) capable of following a 'Magic Bullet''s trajectory but not the details, say, of Ehrlich's 'side-chain' theory. Built around Freud's self-analysis, his arrival at the Oedipus complex, and assertion of infantile sexuality, the narrative disturbs the delicate balance of the classical model by subjectivising and problematising the researcher's drive for knowledge, highlighting obstructions and inhibitions; for example, both Breuer and Freud's reactions to the hazards of 'transference', thus subverting the earlier medical biopics' unambivalent presentation of thought operating on the external world. As Hayman notes of Sartre's version, 'In the first paragraph of his synopsis he sums up what the film is to be about: "A man undertakes to understand other people because this seems the only way to understand himself, and he realises that his researches on other people and on himself can be conducted simultaneously"' (Hayman 1986: 325). Of course the material of Freud's research is more psychically disturbing than that of Pasteur, Ehrlich, Curie or Kenny – germ theory does not demand a traumatic reliving of oedipal relations – but even so, the later film highlights how much the earlier ones close off any ambiguities existing between personal and intellectual life: for instance, the scene where Freud's wife Marthe expresses her distaste for the sexual content of his research underlines by contrast how completely intimate relations in the earlier films exist merely as the support for the researcher's work (the only exception being *Sister Kenny* where the heroine, with the dilemma that a nurse cannot be a married woman, chooses work over marriage, her work's hundreds even thousands of children, over a personal family). Finally, two traditional elements of the biopic are inflected by Huston's film to more destabilising ends than previously. The film's epigraph and final framing statement – both featuring the director's voice – while asserting Freud's greatness do so in the context of the triad of the discoveries of Galileo, Darwin and Freud, subverting the anthropocentrism and humanistic optimism that traditionally drive the genre, while the two 'trial' scenes, especially the lecture near the end of the film where infantile sexuality is announced, end in scandal and rejection, with one man even spitting at Freud, and Freud's colleague Breuer, while defending him, confessing that he cannot accept his theories.

Notes

1   Elsaesser quotes Brecht on Dieterle's biopics, 'Wilhelm Dieterle's grosser buergerlicher figuren' in *Von Deutschland nach Hollywood: William Dieterle 1893-1972*' (Filmfest-

spiele Berlin, 1973). However, Brecht's claim that Warner Bros. abandoned the original Madame Curie project because of the ideological impossibility of the Curies refusing to take out a patent on radium, is somewhat implausible, since the matter is referred to in MGM's film, the product of a more conservative studio.

2 Under the extremes of the law of specification, *Louis Pasteur* and *Magic Bullet* would be noted as a different sub-species of the sub-genre, since, among other specificities, only they deal in dangerous medical experiments on human, and indeed animal, subjects. Since they are the only films of the set that involve vivisection, they are the only ones that develop strategies to soften its effects: such as the heroising of the ex-racehorse used to produce serum in *Louis Pasteur*, Ehrlich's pictures of mice on his wall, his affection for his dachshund, and so forth. Equally the female-centred version of the sub-genre develops individual specificities.

References

Anzieu, D. (1986) *Freud's Self-Analysis*. London: Hogarth Press.

Behlmer, R. (1987) *Inside Warner Brothers (1935–1951)*. London: Weidenfeld & Nicolson.

Cohen-Solal, A. (1987) *Sartre: A Life*. London: Heinemann.

Curie, E. (1938) *Madame Curie*. London: Heinemann.

Custen, G. (1992) *Bio/Pics: How Hollywood Constructed Public History*. Brunswick: Rutgers University Press.

Elsaesser, T. (1986) 'Film History as Social History: The Dieterle/Warner Brothers Bio-Pic', *Wide Angle*, 8, 2, 15–31.

Flinn, T. (1975) 'William Dieterle: The Plutarch of Hollywood', *Velvet Light Trap*, 15, 23–8.

Freud, S. (1956) *An Autobiographical Study*. London: Hogarth Press

Hayman, R. (1986) *Writing Against: A Biography of Sartre*. London: Weidenfeld & Nicolson.

Henderson, B. (1995) *Four More Screenplays by Preston Sturges*. Berkeley: University of California Press, 241–526.

Kaminsky, S. (1978) *John Huston: Maker of Magic*. Boston: Houghton Mifflin.

Kipple, K. F. (ed.) (1993) *The Cambridge World History of Human Disease*. Cambridge: Cambridge University Press.

Kohn, V. (1993) 'Kenny, Elizabeth', *Collier's Encyclopedia*, 14. New York: P. F. Collier, 26–7.

Lowenthal, L. (1944) 'Biographies in Popular Magazines', in P. Lazarsfeld and F. Stanton (eds) *Radio Research, 1942–43*. New York: Duell, Sloan & Pearce.

Madsen, A. (1978) *John Huston*. New York: Doubleday.

Neale, S. (2000) *Genre and Hollywood*. London: Routledge.

Porter, R. (1997) *The Greatest Benefit to Mankind: A Medical History of Humanity from Antiquity to the Present*. London: HarperCollins.

Schopenhauer, A. (1995) 'Appendix: Abstract of Schopenhauer's essay On the Fourfold Root of the Principle of Sufficient Reason', in D. Berman and J. Berman (eds) *The World as Will and Idea*. London: J. M. Dent, 267–8.

Wright, T. R. (1986) *The Religion of Humanity: The Impact of Comtean Positivism on Victorian Britain*. Cambridge: Cambridge University Press.

11

C. A. Morgan III

From *Let There Be Light* to *Shades of Grey*: the construction of authoritative knowledge about combat fatigue (1945–48)

Introduction

In 1945 the US Army released to the general public its official documentary film dealing with subject of combat fatigue in American soldiers. The film was directed by Lt. John Huston and was called *Let There Be Light*.[1] Within weeks of its release, military officials denounced the film as unsuitable for public viewing and withdrew it from circulation.[2] Despite repeated appeals for its release by Huston, Hollywood studio executives and film critics, the military suppressed *Let There Be Light* for the next thirty years.[3]

Having withdrawn *Let There Be Light* from public circulation, the War Department offered John Huston the opportunity to re-shoot his film using actors instead of real patients – a proposal he emphatically declined.[4] The project was given to producer Frank Payne and director Joe Henaberry, and their remake of *Let There Be Light* was released in 1947 under the title *Shades of Grey*. The existence of this film offers the historian an opportunity to examine the way official public knowledge about combat fatigue was crafted, for *Shades of Grey* incorporated certain aspects of *Let There Be Light* and rejected others.

Army officials offered two reasons for the withdrawal of *Let There Be Light*. The first was that the film violated patient confidentiality and Army regulations by portraying actual patients suffering from combat fatigue. The second reason given by Army officials was that the remarkable psychiatric cures portrayed in *Let There Be Light* might encourage veterans who had not experienced such positive responses to treatment to litigate against the government.[5] While these concerns possessed an air of legitimacy, there are reasons for questioning their validity.

First, while the film did portray actual cases of combat fatigue, it complied fully with Army regulations. In August 1945, the Joint Chiefs of Staff issued a memorandum for the production of films that would dispel public misinformation about the nature of combat fatigue. In part, it stated:

> … tremendous educational value may accrue to the benefit of the Army, the public, and ultimately the individual psychiatric patient, through the utilisation of carefully developed motion pictures and photographs of neuropsychiatric activities. This would in some instances, of necessity, include 'identifiable' patients. Therefore, it is recommended that the restriction given above be modified to permit such photos, taken under Army supervision.[6]

Second, while it remains unclear whether Huston obtained written consent forms, it is clear that the Army obstructed his attempts to do so at a later time.[7] When Huston and Hollywood executives offered to re-obtain consent forms from the identifiable patients in the film, they were told the Army could not locate them.[8] That the Army was unable to contact 25 former psychiatric patients living in Long Island, New York, was minimally credible given the fact that the Army had been able to re-contact over 4,000 former patients several months earlier.[9] Further, there is evidence it was the Army doctors who had appeared in *Let There Be Light*, and not the patients, who would not sign consent forms which would have permitted the release of the film.[10]

Finally, the Army's assertion that the fantastic cures depicted in *Let There Be Light* would lead to increased litigation against the government was also suspect. First, Huston had included depictions of cases that did not respond to treatment in the original film.[11] Second, none of the civilian or professional feedback indicates viewers of the film took issue with the psychiatric treatments portrayed.[12] In the end, John Huston confessed in his personal letters that he never understood why his film was banned.

In 1947 the Army released its official 'remake' of *Let There Be Light*, entitled *Shades of Grey*.[13] Thus, the historian is presented with the paradox of the military's support of a particular cinematic portrayal of combat fatigue on the one hand, and its condemnation and suppression of another. An in-depth examination of both films offers the historian a chance to understand what may have been objectionable to the military about *Let There Be Light*, yet acceptable about *Shades of Grey*. Such an analysis may clarify the multiple and possibly dichotomous beliefs about combat fatigue which may have existed at this period in US history. Further, critical analysis of the films may shed light on processes involved in the construction of authoritative scientific knowledge about what was one of the most significant and costly conditions caused by the war.[14]

Over the past decade historians of medicine and science have increasingly viewed film as a legitimate component of historical inquiry.[15] Many scholars in the fields of literary criticism, discourse analysis and political science have suggested that film is a text-base from which critical analyses can emanate.[16] Any filmmaker attempting to portray a mental condition[17] must surmount the challenge of forming a coherent representation of the complex realities of a human being's mental life. In fashioning such a representation the resultant film in-corporates, and bases itself on, certain cultural, ideological or literary presuppositions. As such, a potentially rich field of presuppositions involving mental illness and mental health may be exposed through an analysis of cinematic depictions of combat fatigue, provided such study also focuses on the manner in which these representations were selected or rejected.[18]

Official government films like *Let There Be Light* and *Shades of Grey* were explicitly made to reflect contemporaneous mental health knowledge, and to actively shape such knowledge for physicians, soldiers and civilians alike.[19] Clarification of the messages or beliefs contained in these films represents a fundamental step towards understanding *why* certain messages or beliefs in these films were endorsed or suppressed.[20] Understanding *why* certain mental health messages were censored or promoted provides the historian the opportunity to learn *what* was counted as authoritative knowledge and *why* or *how* that knowledge changed.[21]

Shades of Grey (1947)

Despite a military press release claiming *Shades of Grey* was simply a remake of Huston's film designed to protect patient confidentiality by using actors instead of real patients, critical analysis of the film and its use of source materials indicates otherwise.[22] Of Huston's 55-minute film, *Shades of Grey* retains one minute of original footage and approximately seven minutes of re-enacted scenes based upon original footage.[23] The remaining 60 minutes of footage in *Shades of Grey* are divided evenly between new script material, US Army stock footage, and re-enacted scenes of material taken from an 1944 Army Signal Corps medical film, *Psychiatric Procedures in the Combat Arena*.[24] Thus, *Shades of Grey* is a film that did not remake, but instead replaced, *Let There Be Light* with a very different ideology, focus and emphasis – all the while claiming to be to be a remake of Huston's film.[25]

Analysis and comparison of the footage from *Let There Be Light* and of *Psychiatric Procedures in the Combat Arena* to footage kept, copied and/or discarded by the makers of *Shades of Grey*, offers a fairly direct way of examining factors and presuppositions involved in the creation of official knowledge. *Shades of Grey* was designed to instruct the general public *and* physicians about the nature of war neuroses. As such, the film offered a corrected version of official knowledge on the subject.

To even the casual viewer, it is immediately apparent that *Shades of Grey* is organised in a very different manner than was *Let There Be Light*. Whereas Huston's film took, as its point of departure, the return of military psychiatric casualties to the United States, *Shades of Grey* starts with civilian life. In marked contrast to the opening section of *Let There Be Light* which, through intimate interviews, poignantly underscored the psychological suffering of soldiers, *Shades of Grey* begins with Army stock footage and a narrated segment. This sequence normalises mental distress by equating it with the routine physical ills experienced by men in the army. The following speech is delivered by the narrator as the camera pans over hundreds of regimented troops marching in formation:

Take any section of the United States Army, a tough and rugged body of men. Not a single one of them is 100% healthy. Some have a little sinus trouble. Some have periodic attacks of boils. Others have had repeated attacks of appendicitis which may return in an acute form. More than half have been infected with tuberculosis without even knowing it – but the scars of the infection remain. Not one man in one-hundred has a perfect set of teeth, and each man's body carries millions of germs ready to attack should he be weakened by exposure or fatigue. Even the healthiest of people are not pure white healthy, or the sickest people solid black sick – unless they're dead. Instead, people are somewhere in between, neither white nor black, but some Shade of Grey. Most people are a light shade of grey – a lot of health mixed with a little sickness. It's the same with emotional or mental health. Slight mental disturbances exist in everyone. No one is 100% perfect. Nobody has pure white mental health.[26]

This introduction normalises mental distress in a statistical sense.[27] It also naturalises psychological illness and sets the stage for what will become the over-arching message of the film: war is not the cause of mental illness; it only serves as a stimulus that brings to the surface or uncovers the seeds of mental illness which lurk in everyone. Accordingly, the viewer is next shown scenes of newborn babies in a hospital nursery. The narrator comments:

Foundations of physical and mental health are laid in infancy. A child is born with its lungs and digestive track free of germs. But, as it starts life in the outside world, it admits thousands of them. The newborn baby has very little permanent immunity or resistance to disease, but in fighting and conquering infection, resistance is developed and strengthened. *It's the same with mental disease.* (My emphasis)[28]

Following this, *Shades of Grey* depicts a series of fictionalised accounts of two prototypical little boys named Bill Brown and Joe Smith. Bill Brown (and his mother) represent shining examples of a healthy upbringing. The case of Joe Smith, in contrast, tells the story of a less fortunate child who is destined to develop combat fatigue.

Bill Brown, through a series of vignettes, is shown to have a wise and understanding mother who lets him experience unpleasant events which she believes will strengthen his character. In the first of these vignettes, Bill is seen playing with a large butcher knife. His mother takes it away from him. He cries and protests, but she only smiles, gently shakes her head and returns to her sewing. She leaves Bill to comfort himself with his age-appropriate toys. In the second vignette, a slightly older Bill Brown is challenged by a neighborhood bully who tries to take his bicycle away from him. Bill fights back and successfully wrestles his bike from the hands of the would-be-thief. The narrator tells the viewer Bill's victory is evidence that he has learned to handle aggression and 'resist it'. Subsequent vignettes show Bill Brown playing in the woods with classmates and, by so doing, developing athletic ability. This sequence concludes with the narrator's comment: 'Bill Brown has lost the helpless fears he had as a baby. Deep in the unconscious mind these things [his victories] are remembered.'

Joe Smith, however, is not so lucky. His over-concerned and anxious mother does not allow him to play independently, nor will she let him associate freely with other children. As a result, Joe Smith is unable to learn how to defend himself physically or psychologically. When the neighborhood bully grabs Joe's wagon, Joe sits helpless on the porch and cries for his mother. Scenes from Joe's life in grade school and high school, show the consequences of his upbringing. Joe is unathletic, perpetually fearful of getting his clothes dirty and disinterested in women. The narrator mentions (surprisingly) that in spite of his deficiencies Joe Smith is a good student and speculates that there is a chance, *if he is lucky*, Joe may someday find a low stress job. Immediately following this comment Joe Smith is shown working in an office for his father, Joe Smith, Sr. The sequence concludes on a disquieting note:

Joe Smith is a deep shade of grey. He is by no means a rarity. Today medical professionals estimate that 50–75% of their patients suffer from mental illness.

Of hundreds of thousands of hospital beds, over one-half are occupied by patients with serious mental illness. Medical statistics indicate that of 139,000,000 people in the United States, one in eighteen, or 7.5 million will at some time be treated in a mental hospital. *A far greater number will suffer less serious mental illness* [emphasis narrator]. From the population, the American people, the personnel of the Army is selected.[29]

Thus, the theoretical framework underlying the conceptualisation of combat fatigue becomes clear. In the diagesis of *Shades of Grey* the seeds of mental illness are alarmingly ubiquitous. The population of the United States is permeated with mental illness – an unfortunate fact with which the Army must deal. The military is not responsible for this plague of mental illness, but must make the best of a less than ideal situation, for as the narrator comments: 'If the Army rejected everyone with a trace of mental illness there would be no Army at all!'[30]

Joe Smith and Bill Brown are next seen after induction into the Army. In keeping with the developmental model, each (predictably) has a very different experience during basic training. While Bill Brown adapts quite well, Joe Smith does not. Joe cannot run the obstacle course, lacks the strength to climb barriers and is afraid to jump over a muddy riverbed. Finally, while on the grenade practice range, he is overcome by fear and freezes after pulling the pin on a grenade. Joe trembles, perspires and is unable to throw it. A training officer sees Joe's distress, and grabs the grenade away from him just before it explodes. Joe Smith is relieved of duty and led away to the psychiatrist. In his interview with the psychiatrist, Joe Smith cries. Being forced to spend his nights away from home has filled him with thoughts of suicide and despair.

At this point, *Shades of Grey* shifts from the fictitious character Joe Smith and turns to a series of psychiatric interviews of soldiers in the Italian campaign of 1944. In each, a soldier is questioned by an Army psychiatrist. All but the first of the seven interviews are re-enactments (by actors) and copied from actual patient interviews seen in the 1944 Army Signal Corps Professional Medical Film, *Psychiatric Procedures in the Combat Arena*. The first of the seven interviews is not a re-enactment but is totally fictitious. It shows Bill Brown who, after being knocked out of his fox-hole by a shell burst, has had a mild case of the 'jitters'. The scene is brief and little is said. Bill Brown is offered a cigarette by the psychiatrist and reassured that he will be all right. Within the context of the film, the vignette serves as a transition device as well as a modest acknowledgement that some healthy people may get a mild case of nerves from exposure to combat.

The subsequent six interviews are re-enactments based on real interviews with soldiers on the Italian front in 1944.[31] These are relevant to historical analysis in that while some were reproduced with high fidelity to the original interviews, others contain significant alterations. Despite the claim of 'authenticity and precision in the replication of actual patient scenes', the scenes provide clear evidence that the makers of *Shades of Grey* took liberties with actual historical information.[32] The rewriting and selective editing appears to have been done in order to bring the patient's appearance and experience in line with the theoretical framework espoused by the film.

The six interviews illustrate, visually and verbally, the continuum of mild to severe psychopathology in combat fatigue. In keeping with the film's title and leitmotif, soldiers (actors) who represent mild cases of combat fatigue appear normal and are identified as being 'light grey' in terms of illness; soldiers (actors) representing severe cases are visibly dishevelled, disoriented and dirty. They are said to represent 'darker shades of grey', or more serious mental illness.

The verbal reports of soldiers were also changed. In the original series of interviews, each soldier reports being exposed to a different type of combat trauma (for example, being shot at, having a shell land beside the fox-hole, seeing one's fellow soldier blown to pieces, being actually hit by incoming rounds, and so on) whereas the actors in *Shades of Grey* all report being exposed to very nearly the same combat trauma (being shot at). This departure from the original text of the source film is highly meaningful in that it removes the etiological significance of combat trauma in the development of combat fatigue. In *Psychiatric Procedures in the Combat Arena* the soldiers who were exposed to the most graphic and personally threatening traumatic events (being next to a soldier who was blown-up, being shot) are the most severe cases of combat fatigue. By contrast, the soldiers reporting exposure to less graphic events (being shot at) are the mild cases of combat fatigue.[33]

The rewriting of material underscores the message in *Shades of Grey* that the cause of illness is an individual's psychological make-up, rather than war stress. The remarkable extent to which *Shades of Grey* downplays, or de-emphasises, the emotionally damaging effects of war stress is made even more striking as one notes the film's complete omission of all material from the introductory footage of *Psychiatric Procedures in the Combat Arena* – footage that gives paramount etiologic importance to war stress as a cause for combat fatigue:

America sends its best and strongest men to fight. Those who actually go to the front endure hardships and dangers unequaled by any in their past experiences. Courage, pride and loyalty help sustain them, but there are fierce demands on their emotional resources [during this there are extensive scenes of bomb blasts on the front lines]. Day after day they live in danger [bombs and explosions]. They see their friends cut down [scenes of wounded men being sewn-up by doctors], shattered by shrapnel [scenes of mutilated bodies], and burned by the fires of the enemy [scene of burned bodies]. They see the grinding horror of mutilating death [close-up on decaying dead bodies]. Finally the mounting pressures overwhelm the strongest of personalities. These men are the residue of the battle [scene of soldiers taken to the psychiatric tent]. For every four men wounded, one soldier will be a psychiatric casualty. Some are shaking or crying. More often they are tired and dirty and depressed. They have few words, are unnerved. They are not quitters but are truely ill.[34]

These powerful images of war contrast strikingly with the rather innocuous 'seeds of illness' introduction in *Shades of Grey*. The words of this text, as well as the accompanying imagery, point to war stress, and not developmental conflicts, as the cause of combat fatigue. This footage expresses the thinking and influence of psychiatrist John Appel, head of the Army Mental Hygiene branch.[35] Appel's environmentalist beliefs about combat fatigue were at odds with those of Brig. Gen. William C. Menninger – whose ideology and efforts so powerfully shaped *Shades of Grey*.[36] Like the testimonial footage in *Let There Be Light*, this footage highlighting the horror of war was avoided, and not included in the script for *Shades of Grey*.

As if to further downplay the psychological risk presented by war stress, *Shades of Grey* highlights material that might be used to support the explanatory power of the developmental model vis-à-vis the etiology of combat fatigue (i.e. that frightening experiences or deprivations in childhood lie at the root of adult mental illness).[37] The following sequences, taken from *Shades of Grey* and *Psychiatric Procedures in the Combat Arena*, illustrate, when presented side by side, how the text of a patient's interview was altered by the filmmakers in order to support the theoretical framework of *Shades of Grey* (the psychiatrist's questions are indicated by 'Q'; the patient's responses by 'A'):

Psychiatric Procedures	*Shades of Grey*
Q: Did you ever get into a fight?	Q: Did you ever get into a fight?
A: No Sir.	A: Uh, no Sir, I never, uh, cared
Q: How's that?	to fight. I saw a man killed once
A: I never cared for fighting. I saw	in a street fight. [pause] Head hit
someone killed one time fighting.	the curb. [breathing with difficulty]
Q: Could you tell me about that?	There was blood all over the place.
A: Oh, just an ordinary street fight,	He just lay there. Covered him up.
Sir. One man hit another man. He	I was scared. I was scared to tell
hit his head on a curb. I heard later	my parents. I had nightmares
he had gotten killed.	about it for years.
Q: How did that make you feel?	
A: Made me feel like I shouldn't fight.	
Q: How old were you then?	Q: How old were you then?
A: 'Bout sixteen.	A: 'Bout six.

By embellishing the story with negative emotional sequelae (such as nightmares) the script from *Shades of Grey* transforms the event into a (fabricated) example of the patient's historical failure to master emotions such as fear. This early failure is, in turn, used by the film as a way of explaining the patient's war-time psychiatric distress. By changing the age of the patient from 16 to 6, *Shades of Grey* underscores its main theme that childhood events are the cause of adult mental illness. From the historical interview, the street fight has no relationship to the soldier's psychiatric distress. In fact, within its original context, the story simply shows the soldier had a pre-war life that was largely free of violence.[38] However, for the purposes of *Shades of Grey* the event (witnessing an ordinary street fight) is transformed and becomes proof for the early developmental model of combat fatigue.

It is noteworthy, and ironic – given the Army's accusation that Huston violated patient confidentiality – that at this moment in the film, the creators of *Shades of Grey* breach patient confidentiality. As the fictitious interview draws to a close, the camera zooms in so the audience may witness what the doctor is writing. The film footage cuts to a close up on a patient's identification tag. A soldier's full name, address and diagnosis are boldly displayed on the screen. They are not fictitious, but part of genuine footage taken from the original interview in *Psychiatric Procedures in the Combat Arena*.

The final segment of *Shades of Grey*, depicts the treatment of soldiers with combat fatigue who were sent home to the United States. In this (shortest) section of the film, some original footage from *Let There Be Light* is seen.[39] One of Huston's most memorable sequences depicted the initial meeting between a doctor and patient; in *Shades of Grey* however, the sequence is spliced and used to introduce the case of a veteran who has been cured of combat fatigue. In Huston's film, this innovative footage gave viewers a mesmerising and highly disturbing look at human suffering during war. Under Henaberry's direction and editing, the footage is a transition from sick patients to the slightly comic face of a well-groomed, normal-looking patient (actor) who has been cured – hardly the 'shivering, frightened wrecks'[40] depicted in *Let There Be Light*. In striking contrast to the film it replaced, *Shades of Grey* contains no re-enactment of the patient interviews contained in *Let There Be Light*. Instead, it presents re-made scenes of group therapy, hypnotherapy and of a baseball game. These seem to have been retained because they emphasise the miraculous, curative powers of modern psychiatry and avoid discussions of war trauma.

Shades of Grey concludes with a fanfare of patriotic music and a visual collage of all-American images – soldiers, New York City pedestrians, steel welders, electricians, scientists and watchmakers. The collage culminates in a shot of the Statue of Liberty. As the shot moves in for a close-up, the narrator speaks with great emphasis:

> An army is no stronger than the population from which it is drawn. To keep America strong we must strive to improve the physical and mental health of the whole nation; to deepen understanding of those factors which darken or lighten the all important shades of grey.

At the narrator's words 'lighten the all important shades of grey' Lady Liberty's torch springs to life – benevolently spreading the gospel of mental health to the nation.[41] The theme of nationalism contained in *Shades of Grey* is blatant and unambiguous. Not found in any of the source films, its prominence in *Shades of Grey* begs to be understood within the specific historical context of the production of the film.

The selective survival of messages

Many clues help explain why the military responded so favourably to *Shades of Grey* and so unfavourably to *Let There Be Light*. Briefly put, the evidence suggests that the content of *Shades of Grey* was compatible with long-standing military-culture motifs of heroism and health, as well as contemporaneous political and professional (medical, psychoanalytic, psychiatric) interests, while the content of *Let There Be Light* was not.

Although some accused Huston of making a film that was 'anti-war', it may be more accurate to say that *Let There Be Light* was 'anti-military'. Through its appropriation of soldiers with combat fatigue, Huston's film broke with traditional military images of strength, invulnerability, competence, heroism and beauty. In 1945, depictions of physical weakness, dysfunction or deformity, much less dependency, in men – and in military men in particular – were incompatible with the self-image promoted by the US military.[42] By using visually compelling physical deficits (such as stuttering or paralysis) to represent the internal, less tangible mental distress of veterans, Huston may have compounded the problem his film presented to American military culture.

Support for this idea is found within the structure and content of *Shades of Grey*. Although *Shades of Grey* does briefly note that war stress may contribute to the development of psychological distress in *some* healthy individuals, such persons are never portrayed in a manner that might conform to cultural fantasies of illness (including mental illness). They are never shown to be dependent, debilitated, weak, cowardly or feminine.[43] The character

Joe Smith, who develops combat fatigue, is portrayed as a weak sissy who is dependent on his parents and not interested in women; real soldiers (like Bill Brown) are men who are hearty, strong, independent and heterosexual.[44]

Further, and as evidenced by what was not included in *Shades of Grey*, it seems *Let There Be Light* gave its greatest offence through its powerful and raw examination of the mental anguish incurred by military duty. These images of suffering and dependency could not be officially sanctioned by the government for they ran counter to the spirit of longstanding military codes, and challenged cultural stereotypes of masculinity.[45]

In addition to issues of culture and of masculinity, *Let There Be Light* was incompatible with the agendas of mental health professionals during the 1940s. These agendas were given their most articulate expression in the language and passage of the Neuropsychiatric Institute Act of 1946. It is within the context of this political background that the nationalistic themes and carefully selected representations of combat fatigue in *Shades of Grey* may be most fully appreciated. If the passage of the Act was the penultimate realisation of a vision held by certain members of the American Psychiatric Association, *Shades of Grey* was to become a major vehicle by which this gospel was spread to the population of the United States.

Transcripts of the US Senate hearings on the Neuropsychiatric Institute Act (NP Act) provide direct evidence about how American Psychiatric Association and the Army officially (and publicly) interpreted war-related psychological illness. The arguments presented in the transcripts reveal a great deal about the ends to which the official interpretations were used, and by whom.

The stated purpose of the NP Act was to rectify two main problems: the shortage of personnel trained for mental health work; and the shortage of knowledge about the causes of, and the treatments for, mental illness.[46] Not surprisingly, the largest sections of the NP Act are a series of testimonials, or persuasive arguments, designed to convince the members of the US Senate Subcommittee on Health and Education of these two issues. The individuals who put forward their persuasive arguments were a small but close-knit group of psychiatrists, crusading laymen and federal officials.[47] They were indefatigable, if not outright evangelical, in their approach. An initial budget of $18 million was at stake and each had a vested interest in what was at that time a remarkable sum.

Surg. Gen. Thomas Parran (United States Public Health Service), Brig. Gen. William C. Menninger (Chief, Neuropsychiatric Division, US Army), Dr George S. Stevenson (Medical Director, The National Committee for Mental Hygiene) and Dr Karl Bowman (President, American Psychiatric Association), all shared the common interest of American psychoanalytic psychiatrists: to see psychiatry accepted into the family of Scientific Medicine so as to enjoy the same prestige, respect and admiration.[48] If they were successful in persuading the Senate to approve the NP Act, funding would become available for psychiatric research and for psychiatric residency training programmes.[49] These, in turn, would lead to an increase in scientific publications, the number of practicing psychiatrists and prestige.[50]

The arguments presented by Capt. Francis J. Braceland (Chief, Neuropsychiatric Division, United States Navy), and Brig. Gen. William C. Menninger suggest that the military also stood to gain from the Act in two ways. First, the military would be absolved of responsibility or blame for the prevalence of war neuroses – since these would be laid at the doors of American society and the Veteran's Administration (VA).[51] Second, military institutions would receive funding for psychiatric research.

The needs of the VA, as evidenced by the testimony of Dr Daniel Blain (Chief, Neuropsychiatric Division, Veteran's Administration), were straightforward and dictated by the large number of veterans seeking treatment. VA officials were not interested in explaining the cause of combat fatigue in veterans, but rather, *how* the VA could provide treatment for so large a number of patients. They hoped funding via the NP Act would address this need by increasing the number of psychiatrists.[52]

Non-military, non-VA affiliated and non-physician groups such as the American Psychological Association, the American Association for Psychiatric Social Workers, and the Children's Bureau also stood to profit in that funding for the administration, education, training, treatment and research programmes would also become available to them.[53] Moreover, federally funded research and training programmes offered the professions of psychology and social work some of the prestige enjoyed by medicine.[54]

Thus, multiple agendas – prestige, professional proliferation, institutional support, avoidance of cost – motivated the interest of the participants. However, these motivations could not be overtly acknowledged without invoking the appearance of institutional opportunism. For federal funding to be (quickly) appropriated, the problem would have to be national in importance, and threatening in nature. Accordingly, the language found in the document is terse, and filled with a sense of urgency. The testimonials portray 'America-in-crisis'. There is a sense of danger, and of impending disaster – as real and as deadly to the Nation as cancer or atomic bombs.[55] Through the discourse, alarm and nationalism become tightly linked:

> The stimulation and support of this measure is urgently needed at once, not alone in providing added medical facilities but also to aid this country in the solution of the variety of social problems which confront us on an increasing scale.[56]

> The psychiatric problem pervades every aspect of our lives and collectively these disorders constitute the largest single medical problem which confronts the Nation. The inventory of the health of the Nation's manpower ... leaves no doubt that health is a national resource more vital to our economy than coal, oil or chemical reserves.[57]

> ... if the Congress adopts and sets this kind of bill in motion, there will eventuate not only a great contribution to the future of this branch of medicine, but also the development of surcease from the physical distress of thousands and thousands of our citizens, and a great contribution to the content and effectiveness of millions of persons yet unborn.[58]

Proof for the existence of this psychiatric problem, this 'crisis of mental illness', is the prevalence of combat related nervous disorders in returning Second World War veterans. This prevalence is used, not to indict war stress as a cause for illness, but instead as an indication of mental illness pervading the nation:

> The enormous pressures of the times, the catastrophic world war which ended in victory a few months ago, and the difficult period of reorientation ... have resulted in an alarming increase in the incidence of mental disease and neuropsychiatric maladjustments among our people.[59]

War seems to bring emotional and characterological defects into the foreground because of the tension under which the group is operating, and it focuses a bright light on defects which seemed heretofore in peacetime, not to seem to be so important … I think that it is perhaps time, sir, for us to realise that no matter how rapid the advances which come about in the field of physics or commerce, these will be of little value if unpredictable human behavior is allowed to jeopardise our civilisation, for no matter whether it is in war or in peace, the conduct of our affairs depends in the last analysis on how men behave and what men do, and there has been too little interest in research into the human factors and into interpersonal relationships.[60]

Mental illness does not arise *de novo* or simply out of the blue, but in a large measure it is dependent on the individual's relationship … to society in general.[61]

The challenge for the proponents of the NP Act was to get Senate committee members to embrace the idea of a psychiatric problem national in scope and that relevant funding was necessary to combat. It is likely their efforts would have failed if members of the Senate simply viewed combat fatigue as the delimited problem for the military. Evidence for this concern is seen in their rhetoric which shifts the root cause of combat fatigue from war-trauma to pre-war civilian life. Support for the conscious nature of this strategy is evidenced by the fact that *none* of the most prominent and well-known proponents of the 'Environmentalist' position [that war-trauma, and not latent character flaws, caused combat fatigue] was at the hearings – nor were any of their views represented.[62]

If the absence of such notables as Dr John Appel (Chief, Army Mental Hygiene Preventive Medicine Branch, and who worked on *Let There Be Light* and *Psychiatric Procedures in the Combat Arena*), Roy Grinker and John Speigel (authors of the famous treatise *War Neuroses*)[63] was suspect, it was fortuitous for those at the hearing. Arguments based upon the Environmentalist position would have been incompatible with the official scenario of a nation besieged by latent and ever increasing psychopathology. The National Neuropsychiatric Institute Act was passed.

Conclusions

In March 1946, the rhetoric and arguments put forward by a small group officially transformed combat fatigue from a blight of war, into a barometer of mental illness in America. This official interpretation was imprinted onto thousands of feet of celluloid and disseminated to Americans through the medium of cinema.[64] Although he most certainly did not accomplish this feat on his own, Brig. Gen. W. C. Menninger played an executive role in ensuring this official interpretation of combat fatigue was presented to the American public.[65]

The centrality of Menninger's role is reflected in his activities. During March 1946, Menninger told John Huston that although *Let There Be Light* was 'the very finest motion picture on combat fatigue [that he had] ever seen' it would not be released. Unbeknownst to Huston, during that same month, Menninger was actively promoting the production of *Shades of Grey*.[66] Menninger did his best to insure that *Shades of Grey* and not *Let There Be Light* was the official messenger of truth to the nation. The circumscribed images and messages of *Let There Be Light* were not compatible with the multiple agendas of his cohort of American medical (psychiatric), military and public health officials.

Evidence for the idea that Shades of Grey was largely a political strategy designed to advance the goals of the proponents of the NP Act is robust. However, this 'political strategy' did not occur in an ideological vacuum, nor during a period of relative quiescence. To the contrary, during the 1940s members of the psychiatric community were engaged in a vigorous, and often bitter, debate over the role that psychoanalytic ideologies would play in shaping the direction of the discipline of psychiatry. For individuals such as Menninger, psychoanalytic ideologies represented the means by which the profession of psychiatry would gain authority, prestige and recognition within the medical community and within society. Menninger, and men like him believed that psychoanalysis offered the greatest opportunities for social change and improvement.

Within the context of a war of professional ideologies within the psychiatric community, the production of Shades of Grey can be best appreciated as a 'micro-historical' illustration of at least one means by which this war of ideologies was engaged. Although there may be nothing unique in this analysis about the existence of a 'seed/soil' debate in the 1940s, micro-analysis of these films offers a unique opportunity to observe the concrete ways particular individuals attempted to promote their views. In the production of *Shades of Grey*, it is clear that certain individuals altered and fabricated patient reports and suppressed opposing viewpoints in order to promote their ideology about combat fatigue.

Notes

1 In 1945 John Huston was commissioned to direct *Let There Be Light* for the War Department. This documentary was made to influence public attitudes towards the psychiatric casualties of war. The army hoped that *Let There Be Light* might decrease both stigma and the public's reluctance to employ such veterans. Like the films in the 'Why We Fight' series, Huston's film was originally intended for theatre screenings prior to the main feature. See Stuart Kaminsky's *John Huston: Maker of Magic* (Boston: Houghton Mifflin, 1978); also see 'Section of Medicine', *Proceedings of the Royal Society of Medicine*, 36, 253 (24 Nov 1942); Introduction and Preface to *Let There Be Light* (1946), following opening credits; also see letter to Brig. Gen. William C. Menninger, Army Service Forces, Office of the Surgeon General, dated 15 April 1945: 'the film serves the purpose for which it was conceived and designed – that purpose being to dispel prejudice on the part of the public against service men with a psychoneurotic history', in The Huston papers, Special Collections, Margaret Herrick Library, Beverly Hills, CA.

2 According to Kenneth Royal, Under-Secretary of War, War Department of the United States, after its official withdrawal from release, *Let There Be Light* was classified for official use only. Letter dated 9 September 1946, in The Huston papers, Special Collections, Margaret Herrick Library, Beverly Hills, CA.

3 *Variety*, 7 January 1981, 6. *Time*, 19 January 1981, 80.

4 It is likely Huston's refusal to create a re-enactment film was influenced by the negative experiences he underwent during the filming of *Tunisian Victory* (1944). The film incorporated faked scenes of active combat (filmed in the Arizona desert) and was ridiculed by the servicemen who viewed it. (The Huston papers, Special Collections, Margaret Herrick Library, Beverly Hills, CA.)

5　The War Department may have issued a third reason for suppressing *Let There Be Light* – that (as was the case for *The Battle of San Pietro*) John Huston had 'pulled a fast one' and produced a film that was 'anti-war' in nature. I have been unable to locate official Army documentation of this assertion, only personal letters to Huston (Huston Collection, Margaret Herrick Library, Beverly Hills, CA).

6　JSC/B25, Serial 6116 from The Joint Chiefs of Staff, dated 29 June, 1945. Subject: List of Topics to be Withheld from Publication. Ed. Albert Glass, *Neuropsychiatry in World War II* (1966), Vol. 1, Zone of the Interior. Office of the Surgeon General, Washington, DC, 147.

7　Although Huston maintained he obtained written consent from patients information, a letter he wrote to Brig. Gen. William Menninger suggests that he did not: 'To my knowledge, no motion picture by the military for the military ever entailed the obtaining of signature of individuals photographed.' Excerpt from letter dated 15 April 1945, in The Huston papers, Special Collections, Margaret Herrick Library, Beverly Hills, CA.

8　Letter to Mr. Huston from Arthur L. Mayer, 14 August 1946, in The Huston papers, Special Collections, Margaret Herrick Library, Beverly Hills, CA.

9　The Neuropsychiatric Consult Division, Office of the Surgeon General did a follow up study of enlisted men discharged for combat fatigue before 1 January 1944. Questionnaires were sent to 5,937 former patients. Replies were received from 4,178 (less than 70 per cent). N. Q. Brill, M. C. Tate and W. C. Menninger, *Enlisted Men Discharged from Army Because of Psychoneuroses – A Follow-up Study*. J.A.M.A. 128, June 1945, 633–7.

10　*The New York Post* published an investigative report by Winsted Archer in which Archer provided evidence that of the 122 identifiable persons in the film only 24 were patients – only six of whom needed waivers. Archer also claimed that the refusals to re-sign waivers came from US Army doctors and nurses. *New York Post*, 21 Sept 1946. Clippings in Huston papers, Special Collection, Margaret Herrick Library, Beverly Hills, CA.

11　In the original version of *Let There Be Light*, Huston included a closing shot depicting patients who had not responded to treatment. In the scene, as the patients who have been 'cured' are driven away, the camera closes in on a few patients who remain, behind bars, in the hospital. (Interviews with Frank Payne, November 1996, CAM.)

12　The following excerpts are from letters sent to Huston by individuals who saw his film: 'I have seen hard-bitten neurologists, who have little use for emotional factors in psychiatric disorders, weep on seeing the film. The almost unanimous consensus of opinion is that the film should be shown in public. This comes from professional and non-professional groups alike.' To John Huston, from, Benjamin Simon M.D., Clinical Director, Connecticut State Hospital, 6 May 1946, in The Huston papers, Special Collections, Margaret Herrick Library, Beverly Hills, CA; 'I want to thank you most sincerely for giving me an opportunity to see last night what, in my humble opinion, is in many ways the most outstanding documentary picture ever produced.' To John Huston from W. Karri Davies of Universal International Films, Inc. Rockefellar Center, New York, 6 March 1946, in The Huston papers, Special Collections, Margaret Herrick Library, Beverly Hills, CA; 'I wanted to tell you how moved I was by your film on psychoneurosis … it is a beautiful piece of work, done with great sensitivity and understanding, and warm feelings.' To John Huston from

Reme and de___ [name undecipherable], in The Huston papers, Special Collections, Margaret Herrick Library, Beverly Hills, CA; 'I wish Chekov were alive to see and feel this picture. You have some of the same sharpness, you make people look away from the screen into life. The second time, the picture came through not at all as an Army picture, it just happened to be that, but as just a picture about people in horrible trouble, trying so hard again, being helped, not hurt by science, and making the audience freer and kinder as they watched.' To John Huston, from Ernestine Evans, 6 March 1946, in The Huston papers, Special Collections, Margaret Herrick Library, Beverly Hills, CA.

13 *Reporter*. Friday, 6 February 1948, 3. The producer of *Shades of Grey*, Frank Payne, and *Variety* magazine are both in agreement that *Shades of Grey* was released in 1947. However, the Hollywood *Reporter* indicates that the film was released in 1948. In keeping with the information provided by the film's producer and by his diary, I have used the identified release date '1947' when referring to *Shades of Grey* in this paper.

14 W. C. Porter, 'What has Psychiatry Learned During Present War?', *American Journal of Psychiatry*, 99 (1943), 850–5; W. C. Porter, 'The Military Psychiatrist at Work', *American Journal of Psychiatry*, 98 (1941), 317–23; W. C. Menninger, 'Psychiatric Problems in the Army', *American Journal of Psychiatry*, 123 (1943), 751–4; W. Overholser, 'Psychiatric Casualties of War and Their Treatment', *The New England Journal of Medicine*, 231, 11 (1943), 377–80; Willard Waller, *Veteran Comes Back* (New York: Dryden Press, 1944), 165–6.

15 Martin Pernick, *The Black Stork: Eugenics and the Death of Defective Babies in American Medicine and Motion Pictures Since 1915* (New York and Oxford: Oxford University Press, 1996); Rima D. Apple and Michael W. Apple, 'Screening Science', *Isis*, 84 (1993), 750–4; Michael Shortland, 'Screening History: Towards a history of Psychiatry and Psychoanalysis in the movies', *British Journal for the History of Science*, 20, 4 (Oct 1987), 421–52; Robert Sklar and Charles Musser (eds) *Resisting Images: Essays on Cinema and History* (Philadelphia: Temple University Press, 1990).

16 Michael A. Genovese, 'Art and Politics: The Political Film as a Pedagogical Tool', paper presented at the annual meeting of the American Political Science Association, Chicago, September 1995; Michael A. Genovese, *Politics and the Cinema: An Introduction to Political Films* (Needham Heights, MA: Ginn Press, 1987); Linda Williams, *Viewing Positions: Ways of Seeing Film* (New Brunswick, NJ: Rutgers University Press, 1994).

17 This is not only true of mental conditions, but also true of most anything that one attempts to represent, for in attempting to define an entity, one necessarily excludes some portion of the field of observation. See Michel Foucault, *The Archaeology of Knowledge and the Discourse on Language* (New York: Pantheon Books, 1972), Chapter 2, 'The Original and the Regular', 141–8, 'Knowledge and Ideology', 184–6; David Spurr, *Colonial Discourse in Journalism, Travel Writing and Imperial Administration* (Durham and London: Duke University Press, 1993).

18 In order to better understand the appropriation of combat fatigue in *Let There Be Light* and *Shades of Grey*, several levels of analysis were necessary. First, each film was examined as a text-base from which the dialogue and visual shots could be used to construct a portrait of combat fatigue. I made a deliberate attempt to draw only on material with explicit and referential meaning. I started with the film's text – its grammatical or literal sense – and attempted to supplement it with social/historical background (pre- and post production aspects of each film: director's notes, drafts of

the screenplays, censorship notes, advertisements and film reviews, production staff diaries, and so forth). For an exhaustive clarification of the relationship of this method to the construction of meanings, see David Bordwell, *Making Meaning* (Cambridge, MA, Harvard University Press, 1989).

19 'Consideration be given the fact that tremendous educational value may accrue to the benefit of the Army, the public, and ultimately the individual psychiatric patient, through the utilisation of carefully developed motion pictures and photographs of neuropsychiatric activities. This would in some instances, of necessity, include "identifiable" patients. Therefore, it is recommended that the restriction given above be modified to permit such photos, taken under Army supervision.' – JSC/B25, Serial 6116 from The Joint Chiefs of Staff, dated 29 June 1945. Subject: List of Topics to be Withheld from Publication. Quoted in *Neuropsychiatry in World War II*, Vol. 1 (1966), Zone of the Interior, Albert Glass (ed.) Office of the Surgeon General, Washington, DC, 147 'With regard to the recommendation about photographs and motion pictures, it is strongly believed that great educational value may accrue to the Army, the public, and ultimately the individual psychiatric patient through develoment of motion pictures, photographs of neuropsychiatric activities.' Memorandum of Brig. Gen Stanhope Bayne-Jones, Chairman of the Board of Declassification of Medical and Scientific Reports of the Surgeon General's Office, 3 August 1945, cited in *Neuropsychiatry in World War II*, Vol. 1 (1966), Zone of the Interior, Albert Glass (ed.) Office of the Surgeon General, Washington DC, 148; 'Col. Howard Rusk, of the Convalescent Training Section AAF, spoke in many communities to audiences of as much as 11,000 after showing them films on combat fatigue … which depicted to civilians how and why their returning men might have transient violent gripes.' Glass, 725; *National Neuropsychiatric Institute Act* (1946): hearings before a Subcommittee of the Committee on Education and Labor, United States Senate. 79th Congress, Second Session on S. 1160, 67, 78 (CIS).

20 *National Neuropsychiatric Institute Act* (1946), 67.

21 The circumstances by which *Let There Be Light* was replaced by *Shades of Grey* offer an opportunity to examine ways in which authoritative knowledge about combat fatigue was crafted during the very years that it was thought to be one of the most significant and costly conditions caused by the war. (For more information on the perceived significance and cost to the Nation of Combat Fatigue, see n. 14.)

22 'Army Will Screen Psycho Short: The Army Signal Corps made a decision to re-do Huston's film *Let There Be Light* with professional actors after soldiers who appeared in the film as genuine psycho cases refused to sign releases.' *Variety*, 20 August 1947, 1 (see n. 13).

23 The producer of *Shades of Grey* (Frank Payne) insists that none of Huston's film was used in *Shades of Grey*. However, examination of the two films suggests otherwise. Footage in some sequences is identical. According to Payne the footage is identical by design. He reports that the lighting crew, the film editor and the cinematographer from *Let There Be Light* were also involved in the filming of *Shades of Grey*. (Interview with Frank Payne [CAM], November 1996.) This author remains uncertain.

24 Filmed in the Italian Campaign, 1944–45, edited by Capt. Steven W. Ransom, M.C. Glass, *Neuropsychiatry in World War II* (n. 6). Different versions of *Shades of Grey* are known to exist. The copy of the film given to the National Archives is not identical to the copy owned by the film's producer Frank Payne. Payne's copy of *Shades of Grey*

includes sequences of footage taken from Huston's film *The Battle of San Pietro* (1943). At this time it is unclear how, when, or why this footage was removed from the copy given to the Archives. Payne asserts that the early segment of *Shades of Grey* was used as a brief educational film for officers in training at West Point, NY. Interview with Frank Payne, November, 1996 (CAM).

25 While the films are dramatically different in theory and content, the scrolled introductory segment of *Shades of Grey* is nearly an exact copy of that from *Let There Be Light*. The differences between the two scrolls are found in the lines explaining that to protect patient confidentiality, actors, instead of real patients, were used in the making of the film.

26 *Shades of Grey* (1947).

27 It also provides a potential explanation why there are no black people in the film. I was unable to locate any production materials on the subject of race depiction, however given the prominence of black veterans in Huston's film, and their complete absence in the re-enacted scenes in *Shades of Grey*, it seems feasible that depictions of race were at issue (see n. 43).

28 *Shades of Grey* (1947).

29 *Shades of Grey* (1947).

30 *Shades of Grey* (1947).

31 *Psychiatric Procedures in the Combat Arena* (1944).

32 This is stated in the opening credits of *Shades of Grey*. My use of the term 'actual' does not mean I believe the film captured the experience of soldiers at the front in a totally unbiased manner. The presence of the camera necessarily changes the experience of the doctor/patient interview through its elicitation of self-awareness. In many of the scenes the soldiers scrutinise the camera in a wary manner during their conversations with the doctors.

33 Instead they report more commonly experienced events from a war zone such as being under enemy fire, being in fox-holes for long periods of time or feeling tired, wet and sleep-deprived. *Psychiatric Procedures in the Combat Arena* (1944).

34 *Psychiatric Procedures in the Combat Arena* (1944).

35 The same ideology is in Huston's film *Let There Be Light*. John Appel directed the Army's Public Health programme and was directly involved with Frank Capra (and John Huston) in the production of films by the Office of War Information. Scott Hammen, *John Huston* (Boston: Twayne Publishers, 1985), 19–20. Also see Clayton R. Koppes and Gregory D. Black, *Hollywood Goes to War: How Politics, Profits and Propaganda Shaped World War II Movies* (Berkeley, CA: University of California Press, 1987), 122; and Nathan G. Hale Jr, *The Rise and Crisis of Psychoanalysis in America: Freud and the Americans, 1917–1985* (New York and Oxford: Oxford University Press, 1995), 190.

36 The difference in opinion of the two are seen clearly in changes made in the film-scripts. However, they are also evidenced in the following comments: 'A history of maladjustment in the family or in the individual, contributed to many of the casualties that occurred ... normal personalities' reaction to abnormal stress must have had some predisposition, and this determined their reaction to combat.' W. C. Menninger, 'World War II: Psychoanalytic Warriors', in Nathan G. Hale Jr, *The Rise and Crisis of Psychoanalysis in the United States* (1995). For similar comments, also see *Modern Concepts of War Neuroses*, The Ludwig Kast Lecture, by William C.

Menninger, reprinted from *Bulletin of the New York Academy of Medicine*, Jan. 1945, second series, vol. 22, no. 1, 7–22 (courtesy of Menninger Archives). This contrasts with statements of John Appel: 'It can be said that the mental health of the American soldier was good during WWII. It seems evident that the war had an adverse effect on mental and emotional health. It was the epidemiology studies of the hospital admission rates which showed the direct role of physical danger of the enemy shell fire in *causing* psychiatric disorders' (emphasis mine). Glass, *Neuropsychiatry in World War II* (n. 6). While historian Nathan G. Hale Jr has argued that Menninger supported both the Environmentalist and the Developmentalist positions (Hale 1995: 202), Menninger's directives and behaviour related to the production of *Shades of Grey* show he was officially in the developmentalist camp.

37 Script transformations downplaying combat trauma and emphasising early developmental issues are not the only examples of 'creative writing' in *Shades of Grey*. There are alterations designed to aesthetise the representations of soldiers themselves. For example, a soldier suffering from combat fatigue and amnesia undergoes a sodium amytal interview in order to regain his memory. In the actual patient interview, the soldier cries during the procedure. He appears to experience the amytal interview as extremely painful. In addition, he admits to having executed German POWs after they laid down their weapons and surrendered. The emotions the soldier displays during the amytal interview and his confession about executing German prisoners were unacceptable for public consumption. When this scene was re-done for *Shades of Grey* the soldier does not weep, nor does he report killing Germans. Instead, he is stoic and states that his unit captured some German soldiers who were later taken to the Allied base camp.

38 The patient also reports that he had a steady job prior to the war. This is relevant in that it is implied by the text of *Shades of Grey* that individuals with a predisposition to combat fatigue would have an uneven work history.

39 Frank Payne insists his team shot this scene using the same personnel that appeared in the sequence in Huston's film. If this is true it emphasises the degree to which the military went to make this film appear to be a copy of Huston's film. It also may provide evidence for Huston's belief that it was the physicians, and not the patients, who refused to re-sign consent forms to permit the release of his film. The physicians had stated that they were not permitted, by military policy, to appear on camera, yet somehow this permission has been obtained for *Shades of Grey*. Payne has stated clearly that he did not obtain consent forms, and never did, when filming for the Army.

40 Quoted from Francis McFadden's *Film Review* article in *Harpers Bazaar*, May 1946, 116.

41 A summary of the theory of illness and the messages about combat fatigue contained in *Shades of Grey*: All human beings have the seeds of mental illness lurking within their unconscious mind. Individuals fortunate enough to have had non-anxious or over-coddling mothers, attain, through exposure to adversity, resilience to the stresses and strains of life. While they may get a mild case of the jitters, they do not succumb to combat fatigue. Those who are not so fortunate have less immunity to the demands of life. They are vulnerable and lack the capacity to defend themselves and therefore succumb to combat fatigue and mental illness. The varying degrees of resilience or vulnerability seen among soldiers is a reflection of the innate, developmental differences of each. As one psychiatrist in the film explains to his patients, 'It's not necessary to be

in the war. These kinds of problems have always gone on, in all times, and in all places' (*Shades of Grey*, 1947). The demands of military life and of war are seen only as agents that uncover an individual's inherent deficits, and bring them to light.

42 In fact, this is one of the main storylines of the feature film *The Best Years of Our Lives* (1946) directed by William Wyler. In it a Navy veteran comes to terms with his physical disabilities (the loss of his hands). The character was played by a real veteran double amputee, whose performance won him a special Oscar. A recurrent theme in the film is the severe rift created in the self image of a soldier who finds himself weak, deformed and dependent as a result of war injuries. Huston's film also challenged racial stereotypes. In *Let There Be Light* black veterans lose stereotypical associations linking colour to disease and degeneration. Instead, they are represented positively in the film and are portrayed as being *no* different than their fellow white veterans in terms of childhood developmental difficulties or symptoms of (or susceptibility to) combat fatigue. In fact, the black veterans suffering from symptoms of combat fatigue appear less bizarre than the white veterans and by consequence appear to be less 'crazy'. Interestingly, the film's only depiction of 'a healthy and caring relationship' is that of a black veteran and his wife taking a picnic on the hospital grounds. Thus as the film breaks with racial stereotypes, it breaks with long-standing ideologies of health which associated white with health and beauty and black (or non-white) with disease and ugliness. The boldness of Huston's footage is underscored by the fact that no blacks were included in *Shades of Grey*.

43 While the men depicted in the film may be seen to contemplate giving up, they never do. Not one is a coward – in fact those who are accused of cowardice early in the film are later shown to be even more heroic than the other men. By femininity, I refer to those factors which contrast with the conceptualisations of masculinity – conceptualisations that exclude the expression of emotions or attitudes that are traditionally equated with femininity, such as: an open expression of tenderness, sadness, or crying; concern for the feelings of others and their emotional and attachment needs. These are traditionally downplayed in the military as is most explicitly expressed in boot-camp training where to express emotions (other than aggression and anger) or to display physical weakness or inability is equated with 'non-male imagery'. Derogatory terminology referring to women or homosexual men (sissies, pussies, faggots, queers, and so on) is still routinely manifest in military training. The terminology seems to be used to humiliate and motivate recruits to increase their ability to conform to, and to improve in, military duty. (Personal observations, Camp MacCall, Fort Bragg, NC.)

44 According to the film's producer Frank Payne, 'it was sometimes necessary to overdub the soundtrack because an actor would sound too much like fairy, or [like a] gay. We couldn't have that you know for an Army picture. One actor was really good, but I think that he picked up all that gay talk by hanging out with the nancy-boys [gay men].' Interviews with Frank Payne, December 1996, CAM.

45 Military censorship codes exhibited extensive influence over the portrayal of American dead or wounded – ostensibly to prevent the enemy from assessing the amount of damage inflicted on US troops. However, these censorship codes were unevenly enforced and strongly influenced by the economic status of the War Bond effort. For an exhaustive analysis of this see George H. Roeder Jr, *The Censored War: American Visual Experience During World War Two* (New Haven and London: Yale University Press, 1993). Of note, many of these censorship codes continued to be

149

authoritative knowledge and combat fatigue

enforced after the Second World War and, in some cases, were not lifted until 1980. Personal Communications from Dr Adrianne Noe of the National Museum of Heath and Medicine. John Huston's earlier film, *The Battle of San Pietro*, was also initially banned by the military. The Army feared any individual who witnessed the suffering, the death and destruction portrayed in the film would not want to take part in military duty. (Scott Hammen, *John Huston* (Boston: Twayne Publishers, 1985), chapter 3 'At War', 24). While this charge was not explicitly levelled at *Let There Be Light* it is likely that military officials worried that it held the potential to elicit similar concerns in the American public. See notes 37 and 44.

46 *National Neuropsychiatric Institute Act* (1946), Congressional Information Services (CIS), 1.

47 Surg. Gen. Thomas Parran, United States Public Health Service. Brig. Gen. William C. Menninger, Chief, Neuropsychiatric Division, United States Army. Dr George S. Stevenson, Medical Director, The National Committee for Mental Hygiene. Dr Karl Bowman, President, American Psychiatric Association. Dr Daniel Blain, Chief, Neuropsychiatric Division, Veteran's Administration. Capt. Francis J. Braceland, Chief, Neuropsychiatric Division, United States Navy. John C. Williamson, Assistant Legislative Representative, Veterans of Foreign Wars. Dr C. C. Burlingame, Psychiatrist in Chief, Institute of Living, Hartford, Conn., and Psychiatric Consultant, National Association of Manufacturers. Mrs. Lee Steiner, American Association of Psychiatric Social Workers and Author of 'Where do People Take Their Troubles?' Martha Eliot, M.D., Associate Chief, Children's Bureau. Albert Deutsch, Author of 'The Mentally Ill in America' and Columnist, PM Newspaper. Eugene Mayor, President, National Committee For Mental Hygiene, Editor and Publisher, *The Washington Post*.

48 *National Neuropsychiatric Institute Act* (1946), 70.

49 *National Neuropsychiatric Institute Act* (1946) (CIS), 1–2 (sections 2, 3a, 3b, 3c, 3d, 3f).

50 Ibid., 2 (section 3f), 5, 6.

51 Ibid., 68–9, 70.

52 Ibid., 18, 67, 72.

53 Funding for the Children's Bureau programme would lead to greater emphasis on early development and on age-appropriate experts – pediatricians, child guidance counsellors, child welfare workers. Ibid., 95, 97. Representatives of the American Equity Association, and the American Association of Psychiatric Social Workers approved of the NP Act – yet disapproved what they believed was an attempt on the part of the American Psychiatric Association to 'create psychopathology out of everyday life' and thereby expand the professional domain of psychiatry. Ibid., 97, 98, 114, 147, 167. These sections of the Act provide evidence that is in support of, and consistent with, historian Elizabeth Lunbeck (*The Psychiatric Persuasion: Knowledge, Gender and Power in Modern America*, Princeton: Princeton University Press, 1995), whose work traces, among other things, the transition of psychiatry from a profession of asylum innkeepers to profession charged with guarding the mental health of all citizens.

54 *National Neuropsychiatric Institute Act*, 144, 167.

55 Ibid., 11–13.

56 Ibid., 41.

57 Ibid., 69.

58 Ibid., 7.

59 Ibid., 5.

60 Ibid., 5.

61 Ibid., 64.

62 The Environmentalist position was well-known to psychiatric professionals and had been prominently represented in published articles after the dramatic account of the sinking of the WASP: Commander B. W. Hogan (M.C.) USN, 'Psychiatric Observations of Senior Medical Officer on Board Aircraft Carrier U.S.S. WASP During Action in Combat Areas, At Time of Torpedoing, and Survivors' Reaction'. *American Journal of Psychiatry*, 100 (1943), 90–3.

63 Roy Grinker and John Spiegel, *War Neuroses* (Philadelphia: Blakiston, 1945).

64 I do not say that it was the only one to reach the American public because there is ample evidence, from contemporaneous Hollywood films such as *The Best Years of Our Lives* (1946), that alternative interpretations of combat fatigue were available to civilians. (For more extensive analysis of representations of combat fatigue in American feature films 1940–50, see C. A. Morgan III, 'Captured on Film: The Appropriation of Combat Fatigue in American Feature and Documentary Film' (1996) unpublished thesis, section of the History of Medicine, Yale Graduate School and Yale School of Medicine, New Haven, CT. I do suggest that this version was primary in that it was used for purposes of public and professional education and claimed a greater degree of authority than did Hollywood films.

65 Letter to John Huston from Brig. Gen Menninger, dated 28 March 1946, The Huston papers, Special Collections, Margaret Herrick Library, Beverly Hills, CA.

66 In March 1946, Brig. Gen. W. C. Menninger actively suppressed *Let There Be Light* and simultaneously supported the production of *Shades of Grey*. The Huston papers, Special Collections, Margaret Herrick Library, Beverly Hills, CA; Interview with Frank Payne, producer of *Shades of Grey*, November, 1996 (CAM); Interview with Frank Payne, producer of *Shades of Grey*, December 1996 (CAM).

References

Apple, R. D. and M. W. Apple (1993) 'Screening Science', *Isis*, 84, 750–4.

Bordwell, D. (1989) *Making Meaning*. Cambridge, MA: Harvard University Press.

Brill, N. Q., M. C. Tate and W. C. Menninger (1945) *Enlisted Men Discharged from Army Because of Psychoneuroses – A Follow-up Study*. *J.A.M.A.*, 128 (June), 633–7.

Foucault, M. (1972) *The Archaeology of Knowledge and the Discourse on Language*. New York: Pantheon Books.

Genovese, M. A. (1987) *Politics and the Cinema: An Introduction to Political Films*. Needham Heights, MA: Ginn Press.

_____ (1995) 'Art and Politics: The Political Film as a Pedagogical Tool', paper presented at the annual meeting of the American Political Science Association, Chicago, September 1995.

Glass, A. (ed.) *Neuropsychiatry in World War II* (1966), Vol. 1, Zone of the Interior. Office of the Surgeon General, Washington, DC.

Grinker, R. and J. Spiegel (1945) *War Neuroses*. Philadelphia: Blakiston.

Hale, Nathan G., Jr (1995) *The Rise and Crisis of Psychoanalysis in America: Freud and the Americans, 1917–1985*. New York and Oxford: Oxford University Press.

Hammen, S. (1985) *John Huston*. Boston: Twayne Publishers.

Hogan, B. W. (1943) 'Psychiatric Observations of Senior Medical Officer on Board Aircraft Carrier U.S.S. WASP During Action in Combat Areas, At Time of Torpedoing, and Survivors' Reaction', *American Journal of Psychiatry*, 100, 90–3.

Huston, J. Huston papers, Special Collections, Margaret Herrick Library, Beverley Hills, CA.

Kaminsky, S. (1978) *John Huston: Maker of Magic*. Boston: Houghton Mifflin.

Koppes, C. R. and G. D. Black (1987) *Hollywood Goes to War: How Politics, Profits and Propaganda Shaped World War II Movies*. Berkeley, CA: University of California Press.

Lunbeck, E. (1995) *The Psychiatric Persuasion: Knowledge, Gender and Power in Modern America*. Princeton: Princeton University Press.

Menninger, W. C. (1943) 'Psychiatric Problems in the Army', *American Journal of Psychiatry*, 123, 751–4.

_____ (1995) 'World War II: Psychoanalytic Warriors', in N. G. Hale Jr, *The Rise and Crisis of Psychoanalysis in the United States*. New York: Oxford University Press, 187–210.

Overholser, W. (1943) 'Psychiatric Casualties of War and Their Treatment', *The New England Journal of Medicine*, 231, 11, 377–80.

Pernick, M. (1996), *The Black Stork: Eugenics and the Death of Defective Babies in American Medicine and Motion Pictures Since 1915*. New York and Oxford: Oxford University Press.

Porter, W. C. (1941) 'The Military Psychiatrist at Work', *American Journal of Psychiatry*, 98, 317–23.

_____ (1943) 'What has Psychiatry Learned During Present War?', *American Journal of Psychiatry*, 99, 850–5.

Roeder, G. H., Jr (1993) *The Censored War: American Visual Experience during World War Two*. New Haven and London: Yale University Press.

Shortland, M. (1987) 'Screening History: Towards a history of Psychiatry and Psychoanalysis in the movies', *British Journal for the History of Science*, 20, 4, 421–52.

Sklar, R. and C. Musser (eds) *Resisting Images: Essays on Cinema and History*. Philadelphia: Temple University Press.

Spurr, D. (1993) *Colonial Discourse in Journalism, Travel Writing and Imperial Administration*. Durham and London: Duke University Press.

Waller, W. (1944) *Veteran Comes Back*. New York: Dryden Press.

Williams, L. (1994) *Viewing Positions: Ways of Seeing Film*. New Brunswick, NJ: Rutgers University Press.

12

Jackie Stacey

Imitation of life: the politics of the new genetics in cinema

> If all development is merely an unfolding of pre-existing instructions encoded in the nucleotide sequences of DNA – if our genes make us what we are – it makes perfect sense to set the identification of these sequences as the primary, and indeed ultimate, goal of biology. (Keller 1995: 21)

One of the most significant changes in biomedicine today is the turn to genetics – the science of cell programming. In the continuing search for a 'cure' for cancer and numerous other diseases, genetics seems to promise the solution for which we have all hoped. Scientists now offer preventative diagnosis to future generations, producing the promise of avoiding the diseases of our parents and grandparents. According to recent cultural analysts, conceptions of normal, pathological, desirable and undesirable bodies have been profoundly transformed by the new genetics.[1] We live in the age of the Human Genome Project (HGP), a $3 billion enterprise mapping the genetic make-up of homo sapiens, an age in which DNA is increasingly used as an explanation for human disease and as a means of detecting deviant and criminal behaviour.

José Van Dijck has explored the meaning of the HGP for changing perceptions of disease:

> Assuming that a disposition towards a large number of diseases is stored in the genes, the HGP proposes systematically to apply the tools of molecular biology to the entire complement of DNA in a human cell, on the premise that once we know the complete genetic make-up of the human body, we can diagnose and predict congenital aberrations. (Van Dijck 1998: 119)

The HGP, then, is much more than a concerted effort to inventory the human genome; it entails 'the development, distribution and implementation of a way of thinking about human life' (ibid.). There has been a clear shift in the public perception of genetics since the 1950s, she suggests, 'from an obscure scientific paradigm (genetic engineering) into a preferred solution to a pressing medical problem (genetic therapy)'; thus the cause of 'ever more diseases is purportedly fixed in the genes' (Van Dijck 1998: 7). The place of genetics within biomedicine has become increasingly tightly inscribed, she concludes: 'The HPG stands out as a scientific enterprise with a primarily *medical* goal … the "geneticisation" of society seems to be the flip side of the "medicalisation" of genetics' (Van Dijck 1998: 119–20).

This 'genetic turn' has pointed to the ways in which popular understandings of the new genetics pervade ideas about the human, the body and disease in fiction, film and advertising as well as in more general public debate. Dorothy Nelkin and M. Susan Lindee have argued that the gene has become a cultural icon whose determining power is acclaimed across popular forms: 'In supermarket tabloids and soap operas, in television sitcoms and talk shows, in women's magazines and parenting advice books, genes appear to explain obesity, criminality, shyness, directional ability, intelligence, political leanings and preferred styles of dressing' (Nelkin & Lindee 1995: 2). What is significant for Nelkin and Lindee is the way in which this entity that seems to be a purely biological structure, 'a sequence of deoxyribonucleic acid (DNA) that, by specifying the composition of a protein, carries information that helps form living cells and tissues' has so rapidly and pervasively also become a powerful symbol with an 'almost magical force' (Nelkin & Lindee 1995: 2).

Histories of science fiction have demonstrated how anxieties about the ethics of new developments in science, medicine and now genetics, have been repeatedly rehearsed through familiar visual and narrative conventions.[2] Although audiences obviously recognise the fictional status of film, the cinema is a frequently cited source of public understanding of science; and although there is widespread belief in the potential to clone humans in the twenty-first century, the current claims that a cloned embryo has now been implanted in a human female operate on a cultural register somewhere between science and science fiction.

Gattaca (Andrew Nichol, 1997) questions the desirability of genetic perfection. In its dystopian world, 'valids' (those selected from genetically superior embryos) occupy high-status positions, valued for their exceptional intellectual and physical attributes, while those not pre-selected, the 'in-valids' (a term with obvious connotations of physical inferiority) constitute a low-status labour force of workers doing menial tasks. The inequalities that result from genetic selections are presented most sharply in the space agency, Gattaca, which nightmarishly presents a new form of segregated workforce whose fate is separated from race, class and gender: even white middle-class men like the protagonist, Vincent (Ethan Hawke), can be destined for repetitive, menial labour through their genetic inferiority.[3] Vincent is seen as a 'degenerate', using a 'borrowed ladder' (the impersonation of a valid) to overcome the social exclusions resulting from his genetic predisposition. *Gattaca* casts a critical gaze upon the smooth surface of bodily perfection achieved in a world of genetic selection to fictionalise the dangers of scientific intervention at the genetic level. It cautions against the political and ethical wisdom of ruling out disease and vulnerability through genetic screening and engineering.

Contemporary cinematic explorations of the threat of the new genetics are always operating within a culture which continues to glance nervously backwards to the historical precedents in which genetics and eugenics were synonymous. Fears about the uncomfortable intersection of genetics with politically dubious versions of eugenics associated with right-wing or fascist social programmes are never far away: in *Gattaca* the fantasy of a genetically perfect 'super race' echoes familiar eugenic state policies from past eras. Unlike a number of films about genetics which connect the horrors of genetic engineering directly to the legacy of Nazism (such as *Boys from Brazil*, Franklin Schaffner, 1978), *Gattaca* poses a challenge to what was referred to as the 'positive version of eugenics' in late nineteenth- and early twentieth-century debates. This is a world in which the eugenicists' vision of merging 'a body of scientific knowledge *and* a policy programme' has taken place (Burdett, in Bland & Doan 1998: 166). In the 1920s and 1930s numerous intellectuals were involved in the Eugenics Society in Britain, aiming to capitalise on the 'link between Social Reform of the past ... and the Social Hygiene of the future, which is authorised to deal adequately with the conditions of life because it has its hands on the sources of life' (Havelock Ellis 1912, reprinted in Bland & Doan 1998: 178). Here, the idea of eugenics as a social practice could mean 'positive eugenics', 'promoting the fertility of superior, healthy and useful stocks', alongside 'negative eugenics', 'restricting through voluntary measures the multiplication of those who suffer from hereditary infirmities' (*The Eugenics Review*, 1935, reprinted in Bland & Doan 1998: 185). The category of 'degenerate' was a contested one but included a range of people from 'criminals, lunatics and imbeciles' to 'alcoholics and opium eaters' (August Forel 1906, in Bland & Doan 1998: 168). These 'visionary' utopias of a genetically controllable social reform programme became discredited following the alignment of genetic experimentation with fascist politics in Nazi Germany.

Gattaca shows a society built upon the principle of 'positive eugenics'; the success of the system depends upon scientific intervention to ensure the birth of the maximum number of babies with the most perfect genetic combination available chosen from a number of screened embryos. The social structure engineered to continue this eugenic vision using visual screening techniques restricts the access of degenerates to significant positions within society and promotes the swift rise of the chosen ones. Paradoxically, the system depends upon the continuing reproduction of in-valids to do the low-status, menial work of servicing their superiors. Just as the system in *Metropolis* (Fritz Lang, 1926) depends upon the obedience of the worker-drones, so the smooth running of society in *Gattaca* depends upon the drone labour of the in-valids in their blue overalls cleaning up after their smartly dressed white-collar superiors have left the space station. Thus, although the film creates a world which holds back from the threshold of more directly fascist associations, it nevertheless poses the ethical and political problems of a geneticised culture through an exploration of issues surrounding a 'positive eugenics'.

In his broad-ranging, important consideration of the film, David Kirkby claims that, as a story of a successful conspiracy against institutionalised eugenicist discrimination, '*Gattaca* is a bioethical text that brings the issues associated with gene therapy to the public before the new eugenics becomes a reality ... *Gattaca*'s approach is not only unique among bioethics texts; it is *virtually alone among recent popular-culture narratives in its rejection of the genetic-determinist ideology*' (Kirkby 2000: 211–12, my emphasis). Kirkby's in-depth analysis of the film emphatically celebrates its progressive genetic politics. Whilst this reading is full of insight into the complex relationship between science, science fiction and bioethics, there is nevertheless something much more ambiguous at stake in this film. Drawing on feminist work about the gendering of desire both in science and in the cinema,

I shall interrogate the tensions between the film's critique of a genetically determinist dystopia and its highly conventional forms of masculine fantasy which might inadvertently reinforce many of the values of such genetic perfectionism.

'My resumé was in my cells'

Gattaca exposes the dangers of genetic engineering through its exploration of the possibilities of genetic disguise; cultural cloning is used to highlight the absurdities of genetic determinism. The protagonist, Vincent, successfully impersonates the more genetically desirable Jerome (Jude Law), who, since an accident, is wheelchair-bound and can no longer be the top athlete he once was. Jerome's genetic perfection is sold as a commodified identity to Vincent, who develops elaborate rituals of shedding his own genetic traces (skin, hair, nails) and adopting Jerome's (blood, hair, urine) on a daily basis. Using his acquired expertise in sartorial disguise, physical alteration and prosthetic DNA, combined with the labour and ingenuity of Jerome, Vincent constitutes himself as an imposter clone of genetic perfection. Disguise is mobilised to challenge genetic determinism, placing the threat of discovery at the heart of the narrative structure. Every time he enters the space station, Vincent's genetic identity is screened, so Vincent has to become master of the image and master of deception. His disguise as Jerome presents a cinematic vision of cloning, in which the technologies of imitation are set in battle against the technologies of genetic engineering and genetic screening.

The attempt to defy the predictions of a genetically determinist dystopian society is presented through a story of sibling rivalry. Motivated by filial competition with Anton, his younger, supposedly genetically superior, brother, who supersedes him in his father's favour, Vincent uses his ingenious disguise to fulfil his ambitions to become a space engineer and eventually an astronaut at the space station, Gattaca. Anton's role as the detective who uses genetic screening to fight crime contributes to the narrative tension, particularly when a murder at Gattaca requires him to screen all its employees, including his brother, Vincent. This story of sibling rivalry and paternal rejection, as Susan George (2001) has argued, is predicated upon a maternal exclusion. *Gattaca*, she points out, stages a battle over paternal inheritance where the mother is the scarcely visible symbol of humanity and hope, lacking authority when faced with the father, the scientists and the state. Although Vincent's mother's prediction about her genetically defective newborn son is prescient ('you'll do something', she assures him), her place remains marginal. Ultimately, the film tests competing powers of patriarchal authority (the family, science, business, the law). Femininity in general may threaten to disturb the outcome of these power struggles but, ultimately, remains incidental by comparison with the compelling force of intra-masculine dynamics.

Gattaca's challenge to the predictive power of genetic determinism is articulated through a competition between different modes of masculinity.[4] In the filial battle to test whether he can outdo his younger brother Anton, Vincent repeatedly attempts to exert his individual willpower over biological predisposition. In an early scene, Vincent is shown in sepia flashback as a boy lacking the toughness and drive of his genetically-selected brother: Vincent is fragile, wears glasses and, although two years older, is shorter than Anton. We hear that he has a 99 per cent chance of heart disorder and a predicted life expectancy of 30.2 years. Periodically throughout their childhood, the brothers test their relative strength in a ritual swimming contest, a traditional test of masculine willpower which they call 'the chicken run'.[5] Although Anton has always beaten Vincent, who had had to turn round and swim back first, we see one occasion on which Vincent is not only triumphant, but has to rescue Anton. As if the shock of success requires this achievement to be revisited for Vincent to embody fully its potentialising power, the chicken run is repeated once more later in the film, after Vincent has outwitted his brother in a professional deception. Like the classic traumatic event which is repeatedly revisited by the patient in an attempt to come to terms with the shock of its severity, the match is returned to as the symbolic ritual of re-establishing Vincent's masculine superiority.[6] Vincent's masculinity is anchored in an increasing sense of his superior physical and intellectual capacity, evinced by his sheer determination and willpower.

In testing the authenticity of the genetically valid and in-valid categories of masculinity, the threat of the feminine is invoked through a conventional iconography of Man versus Nature.[7] In both scenes, the two male bodies, extended in competition, are shown in long shot from aerial and underwater positions, emphasising the scale of their task, the distance they have to swim back, and the force of the sea against their attempt to master it. Unlike the rest of the film, in which the crisp blue, white and grey metallic combinations produce a visual style which marks out clear boundaries, shiny surfaces and demarcated split levels to convey a sense of 'man's' technological control over his environment, these scenes show greenish-brown, murky sea water full of tangled weed. The underwater shots in particular convey a claustrophobic sense of entrapment. The contrast to the antiseptic interiors of *Gattaca* could not be more pronounced. Like a cliché of 'man overcoming nature in order to control it', the battle with the elements in the swimming match ritual places masculinity in opposition to a sense of natural chaos. In overcoming the threat of the masculine competitor (by exposing him as an impostor in his claim to superior 'valid' status), Vincent also conquers the threat of nature as the feminine when he surfaces, triumphant, from its potentially engulfing power.

The association of the sea with femininity is extended to include heterosexuality later in the film when Vincent becomes lovers with his colleague, Irene (Uma Thurman). Moving away from the safe, predictable space of Jerome's apartment, he goes home to Irene's place, which has a spectacular location, overlooking the sea. In contrast to Jerome's private, enclosed living space, Irene's apartment is exposed, open to the elements of light, sea breeze and the sounds of the beach. As Vincent and Irene make love on the bed, the crashing waves are shown through clichéd edits cutting between sexual passion and elemental intensity. In the morning, Vincent, robbed of his usual routines and technologies, is shown standing naked on the beach, scrubbing himself with the rough pebbles to remove all traces of his own DNA. Vincent's desire for Irene has returned him to the potential chaos of nature and threatened his control over his future, for which the precision of his technology is necessary for his successful impersonation of Jerome. Throughout the film, his desire for Irene repeatedly compromises both the mutual trust in his relationship with Jerome, and his own control over the highly technologised genetic disguise.

In *Gattaca*, techno-scientific and biomedical prediction offer a fantasy of controlling the meaning of 'life itself'.[8] The repression required for perfection to surface is turned into a science. The maternal body, and nature more generally, are displaced by the genetic selection of embryos before they are implanted into the woman's body, rendering the mother marginal to reproduction (George 2001). The conflict between the two brothers is emphasised in the contrasting scenes of their origin stories, as narrated in flashback from Vincent's point of view. Whilst Vincent's own conception is played to comic effect in its brevity, inelegance and nostalgia for spontaneous sexual misbehaviour (a rocking 1950s Buick shows evidence of a couple having sex on the back seat of the car, under the sign of the swinging crucifix), Anton's selection scene is a clinical meeting of formally-dressed parents and scientists in a laboratory choosing the best embryo against the background of a DNA-shaped staircase. Vincent's very physical birth scene, with the sweat, pain and cries of his mother in labour, also contrasts with the genetic selection of Anton in which four embryos appear together on a computer screen in a scene of calm deliberation and rational choice. Vincent's parents must agree to the suggested selection of the chosen one: the singular promise of embodied perfection. The geneticist (like the manager at the company who will later reject Vincent as an in-valid before the job interview begins) is black, suggesting the separation of eugenics from its racist past and cautioning against the new hierarchies beyond race which genetic engineering might produce. He reads out the list of desired traits that Vincent's parents have requested be pre-selected: 'you have specified hazel eyes, dark hair and…' he smiles wryly, hesitating for a moment before completing the list, 'fair skin'. To their own choices of physical characteristics, the geneticist has added a list of scientifically-eliminated 'potentially prejudicial pre-dispositions': 'tendency to baldness, myopia, alcoholism and addictive susceptibility, a propensity for violence, obesity, etcetera'. The display of the four embryos on the screen alongside the recitation of the genetic information transforms reproduction from a risky human adventure into a fantasy of an exact, predictable science. When Vincent's parents protest at this level of genetic scrutiny, the geneticist tells them, 'this child is still you, simply the best of you; you could conceive naturally a thousand times and never get such results'. At Vincent's birth scene, the father retracts his desire to name his first son after himself (Anton), but at his younger son's conception, the name is finally bestowed as a marker of paternal approval in the expectation of an appropriate masculine genealogical descent. There is no scene of Anton's birth, emphasising the clinical, clean nature of this scientific creation. With this shift from nature (and religion) to science and medicine, reproduction becomes a form of authorship, as the biomedical subject becomes the originator of meaning, and paternity takes on the art of science.[9]

Genes as the active agents of life

The brothers come to represent two conflicting models of the relationship between biological and cultural design. Each stands for a different philosophy: genetic determinism versus social interactionism. Given Vincent's ultimate success in his quest to defy the laws of genetic pre-selection, we might conclude that he personifies the triumph of culture over biology. But the film is more ambiguous. To illustrate this, I want to make a sideways move into the history of genetics itself and examine *Gattaca* in relation to the metaphors through which genetic theory has produced accounts of the gene. The competing, and sometimes paradoxical, 'values' of *Gattaca* might be read through an encounter between two versions of genetics: the discourse of gene action and the discourse of gene activation, as defined by Evelyn Fox Keller (1995). Keller offers an account of the guiding metaphors of the discourses of genetics in the twentieth century in which the discourse of 'gene action' – the utter confidence in the power, autonomy and agency of genes – is gradually, though unevenly, overtaken by the more adequate discourse of 'gene activation' – a more interactive model of the gene in the context of the whole organism. Although there was an eventual modification of gene action by gene activation theory, emphasising the whole organism as an activating environment, developments in genetics continued to be influenced by the discourse of gene action throughout the twentieth century.

For Keller, the metaphors through which the gene is brought to life in these discourses signify a wider set of ideological and epistemological concerns. Within gene action theory, the gene, as the 'primary agent of life', is attributed the power of a self-sufficient system (Keller 1995: 3). This discourse 'postulates discrete, self-perpetuating, stable bodies – the genes – resident in the chromosomes, as hereditary materials. *This means, of course, that the genes are the primary internal agents controlling development*' (R. A. Brink, 1927, quoted in Keller 1995: 7; original emphasis). The attribution of agency is rooted in a version of the gene as a self-regulating system with its own effects: for example, H. J. Muller writes of the gene's most remarkable property, 'specific autocatalysis' (self-replication) and its ability 'to mutate without losing its specific autocatalytic power' (Muller 1926, quoted in Keller 1995: 8). The gene is conceptualised as a closed system able to replicate itself miraculously with no outside assistance: '[Genes] must contain not only the plan for executing the development of the organism but also must "somehow contain the means of putting [this plan] into operation"' (Schroedinger 1944, quoted in Keller 1995: xvi):

> The approach of genetics … is to ask about blueprints, not machines; about decisions, not mechanics; about information and history. In the factory analogy, genetics leaves the greasy machines and goes to the executive suite, where it analyses the planners, the decision makers, the computers, the historic records … Biologists needed to find the cell's brain. (Baltimore 1984, quoted in Keller 1995: 26–7)

For Keller, the dogmatic focus of gene action theory (over other biological explanations of development such as embryology) was problematic, because it leaves no room for environmental influences (Keller 1995: xv). The twentieth-century triumph of genetic theories of inheritance over biological investigation of embryo development – in which the whole organism plays a role – has a more or less explicitly gendered agenda: 'What is specifically eclipsed in the discourse of gene action is the cytoplasmic body, marked simultaneously by gender, by international conflict and by disciplinary politics' (ibid.). Like the masculine subject, imagining himself to be autonomous and unaffected by his surroundings (in contrast to his more relational, interactive feminine counterpart), this model is one of singularity and agency. Such a theory, she argues,

> had established a spatial map that lent the cytoplasm scientific invisibility (at least to geneticists – 'indifferent' was how Morgan described the cytoplasm) and a temporal map that defined the moment of fertilisation as origin, with no meaningful time before fertilisation. This schema offered neither time nor place in which to conceive of the egg's cytoplasm as exerting *its* effects. (Keller 1995: 24)

This highly-gendered mapping of activity onto the gene and passivity onto the cytoplasm relates closely to broader assumptions about the maternal and paternal contribution to reproduction and inheritance. Such attributions need to be understood within a context in which the metaphors used in biological discourse to describe sexual reproduction had long carried a host of ideological underpinnings.[10] Of particular influence here was the way in which sexual reproduction and fertilisation were metaphors for how the cell was seen. Since the female gamete, the egg, was larger and contained more cytoplasm than

159

the male gamete, the sperm, which was almost pure nucleus, a gendering of the internal components of the cell itself followed: the nucleus was considered male and the cytoplasm female. In summary, 'it is thus hardly surprising to find that in the conventional discourse … *cytoplasm* is routinely taken to be synonymous with *egg* … [and] the nucleus was often taken as a stand-in for the sperm' (Keller 1995: 39). According to the stereotypical ascriptions of activity to masculinity and passivity to femininity, the relative contributions attributed to the nucleus and the cytoplasm in inheritance 'invariably reflect older debates about the relative importance (or activity) of maternal and paternal contributions to reproduction, where the overwhelming tendency has been to attribute activity and motive force to the male contribution while relegating the female contribution to the role of the passive, facilitating environment' (Keller 1995: 39–40).

Political readings

If we take from Keller's beautifully articulated historical account a sense of tension between the gene as autopoetic, self-generating and governing system on the one hand, and the gene as dialectically and relationally embedded mode of contextualised communication on the other, we might consider *Gattaca*'s relationship to the politics of genetics in a number of ways. It is perfectly possible to read the film as an enactment (if a critical one) of certain elements of genetic discourse. The most obvious reading might be to map the filial competition onto the discursive conflict in the history of genetics itself. The two brothers could be read as embodiments of those conflicting principles: Anton as the personification of gene action theory, policing the rigid hierarchies of genetic determinism, and Vincent as the figure of challenge to such rigidity, proving that the environment can influence the gene's internal codes and that genetic prescriptions can be overcome through ingenuity.

Similarly, the *mise-en-scène*, which emphasises symmetry and balance, could be seen as the visual aesthetics of gene action theory, whilst other aspects of the film, which seem to defy the laws of such predictable ordering, might push against such values. For if the presentation of the space station is governed by an architectural and organisational logic of 'gene action', in which genes have predictable effects and are immune to the influences outside their self-governing systems, this is not the case in the rest of *Gattaca*. This sense of perfection and harmony is staged only to be successfully challenged by Vincent and Jerome's brilliantly engineered deception. The invention of the new Jerome, combining Vincent's ambition with the old Jerome's perfect DNA, proves the Director's confident 'gene action worldview' to be fatally flawed. Indeed, the discovery that the Director, whose genetic profile indicated that he did not have 'a violent bone in his body', is in fact a murderer undermines the very fantasy of predictability and governability of the space station itself.

Whilst it is tempting to read the film's challenge to genetic determinism as parallel to the success of gene activation theory in finally breaking down the rigidities of the discourse of gene action, a counter reading also has a powerful pull. For Vincent's challenge to the system in *Gattaca* inscribes him unquestionably within the very discourse of gene action theory he might in some ways seem to counter. To read the brothers in relation to these competing versions of genetic discourse is to overlook the crucial ways in which the construction of Vincent as the source of narrative agency places him within a cinematic discourse drawing upon the same metaphors that Keller identifies in the discourse of 'gene action theory'. Like the gene in this account, Vincent can be seen to be the agent in control of the narrative, to be the origin of causal effects and even to mutate (into Jerome) without losing his specific, self-replicating power; like the gene in this theory, Vincent is attributed some miraculous properties that enable him always to find the means to execute his plans.

Following this analogy, there may seem to be a perfect match between the fantasy of masculine autonomy in the highly influential gene action theory and the form of narrative agency in *Gattaca*. Vincent's apparent invincibility constructs a fantasy of masculine autonomy that is widely recognisable; paradoxically, we thus see traces of its influence in the genetic science of which the film is otherwise so critical. This reading throws a rather different light on such critical celebrations as Kirkby's, which sees the film as a unique counter-argument to the general acceptance of genetic determinism in popular culture. Might we not instead conclude that, through insisting on this traditional narrativisation of masculinity, *Gattaca* reinstates at a structural level precisely the ideology it seeks to undermine at the more explicitly thematic one?

And yet, although the narrative is structured around Vincent's desire to achieve heroic status, Vincent never fully inhabits 'valid' masculinity, he never fully becomes the author of his new identity as Jerome.[11] Even as he stands on the threshold of success in the final scene of the film, the power of his agency is questioned: the doctor carries out an unexpected urine test before boarding, for which Vincent has not brought the usual substitute sample of Jerome's urine, and he is thus forced to produce his own sample in front of the doctor. But it is not the subsequent urine test which reveals Vincent as an imposter, but rather his betrayed left-handedness – not science but culture. The doctor, it transpires, has seen the truth of his identity from the beginning. Forcing Vincent to listen to the story of his in-valid son who would like to work at Gattaca, the doctor casually replaces Vincent's ID card with Jerome's on his monitoring screen. In the end, the threat to expose Vincent's elaborate impersonation comes from a father with the power to prohibit, who decides not to, because he wants a sign of hope for his own in-valid son in the future. He is the good father who, unlike Vincent's own who rejected him for his genetic inferiority, recognises human potential in vulnerability and wishes to protect the imperfection that *is* human nature. Against the eugenicist values of Gattaca, hope lies in the figure of the doctor whose humanity comes from a compassion borne of proximity to genetic invalidity. Vincent walks alone down the tunnel to the rocket, taking his place (reborn) amongst the valids travelling together into the future.

In the same way that the narrative structure and agency are ambiguous, so are the modes of cinematic spectatorship operating in *Gattaca*. To some extent, they conform to the traditional structures of identification with the masculine hero: the use of flashback to establish the protagonist's point of view, guided through his voiceover; the use of close-up shots of the substituted hairs and skin fragments at his work terminal at Gattaca to offer an intimate knowledge of his secret activities and deceptions; the use of point-of-view shots to align our vision with his. Thus, the spectator is often positioned in direct contrast to the subjects of scientific, legal and corporate authority in the film; in a pleasurable reversal of power, the spectator position seems to fulfil the panoptic fantasy of the thwarted authorities. These modes of spectatorship produce the pleasure of both reassurance and critique: the close-up shots of Vincent's body offer a sense of knowing the truth about his disguise (in contrast to the police and the corporate officials who do not see what is right in front of them). They show the eugenicist authorities being duped by their own screening technologies. Turning their domestic apartment into a stylish cloning laboratory, Vincent and Jerome succeed in an elaborate deception which plays the blind spots of the scientific gaze back to the corporate authorities at Gattaca, dodging the scrutiny of that gaze by hiding in the shadows of its own occlusions. The spectator is invited to hide with them.

But the film's own awareness of this as a convention of masculinity confounds its straightforward alignment with spectatorial pleasure, for the twist to the status of the image in the age of the new genetics problematises the apparently omnipotent male gaze. The authorities are so sure of the infallibility of their techniques of surveillance that no one actually *looks* at photographs any more. The broker says to Vincent, who is sceptical about his physical resemblance to Jerome: 'When was the last time anybody looked at a photograph? You could have my photograph on your name tag, for Christ's sake.' Whilst intended for social regulation, the ubiquity of imaging and other surveillance technologies opens up new possibilities for disguise in the culture of the copy (Schwartz 1996). Indeed, this paradox is thrown back on the cinema audience, who perhaps do not notice that the large photograph, supposedly of Jerome (against which Vincent matches himself, having completed his disguise) actually looks more like a morphed image of them both. As Vincent becomes Jerome's clone, their photographs are merged to produce a composite image of their two faces.

The 'composite' photograph indicates another problem with the reading of Vincent's masculinity as self-sufficient and effective: for it is not one *but two* men whose labour produces the composite masculinity of the new Jerome. If I might push the reading of the film through the analogy with the metaphors identified by Keller one stage further, the conspiracy to defy the laws of genetic determinism in the film is a collaboration much better captured by the metaphors of the discourse of 'gene activation theory' which 'shifts the locus of control from the genes themselves [to] the more complex biochemical dynamics … of cells in constant communication with each other' (Keller 1995: 28). An analysis of the construction of masculinity in the film needs to move beyond a focus on Vincent as autonomous narrative agent to examine the dynamics of the collaboration between Vincent and Jerome in which they are mutually dependent. Vincent adopts Jerome's image; Jerome continues to produce his own bodily fragments and samples for use by Vincent. Any reading of the politics of the apparently traditional masculine drive at the film's heart must take account of the intimate bond between the two male characters which arguably 'queers' any straightforward reproduction of gendered and sexual codes.[12]

To return to Kirkby's celebration of *Gattaca*'s bioethical progressivism with which this analysis began, although this reading seemed convincing to me at first, just at the moment when a conclusive argument about the film's politics drew temptingly near, yet another counter-reading seemed to present itself. Particularly when questions of its constructions of gender come into the frame, tensions develop between the supposedly progressive bio-ethical stance of the film's obvious critique of genetic determinism and the ways in which the masculinity (through which such a challenge is cinematically driven) implicitly reinforce almost the opposite values. This is not to say that the film is 'progressive' about genetics, but 'conservative' about gender (and as I hope to have shown, these adjectives may disguise as much as they reveal), because what Keller's intervention enables us to see is the ways in which the scientific metaphors through which genetics has historically developed are themselves already gendered. In demonstrating so eloquently how metaphor operates within the production of genetic knowledge, Keller confirms that science and medicine are shot through with culture. Borrowing Keller's mapping of the competing metaphors through which the gene is narrativised and attributed agency in scientific discourse, enables us to approach the cinematic configuration of genetics through a lens which highlights the symbolism of the gene. If read as a symbolic fantasy, the attribution of progressivism to genetics in *Gattaca* seems more problematic.

My analysis of *Gattaca* is indicative of the more general question of how to read the politics of the new genetics at the cinematic level: how can we read its ideological position on genetics in its narrative structure and closure, in its *mise-en-scène*, in its masculine desires and in its modes of spectatorship? And what tensions and contradictions might be found in reading the cultural and political values of these different textual elements? Furthermore, it is not simply a question of interpreting the meaning of the complex convergence of these filmic components; there is also the challenge of specifying exactly what kind of political critique the film makes of these new genetic technologies: is *Gattaca* critical of the eugenic underpinnings of genetics, of their justification of social inequalities, of the technologies and knowledges themselves, or only of their biomedical implementation? Is this a dystopian science fiction film warning its audience of what might happen if the technologies got into the wrong hands or were combined with the wrong social philosophies, or is it a rejection of our technologised future more generally? This reading has demonstrated the complexity of answering these questions in relation to the new genetics. This is not to point towards the impossibility or futility of interpretation, of securing what we might call a 'textual ethics', but rather to caution against the attribution of political values to a film about genetic determinism without pushing at the textual contradictions which might produce a more ambiguous conclusion.

Notes

1   For important analyses of popular cultural constructions of the gene: see Nelkin & Lindee 1995; Turney 1998; van Dijck 1998; Franklin 2000.

2   For a detailed historical survey of the genre of science fiction film: see in particular Sobchack 1987; Tudor 1989; King & Krzywinska 2000; Telotte 2001; Newman 2002; Wood 2002; Redmond 2004.

3   As Kaja Silverman (1991) has argued in relation to *Blade Runner* (Ridley Scott, 1982), slavery separated from race provides a fertile fantasy for the threat of replication in science fiction film.

4   There is now a vast literature building on the construction of masculinity in visual representation. For example see Cohan & Harks 1993; Kirkham & Thumim 1993; Tasker 1993; Lehman 2001; Holmlund 2002.

5   This ritual test of masculinity moves the brothers' relationship into the realm of the mythical, referencing other fraternal battles, such as the Biblical 'Cane and Abel' story, or the swimming contest between Cassius and Caesar in which, having challenged Cassius, Caesar then has to be rescued by him; see Shakespeare's *Julius Caesar* (Act I, Scene 2).

6   For a discussion of the structure of the trauma narrative, see Caruth 1995.

7   Drawing on feminist critiques of new reproductive technologies, Susan George (2001) has argued that the mother is repressed in *Gattaca* in ways typical of patriarchal fantasies of technologised motherhood.

8   For a discussion of 'life itself' in the context of the new genetics, see Sarah Franklin (2000: 188–227).

9   Rosi Braidotti offers a critique of how fantasies of reproductive technologies in science

fiction film have produced the reinvention of a paternity which allows the exclusion of women from reproduction (Braidotti 2002: 222–63).

10 For example, Emily Martin's now classic article on the cultural values placed on scientific accounts of the different roles of the egg and the sperm in the process of fertilisation (Martin 1991).

11 I have argued elsewhere that *Gattaca* 'queers' traditional notions of desire and kinship, see Stacey 2005, forthcoming.

12 The significance of the queer dynamics in *Gattaca* is reinforced by Jude Law's appearances in other films more explicitly concerned with homosexuality around the same time, such as *Bent* (1997), *Wilde* (1997) and *The Talented Mr Ripley* (1999). In the latter, Law plays Dickie Greenleaf, a character who is also idolised and impersonated.

References

Bland, L. and L. Doan (eds) (1998) *Sexology Uncensored: The Documents of Sexual Science*. Oxford: Polity Press.

Braidotti, R. (2002) *Metamorphoses: Towards a Materialist Theory of Becoming*. Cambridge: Polity Press.

Caruth, C. (ed.) (1995) *Trauma: Explorations in Memory*. London and Baltimore: Johns Hopkins University Press.

Cohan, S. and I. R. Harks (eds) (1993) *Screening the Male: Exploring Masculinities in Hollywood Cinema*. London: Routledge.

Franklin, S. (2000) 'Life itself' in Sarah Franklin, Celia Lury and Jackie Stacey. *Global Nature, Global Culture*. London: Sage, 188–227.

George, S. (2001) 'Not exactly "Of Woman Born"', *Journal of Popular Film and Television*, 29, 4, 177–83.

Halberstam, J. (1998). *Female Masculinity*. Durham: Duke University Press.

Holmlund, C. (2002). *Impossible Bodies: Femininity and Masculinity at the Movies*. London: Routledge.

Keller, E. F. (1995) *Refiguring Life: Metaphors of Twentieth-Century Biology*. New York: Columbia University Press.

King, G. and T. Krzywinska (2000) *Science Fiction Cinema: From Outerspace to Cyberspace*. London: Wallflower Press.

Kirkby, D. (2000) 'The New Eugenics in Cinema: genetic determinism and gene therapy in GATTACA', *Science Fiction Studies*, 27, 2, 193–215.

Kirkham, P. and J. Thumim (eds) (1993) *You Tarzan: Masculinity, Movies and Wen*, London: Lawrence and Wishart.

Kuhn, A. (ed.) (1990) *Alien Zone: Cultural Theory and Contemporary Science Fiction Cinema*. London: Verso.

_____ (ed.) (1999) *Alien Zone II: The Spaces of Science Fiction Cinema*. London: Verso.

Lehman, P. (ed.) (2001) *Masculinity: Bodies, Movies, Culture*. New York: Routledge.

Martin, E. (1991) 'The egg and the sperm: how science has constructed a romance based on stereotypical male-female sex roles', *Signs*, 16, 3, 485–501.

Nelkin, D. and M. S. Lindee (1995) *The DNA Mystique: The Gene as a Cultural Icon*. New York: W. H. Freeman.

Newman, K. (ed.) (2002) *Science Fiction/Horror: A Sight and Sound Reader*. London: British Film Institute.

Penley, C., E. Lyon, L. Spigel, and J. Bergstrom (eds) (1991) *Close Encounters: Film, Feminism, and Science Fiction*. Minneapolis: University of Minnesota Press.

Redmond, S. (2004) *Liquid Metal: The Science Fiction Film Reader*. London: Wallflower Press.

Schwartz, H. (1996) *The Culture of the Copy: Striking Likenesses, Unreasonable Facsimiles*. New York: Zone Books.

Silverman, K. (1991) 'Back to the Future', *Camera Obscura*, 27, 109–32.

Sobchack, V. (1987) *Screening Space: The American Science Fiction Film*. New Brunswick, NJ: Rutgers University Press.

Stacey, J. (2005) 'Masculinity, Masquerade and Genetic Disguise: *Gattaca*'s Queer Visions', *Signs*, 30, 2.

Tasker, Y. (1993) *Spectacular Bodies: Gender, Genre and the Action Cinema*. London: Routledge.

Telotte, J. P. (1999) *A Distant Technology: Science Fiction Film and the Machine Age*. Hanover: Wesleyan University Press.

_____ (2001) *Science Fiction Film*. Cambridge: Cambridge University Press.

Tudor, A. (1989) *Monsters and Mad Scientists: A Cultural History of the Horror Movie*. Oxford: Blackwell.

Turney, J. (1998) *Frankenstein's Footsteps: Science, Genetics and Popular Culture*. New Haven and London: Yale University Press.

Van Dijck, J. (1998) *Imagenation: Popular Images of Genetics*. New York: New York University Press.

Wood, A. (2002) *Technoscience in Contemporary American Film: Beyond Science Fiction* (Manchester: Manchester University Press).

Bibliography

Altman, D. (1986) *AIDS and the New Puritanism*. London: Pluto Press.

Anzieu, D. (1986) *Freud's Self-Analysis*. London: Hogarth Press.

Apple, R. D. and M. W. Apple (1993) 'Screening Science', *Isis*, 84, 750–4.

Arms, S. (1975) *Immaculate Deception: A New Look at Women and Childbirth in America*. Boston: Houghton Mifflin.

Armstrong, D. (1982) 'The doctor-patient relationship: 1930–1980', in P. Wright and A. Treacher (eds) *The Problem of Medical Knowledge: Examining the Social Construction of Medicine*. Edinburgh: Edinburgh University Press, 109–22.

Aspinall, S. (1983) 'Women, realism and reality in British films 1943–53', in J. Curran and V. Porter (eds) *British Cinema History*. London: Weidenfield and Nicolson, 272–93.

Atwood, M. (1990) 'Giving birth', in W. Martin (ed.) *We Are the Stories We Tell*. New York: Pantheon, 134–49.

Aubourg, P., C. Adamsbaum, M.-C. Lavallard-Rousseau, F. Rocchiccioli, N. Cartier, I. Jambaque, C. Jakobezak, A. Lemaitre, F. Boureau, C. Wolf and P.-F. Bougneres (1993) 'A two-year trial of oleic and erucic acids ("Lorenzo's oil") as treatment for adrenomyeloneuropathy', *New England Journal of Medicine*, 329, 11, 745–52. Available at: http://content.nejm.org/cgi/content/full/329/11/745 (18 January 2004).

Balsalmo, A. (1995) 'Forms of technological embodiment: reading the body in contem-porary culture', in M. Featherstone and R. Burrows (eds) *Cyberbodies/Cyberspace/Cyberpunk: Cultures of Technological Embodiment*. London: Sage, 215–37.

Bandolier Extra (2002) *Lorenzo's Oil for Adrenoleukodystrophy and Adrenomyeloneuropathy* Available at: http://www.jr2.ox.ac.uk/bandolier/booth/neurol/lorenz.html (18 Oct-ober 2003).

Barker, M., J. Arthurs and R. Harindranath (2001) *The Crash Controversy: Censorship Campaigns and Film Reception*. London: Wallflower Press.

Barr, C. (2001) 'Madness, madness!': the brief stardom of James Donald', in B. Bab-ington (ed.) *British Stars and Stardom: From Alma Taylor to Sean Connery*. Manchester: Manchester University Press, 155–66.

_____ (2003) 'The national health: Pat Jackson's *White Corridors*', in I. MacKillop and N. Sinyard (eds) *British Cinema of the 1950s: A Celebration*. Manchester: Manchester University Press, 64–73.

Barthes, R. (1974) *S/Z: An Essay*, trans. Richard Miller. New York: Hill and Wang.

Bataille, G. (2001) *Eroticism*. London: Penguin.

Bathrick, S. K. (1977) 'Ragtime: the horror of growing up female', *Jump Cut*, 14, March, 9–10.

Bauman, Z. (1992a) *Mortality, Immortality and Other Life Strategies*. Cambridge: Polity Press.

_____ (1992b) *Imitations of Postmodernity*. London: Routledge.

_____ (1993) *Postmodern Ethics*. London: Blackwell.

Beauchamp, T. A. and J. F. Childress (1994) *Principles of Biomedical Ethics*. New York: Oxford University Press.

Behlmer, R. (1987) *Inside Warner Brothers (1935–1951)*. London: Weidenfeld & Nicolson.

Berenstein, R. (1990) 'Mommie Dearest: *Aliens, Rosemary's Baby* and mothering', *Journal of Popular Culture*, 24, 2, 55–73.

Bergson, H. (1911a) *Creative Evolution*. New York: Henry Holt.

_____ (1911b) *Laughter: An Essay on the Meaning of the Comic*. London: Macmillan.

Bibring, G. L. (1959) 'Some considerations of the psychological process in pregnancy', *The Psychoanalytic Study of the Child*, 14, 113–21.

Black, Sir D., J. N. Morris, C. Smith, P. Townsend (1982) *Inequalities in Health: The Black Report*. Harmondsworth: Penguin.

Bland, L. and L. Doan (eds) (1998) *Sexology Uncensored: The Documents of Sexual Science*. Oxford: Polity Press.

Blier, B. (1986) 'Les mots et les choses: entretien avec Bertrand Blier' (interview by Pascal Bonitzer and Serge Toubiana), *Cahiers du Cinéma*, 382.

Bloor, D. (1991) *Knowledge and Social Imagery*. Chicago: University of Chicago Press.

Boon, T. M. (1993) 'The smoke menace: cinema, sponsorship, and the social relations of science in 1937', in M. Shortland (ed.) *Science and Nature. BSHS Monograph* 8. Oxford: BSHS, 57–88.

_____ (1997) 'Agreement and disagreement in the making of *World of Plenty*', in D. Smith (ed.) *Nutrition in Britain: Science, Scientists and Politics in the Twentieth Century*. London: Routledge, 166–89.

_____ (1999) *Films and the Contestation of Public Health in Interwar Britain*. Unpublished PhD dissertation, University of London.

_____ (2000) '"The shell of a prosperous age": history, landscape and the modern in Paul Rotha's *The Face of Britain* (1935)', in C. Lawrence and A. Mayer (eds) *Regenerating England: Science, Medicine and Culture in the Interwar Years. Clio Medica* 60. Amsterdam: Rodopi, 107–48.

_____ (2004) 'Industrialisation and catastrophe: the Victorian economy in British film documentary, 1930–50', in M. Wolff and M. Taylor (eds) *The Victorians Since 1901: Histories, Representations and Revisions*. Manchester: Manchester University Press.

Bordwell, D. (1986) *Narration in the Fiction Film*. London: Routledge.

_____ (1989) *Making Meaning*. Cambridge, MA: Harvard University Press.

Boss, P. (1986) 'Vile bodies and bad medicine', *Screen*, 27, 1, 14–24.

Brackenbury, H. (1935) *Patient and Doctor*. London: Hodder and Stoughton.

Braidotti, R. (2002) *Metamorphoses: Towards a Materialist Theory of Becoming*. Cambridge: Polity Press.

Brill, N. Q., M. C. Tate and W. C. Menninger (1945) *Enlisted Men Discharged from Army Because of Psychoneuroses – A Follow-up Study. J.A.M.A.*, 128 (June), 633–7.

British Commercial Gas Association. (1939) *Modern Films on Matters of Moment* (cat-alogue). London: BCGA.

Brody, H. (1987) *Stories of Sickness*. Yale University Press: London.

Brophy, P. (1986) 'Horrality: the textuality of Contemporary Horror Films', *Screen*, 27, 1, 2–13.

Brunovska Karnick, K. and H. Jenkins (1995) *Classical Hollywood Comedy*. New York: Routledge.

Bury, M. (1982) 'Chronic illness as biographical disruption', *Sociology of Health & Illness*, 5, 2, 168–95.

Cahill, K. M. (1983) *The AIDS Epidemic*. New York: St Martin's Press.

Carroll, N. (1981) 'Nightmare and the horror film: the symbolic biology of fantastic beings', *Film Quarterly*, 34, 3, 16–25.

_____ (1990) *The Philosophy of Horror or Paradoxes of the Heart*. New York and London: Routledge.

Caruth, C. (ed.) (1995) *Trauma: Explorations in Memory*. London and Baltimore: Johns Hopkins University Press.

CCHE (1939) *Health Education Year Book*. London: CCHE.

Chapetta, R. (1969) '*Rosemary's Baby*', *Film Quarterly*, 22, Spring, 35–8.

Chapman, R. L. (1987) *New Dictionary of American Slang*. London: Macmillan.

Chesler, P. (1979) *With Child: A Diary of Motherhood*. New York: Thomas V. Crowell.

Chester, L. (ed.) (1989) *Cradle and All: Women Writers on Pregnancy and Childbirth*. Boston and London: Faber and Faber.

Cilliers, P. (1998) *Complexity and Postmodernism*. London: Routledge.

Clifford, G. (1974) *The Transformations of Allegory*. London and Boston: Routledge and Kegan Paul.

Cohan, S. and I. R. Harks (eds) (1993) *Screening the Male: Exploring Masculinities in Hollywood Cinema*. London: Routledge.

Cohen-Solal, A. (1987) *Sartre: A Life*. London: Heinemann.

Combs, R. (1976) '*Shivers*', *Monthly Film Bulletin*, 43, 506.

Cook, P. (1986) '*Mandy*: daughter of transition', in C. Barr (ed.) *All Our Yesterdays: 90 Years of British Cinema*. London: British Film Institute, 355–61.

_____ (1996) *Fashioning the Nation: Fashion and Identity in British Cinema*. London: British Film Institute.

Corrigan, P. (1983) 'Film entertainment as ideology and pleasure: a preliminary approach to a history of audiences', in J. Curran and V. Porter (eds) *British Cinema History*. London: Wiedenfeld and Nicolson, 24–35.

Creed, B. (1986) 'Horror and the monstrous feminine: an imaginary abjection', *Screen*, 27, 1, 44–71.

_____ (1993) *The Monstrous Feminine: Film, Feminism, Psychoanalysis*. London and New York: Routledge.

_____ (1998) 'The *Crash* debate: anal wounds, metallic kisses', *Screen*, 39, 2, 175–9.

Crew, T. (1935) *Health Propaganda, Ways and Means*. Leicester: Bell.

Crimp, D. (ed.) (1988) *AIDS: Cultural Analysis/Cultural Activism*. Cambridge: MIT Press.

Cumston, C. G. (1926) *An Introduction to the History of Medicine: From the Time of the Pharaohs to the End of the XVIIIth Century*. London: Kegan Paul, Trench and Trübner.

Curie, E. (1938) *Madame Curie*. London: Heinemann.

Curtis, L. R. and Y. Caroles (1985) *Pregnant and Lovin' It*. Los Angeles and San Francisco: Price/Stern.

Custen, G. (1992) *Bio/Pics: How Hollywood Constructed Public History*. Brunswick: Rut-gers University Press.

Daley, A. (1959) 'The Central Council for Health Education: the first twenty-five years', *Health Education Journal*, 17, 24–35.

Daley, W. A. (1924) 'The organisation of propaganda in the interests of public health', *Public Health*, (September), 305–13.

Dally, A. (1983) *Inventing Motherhood: The Consequences of an Ideal*. New York: Schocken.

Daly, B. O. and M. T. Reddy (eds) (1991) *Narrating Mothers: Theorizing Maternal Subjectivities*. Knoxville: University of Tennessee.

Dans, P. E. (2000) *Doctors in the Movies: Boil the Water and Just Say Aah*. Bloomington: Medi-Ed Press.

Darke, P. (1994) '*The Elephant Man* (David Lynch, EMI Films, 1980): an analysis from a disabled perspective', *Disability and Society*, 9, 3, 327–42.

_____ (1998) 'Understanding cinematic representations of disability', in T. Shakespeare (ed.) *The Disability Reader*. London: Cassell, 181–97.

Deutsch, H. (1945) *The Psychology of Woman*, Vol. III. New York: Grune and Stratton.

Dick, B. F. (ed.) (1981) *Dark Victory*. Wisconsin: University of Wisconsin Press.

Dingwall, R., A. M. Rafferty and C. Webster (1988) *An Introduction to the Social History of Nursing*. London: Routledge.

Docherty, D., D. Morrison and M. Tracey (1987) *The Last Picture Show? Britain's Changing Film Audiences*. London: British Film Institute.

Dyer, R. (1993) *Brief Encounter*. London: British Film Institute.

_____ (1997) *White*. London: Routledge.

Ebert, R. (1996) Review of *Bob Flanagan Supermasochist*, originally published in *Chicago Sun Times*. Available at: http://www.suntimes.com/ebert/ebert_reviews/1997/12/12051.html

Edwards, N. (1975) 'The parasite murders', *Cinema Canada*, 22, 44–5.

Ehrenreich, B. (1973) *Witches, Midwives, and Nurses: A History of Woman Healers*. Old Westbury, NY: The Feminist Press.

Ellis, J. (1978) 'Art, culture, quality: terms for a cinema in the forties and seventies', *Screen*, 19, 3, 9–49.

_____ (1996) 'The quality film adventure: British critics and the cinema, 1942–1948', in A. Higson (ed.) *Dissolving Views: Key Writings on British Cinema*. London: Cassell, 66–93.

Elsaesser, T. (1986) 'Film History as Social History: The Dieterle/Warner Brothers Bio-Pic', *Wide Angle*, 8, 2, 15–31.

Engels, F. (1993) *The Condition of the Working Class in England in 1844*. Oxford: Oxford University Press.

Ephron, N. (1978) 'Having a baby after 35', *New York Times Magazine* (26 November), 28–9, 86, 88–9.

Evans, W. (1984) 'Monster movies: a sexual theory', in B. K. Grant (ed.) *Planks of Reason: Essays on the Horror Film*. Metuchen, NJ and London: Scarecrow Press, 53–64.

Flinn, T. (1975) 'William Dieterle: The Plutarch of Hollywood', *Velvet Light Trap*, 15, 23–8.

Foot, M. (1962) *Aneurin Bevan: A Biography, vol. one 1897–1945*. London: MacGibbon & Kee.

Forbes, T. R. (1966) *The Midwife and the Witch*. New Haven and London: Yale University Press.

Foucault, M. (1972) *The Archaeology of Knowledge and the Discourse on Language*. New York: Pantheon Books.

_____ (1973) *The Birth of the Clinic: An Archaeology of Medical Perception*. New York: Vintage.

_____ (1977) *Discipline and Punish*. London: Allen Lane.

Franklin, S. (2000) 'Life itself' in Sarah Franklin, Celia Lury and Jackie Stacey. *Global Nature, Global Culture*. London: Sage, 188–227.

French, K. (1993) 'Introduction', in *The Marx Brothers: Monkey Business, Duck Soup and A Day at the Races*. London: Faber.

Freud, S. (1956) *An Autobiographical Study*. London: Hogarth Press

_____ (1966) *Complete Psychoanalytical Works*. London: Cassell.

Genovese, M. A. (1987) *Politics and the Cinema: An Introduction to Political Films*. Needham Heights, MA: Ginn Press.

_____ (1995) 'Art and Politics: The Political Film as a Pedagogical Tool', paper presented at the annual meeting of the American Political Science Association, Chicago, September 1995.

George, S. (2001) 'Not exactly "Of Woman Born"', *Journal of Popular Film and Television*, 29, 4, 177–83.

Geraghty, C. (2000) *British Cinema in the 1950s: Gender, Genre and the New Look*. London: Routledge.

Gilliatt, P. (1968) 'Anguish under the skin', *New Yorker* (15 June), 87–9.

Gilman, S. L. (1988) *Disease and Representation: Images of Illness From Madness to AIDS*. Ithaca: Cornell University Press.

Glass, A. (ed.) *Neuropsychiatry in World War II* (1966), Vol. 1, Zone of the Interior. Office of the Surgeon General, Washington, DC.

Gledhill, C. (ed.) (1987) *Home is Where the Heart Is: Studies in Melodrama and the Woman's Film.* London: British Film Institute.

____ (1996) 'An abundance of understatement': documentary, melodrama and romance', in C. Gledhill and G. Swanson (eds) *Nationalising Femininity: Culture, Sexuality and British Cinema in the Second World War.* Manchester and New York: Manchester University Press, 213–29.

Grant, B. K. (ed.) (1984) *Planks of Reason: Essays on the Horror Film.* Metuchen, NJ and London: Scarecrow Press.

Grant, M. (1998) 'Crimes of the future', *Screen*, 39, 2, 180–5.

Greenhalgh, T. and B. Hurwitz (eds) (1998) *Narrative Based Medicine.* London: B. M. J. Books.

Grinker, R. and J. Spiegel (1945) *War Neuroses.* Philadelphia: Blakiston.

Grover, J. Z. (1988) 'AIDS: keywords', in D. Crimp (ed.) *AIDS: Cultural Analysis/Cultural Activism.* Cambridge: MIT Press, 17–30.

Halberstam, J. (1998). *Female Masculinity.* Durham: Duke University Press.

Hale, Nathan G., Jr (1995) *The Rise and Crisis of Psychoanalysis in America: Freud and the Americans, 1917–1985.* New York and Oxford: Oxford University Press.

Hall, L. and R. Porter (1995) *Facts of Life: The Creation of Sexual Knowledge in Britain, 1650–1950.* New Haven: Yale University Press.

Hall, S. (1981) 'Notes on deconstructing "The Popular"', in R. Samuel (ed.) *People's History and Socialist Theory.* London and Boston: Routledge and Kegan Paul, 227–40.

Hallam, J. (1996) 'Nursing an image: the Sue Barton stories', in S. Sceats and G. Cunning-ham (eds) *Image and Power: Women in Twentieth Century Fiction.* London: Longmans, 91–102.

____ (2000) *Nursing the Image: Media, Culture and Professional identity.* London: Routledge.

Hallam, J. with M. Marshment (2000) *Realism and Popular Cinema.* Manchester and New York: Manchester University Press.

Halliwell, L. (1989) *Halliwell's Film Guide.* 7th Edition, London and New York: Paladin Grafton.

Hammen, S. (1985) *John Huston.* Boston: Twayne Publishers.

Hancock, G. and E. Carim (1986) *AIDS: The Deadly Epidemic.* London: Victor Gollancz.

Harper S. (2000) *Women in British Cinema: Mad, Bad and Dangerous to Know.* London, Continuum.

Haskell, M. (1974) *From Reverence to Rape: The Treatment of Women in the Movies.* Mid-dlesex and Baltimore: Penguin.

Hayman, R. (1986) *Writing Against: A Biography of Sartre.* London: Weidenfeld & Nicolson.

Hazlitt, W. (1855) *Essays on English Comic Writers.* London: George Bell.

Henderson, B. (1995) *Four More Screenplays by Preston Sturges.* Berkeley: University of California Press, 241–526.

Hoberman, J. (1987) 'The Other, Woman', *Village Voice*, 1 December, 68.

Hogan, B. W. (1943) 'Psychiatric Observations of Senior Medical Officer on Board Aircraft Carrier U.S.S. WASP During Action in Combat Areas, At Time of Torpedoing, and Survivors' Reaction', *American Journal of Psychiatry*, 100, 90–3.

Holmlund, C. (2002). *Impossible Bodies: Femininity and Masculinity at the Movies.* London: Routledge.

Hopkins, H. (1963) *The New Look.* London: Secker and Warberg.

Houston, B. and M. Kinder (1968–69) '*Rosemary's Baby*', *Sight and Sound*, 38, 1, 17–19.

Hunt, L. M. (2000) 'Strategic suffering: illness narratives as social empowerment among Mexican cancer patients', in C. Mattingly and L. G. Garro (eds) *Narrative and the Cultural Construction of Illness and Healing.* London: University of California Press, 90.

Huston, J. Huston papers, Special Collections, Margaret Herrick Library, Beverley Hills, CA.

Hydén, L.-C. (1997) 'Illness and narrative', *Sociology of Health and Illness*, 19, 1, 48–69.

Jackson, P. (1999) *A Retake Please!: Nightmail to Western Approaches.* Liverpool: Liverpool University Press.

James, C. (1990) 'The high art of horror films can cut deep into the psyche', *New York Times* (27

May), Section 2, 1, 15.

Jones, A. (1990) 'Brian Yuzna's *Society*'. *Starburst*, 140, 9–12.

Jones, A. H. (2000) Medicine and the movies: *Lorenzo's Oil* at century's end', *Annals of Internal Medicine*, 133, 7, 567–71. Available at: http://www.annals.org/cgi/content/full/133/7/567 (4 February 2004).

Jordan, M. (1983) 'Carry On: follow that stereotype', in J. Curran and V. Porter (eds) *British Cinema History*. London: Weidenfield and Nicolson, 312–27.

Kalisch, B. and P. Kalisch (1982) 'The image of the nurse in motion pictures', *American Journal of Nursing*, 82, 4, 605–12.

_____ (1987) *The Changing Image of the Nurse*. California: Addison-Wesley.

Kaminsky, S. (1978) *John Huston: Maker of Magic*. Boston: Houghton Mifflin.

Karpf, A. (1988) *Doctoring the Media*. London and New York: Routledge.

Keller, E. F. (1995) *Refiguring Life: Metaphors of Twentieth-Century Biology*. New York: Columbia University Press.

Kemp, P. (1991) *Lethal Innocence: The Cinema of Alexander Mackendrick*. London: Methuen.

King, G. (2002) *Film Comedy*. London: Wallflower Press.

King, G. and T. Krzywinska (2000) *Science Fiction Cinema: From Outerspace to Cyberspace*. London: Wallflower Press.

Kipple, K. F. (ed.) (1993) *The Cambridge World History of Human Disease*. Cambridge: Cambridge University Press.

Kirkby, D. (2000) 'The New Eugenics in Cinema: genetic determinism and gene therapy in GATTACA', *Science Fiction Studies*, 27, 2, 193–215.

Kirkham, P. and J. Thumim (eds) (1993) *You Tarzan: Masculinity, Movies and Wen*, London: Lawrence and Wishart.

Kitzinger, S. (1978) *Women as Mothers*. New York: Random House.

Klobas, L. (1988) *Disability Drama in Television and Film*. Jefferson, NC: McFarland & Co.

Koestler, A. (1964) *The Act of Creation*. London: Hutchinson.

Kohn, V. (1993) 'Kenny, Elizabeth', *Collier's Encyclopedia*, 14. New York: P. F. Collier, 26–7.

Koppes, C. R. and G. D. Black (1987) *Hollywood Goes to War: How Politics, Profits and Propaganda Shaped World War II Movies*. Berkeley, CA: University of California Press.

Kristeva, J. (1982) *Powers of Horror: An Essay on Abjection*, trans. Leon S. Roudiez. New York: Columbia University Press.

Krutnik, F. and S. Neale (1990) *Popular Film and Television Comedy*. London: Routledge.

Krzywinska, T. (1999) 'Cicciolina and the dynamics of transgression and abjection in explicit sex films', in M. Aaron (ed.) *The Body's Perilous Pleasures: Dangerous Desires and Contemporary Culture*. Edinburgh: Edinburgh University Press, 188–209.

Kübler-Ross, E. (1970) *On Death and Dying*. London: Tavistock Publications.

Kuhn, A. (1988) *Cinema, Censorship and Sexuality, 1909–1925*. London: Routledge.

_____ (ed.) (1990) *Alien Zone: Cultural Theory and Contemporary Science Fiction Cinema*. London: Verso.

_____ (1995) *Family Secrets: Acts of Memory and Imagination*. London: Verso.

_____ (1999a) '*Crash* and film censorship in the UK', *Screen*, 40, 4, 448–50.

_____ (ed.) (1999b) *Alien Zone II: The Spaces of Science Fiction Cinema*. London: Verso.

Leayman, C. D. (1976) '"They Came from Within": Siegel's "Pods" have in fact won out', *Cinefantastique*, 5, 3, 22–3.

Lebas, E. (1995) '"When every street became a cinema": the film work of the Bermondsey Borough Council's Public Health Department', *History Workshop Journal*, 39, 42–66.

Lehman, P. (ed.) (2001) *Masculinity: Bodies, Movies, Culture*. New York: Routledge.

Leifer, M. (1980) *Psychological Effects of Motherhood: A Study of First Pregnancy*. New York: Praeger.

Levin, I. (1967) *Rosemary's Baby*. New York: Random House.

Lewis J. (1992) *Women in Britain since 1945*. Oxford: Blackwell.

Liley, H. M. and B. Day (1968) 'The inside story of your baby's life before birth', *Expecting* (A Guide for Expectant Mothers Published by *Parent's Magazine*) (Fall).

Lloyd, C. (1986) *Explanation in Social History*. Oxford: Blackwell.

Longmore, P. (1986) 'Screening stereotypes: images of disabled people in television and motion pictures', in A. Gartner and T. Joe (eds) *Images of the Disabled/Disabling Images*. New York: Praeger, 65–78.

Lothe, J. (2000) *Narrative in Fiction and Film*. Oxford: Oxford University Press.

Low, R. (1979a) *Documentary and Educational Films of the 1930s*. London: George Allen and Unwin.

____ (1979b) *Films of Comment and Persuasion of the 1930s*. London: George Allen and Unwin.

Lowenthal, L. (1944) 'Biographies in Popular Magazines', in P. Lazarsfeld and F. Stanton (eds) *Radio Research, 1942–43*. New York: Duell, Sloan & Pearce.

Luckin, B. (1990) *Questions of Power: Electricity and Environment in Interwar Britain*. Manchester: Manchester University Press.

Lunbeck, E. (1995) *The Psychiatric Persuasion: Knowledge, Gender and Power in Modern America*. Princeton: Princeton University Press.

Lyotard, J.-F. (1984) *The Postmodern Condition*. Manchester: Manchester University Press.

Madsen, A. (1978) *John Huston*. New York: Doubleday.

Malleson, A. (2002) *Whiplash and Other Useful Injuries*. Montreal and Kingston: McGill-Queen's University Press.

Maltby, R. (1983) *Harmless Entertainment: Hollywood and the Ideology of Consensus*. Metuchen, NJ: Scarecrow Press.

Martin, E. (1991) 'The egg and the sperm: how science has constructed a romance based on stereotypical male-female sex roles', *Signs*, 16, 3, 485–501.

Marx Brothers (1993) *The Marx Brother: Monkey Business, Duck Soup and A Day at the Races*. London: Faber.

McGrath, R. (1990) 'Dangerous liaisons: health, disease and representation', in T. Boffin and S. Gupta (eds) *Ecstatic Antibodies: Resisting the AIDS Mythology*. London: Rivers Oram Press, 142–55.

McKay, P. (1988) 'Fatal Attraction', *Evening Standard*, 7 March.

McMahon, M. (1991) 'Nursing histories: reviving life in abandoned selves', *Feminist Review*, 37, 22–37.

Menninger, W. C. (1943) 'Psychiatric Problems in the Army', *American Journal of Psychiatry*, 123, 751–4.

____ (1995) 'World War II: Psychoanalytic Warriors', in N. G. Hale Jr, *The Rise and Crisis of Psychoanalysis in the United States*. New York: Oxford University Press, 187–210.

Moser, H. W. (1999) 'Treatment of X-linked adrenoleukodystrophy with Lorenzo's oil' [Editorial], *Journal of Neurology, Neurosurgery and Psychiatry*, 67, 279–80. Available at: http://jnnp.bmjjournals.com/cgi/content/full/67/3/279 (4 February 2004).

Murray, S. A., K. Boyd, M. Kendall, A. Worth, T. F. Benton, H. Clausen (2002) 'Dying of lung cancer or cardiac failure: prospective qualitative interview study of patients and their carers in the community', *British Medical Journal*, 325, 929–32.

Neale, S. (2000) *Genre and Hollywood*. London: Routledge.

Neagle, A. (1958) 'Portraying Edith Cavell and other nurses', *Nursing Mirror*, 10, 1–11.

Nelkin, D. and M. S. Lindee (1995) *The DNA Mystique: The Gene as a Cultural Icon*. New York: W. H. Freeman.

Newman, G. (1925) *Public Education in Health*. London: HMSO.

Newman, K. (1989) 'Skin Deep', *Monthly Film Bulletin*, 56, 215.

____ (ed.) (2002) *Science Fiction/Horror: A Sight and Sound Reader*. London: British Film Institute.

Nichols, B. (1976/77) 'Documentary theory and practice', *Screen*, 17, 4, 34–48.

Nillson, L. (1965) 'Drama of life before birth', *Life*, 58, 17, 30 April.

Norden, M. (1994) *The Cinema of Isolation*. New Brunswick, NJ: Rutgers University Press.

Odone A. (2003) *The Myelin Project Progress Report, December 8 2003*. Available at: http://www.myelin.org/12082003.htm (9 March 2004).

Odone, A. and M. Odone (1994) 'More on Lorenzo's Oil' [Letter]. *New England Journal of Medicine*, 330, 26, 1904–5. Available at: http://content.nejm.org/cgi/content/short/330/26/1904 (3 February 2004).

Oliver, M. (1998) 'Review of *The Sexual Politics of Disability*', *Disability and Society*, 13, 1, 150–2.

Orwell, G. (1986) *The Road to Wigan Pier*. London: Secker and Warburg.

Overholser, W. (1943) 'Psychiatric Casualties of War and Their Treatment', *The New England Journal of Medicine*, 231, 11, 377–80.

Parsons, T. (1951) *The Social System*. Glencoe, IL: Free Press.

Paul, W. (1994) *Laughing Screaming: Modern Hollywood Horror and Comedy*. New York: Columbia University Press.

Pearson, D. (1982) 'Speaking for the common man: multi-voice commentary in *World of Plenty* and *Land of Promise*', in P. Marris (ed.) *Paul Rotha*. London: BFI, 64–85.

Penley, C., E. Lyon, L. Spigel, and J. Bergstrom (eds) (1991) *Close Encounters: Film, Feminism, and Science Fiction*. Minneapolis: University of Minnesota Press.

Pernick, M. (1996), *The Black Stork: Eugenics and the Death of Defective Babies in American Medicine and Motion Pictures Since 1915*. New York and Oxford: Oxford University Press.

Pirandello, A. (1960) *On Humour*, trans. A Iliano and D. Testa. University of North Carolina Press: Chapel Hill.

Polan, D. (1984) 'Eros and syphilization: the contemporary horror film', in B. K. Grant (ed.) *Planks of Reason: Essays on the Horror Film*. Metuchen, NJ and London: Scarecrow Press, 201–11.

Porter, R. (1997) *The Greatest Benefit to Mankind: A Medical History of Humanity from Antiquity to the Present*. London: HarperCollins.

Porter, W. C. (1941) 'The Military Psychiatrist at Work', *American Journal of Psychiatry*, 98, 317–23.

_____ (1943) 'What has Psychiatry Learned During Present War?', *American Journal of Psychiatry*, 99, 850–5.

Randall, R. S. (1979) 'Censorship: from *The Miracle* to *Deep Throat*', in T. Balio (ed.) *The American Film Industry*. Madison: University of Wisconsin Press, 432–57.

Redmond, S. (2004) *Liquid Metal: The Science Fiction Film Reader*. London: Wallflower Press.

Rich, A. (1986) *Of Woman Born: Motherhood as Experience and Institution*. New York and London: W. W. Norton.

Richards, J. (1984) *The Age of the Dream Palace*. London: Routledge and Kegan Paul.

Richards, J. and D. Sheridan (eds) (1987) *Mass-Observation at the Movies: Cinema and Society*. London: Routledge.

Riessman, C. K. (2002) 'Illness narrative and performance', unpublished presentation given at 'Narrative and Health Workshop', 14 November 2002, King's College, Cambridge.

Robinson, C. (1986) 'Casey Robinson: master adaptor' (interview with Joel Greenberg), in P. McGilligan (ed.) *Backstory: Interviews with Screenwriters of Hollywood's Golden Age*. Berkeley: University of California Press, 301.

Rodley, C. (ed.) (1993) *Cronenberg on Cronenberg*. London: Faber.

Roeder, G. H., Jr (1993) *The Censored War: American Visual Experience during World War Two*. New Haven and London: Yale University Press.

Rogers, N. (1989) 'Germs with legs: flies, disease and the New Public Health', *BHM*, 63, 599–617.

Rogin, M. P. (1987) *Ronald Reagan, the Movie, and Other Episodes in Political Demonology*. Berkeley and Los Angeles: University of California Press.

Rotha, P. (1936) *Documentary Film*. London: Faber.

_____ (1973) *Documentary Diary: An Informal History of the British Documentary Film, 1928–1939*. London: Secker and Warburg.

Rowson, S. (1936) 'A statistical survey of the cinema industry in Great Britain in 1934', *Journal of the Royal Statistical Society*, 99, 67–129.

Russell, C. (1995) *Narrative Mortality: Death, Closure and New Wave Cinemas*. London: University of Minnesota Press.

Samson, C. (1999) 'Biomedicine and the body', in C. Samson (ed.) *Health Studies: A Critical and*

Cross-Cultural Reader. Oxford: Blackwell, 3–21.

Sarris, A. (1968) (review). *The Village Voice*, 25 July, 37.

Schmidt, C. G. (1984) 'The group-fantasy origin of AIDS', *Journal of Psychohistory*, 12, 37–78.

Schopenhauer, A. (1995) 'Appendix: Abstract of Schopenhauer's essay On the Fourfold Root of the Principle of Sufficient Reason', in D. Berman and J. Berman (eds) *The World as Will and Idea.* London: J. M. Dent, 267–8.

Schüklenk, U. (2000) 'An Introduction to bioethics', in C. Ernest (ed.) *Principled Choices: Medical Ethics in South Africa.* Johannesburg: The Center for the Study of Violence and Reconciliation, 7–13.

Schwartz, H. (1996) *The Culture of the Copy: Striking Likenesses, Unreasonable Facsimiles.* New York: Zone Books.

Seale, C. (2000) 'Resurrective practice and narrative', in M. Andrews, S. D. Sclater, C. Squire and A. Treacher (eds) *Lines of Narrative: Psychosocial Perspectives.* London: Routledge, 36.

Shakespeare, T. (1994) 'Cultural representation of disabled people: dustbins for dis-avowal?', *Disability and Society*, 9, 3, 283–300.

____ (1999) 'Art and lies: representations of disability on film', in M. Corker and S. French (eds) *Disability Discourse.* Buckingham: Open University Press.

Shakespeare, T. K. Gillespie-Sells, D. Davies (1996) *The Sexual Politics of Disability: untold desires.* London: Cassell.

Shortland, M. (1987) 'Screening History: Towards a history of Psychiatry and Psycho-analysis in the movies', *British Journal for the History of Science*, 20, 4, 421–52.

____ (1989) *Medicine and Film: A Checklist, Survey and Research Resource.* Oxford: Wellcome Institute for the History of Medicine.

Sikov, E. (1989) *Screwball: Hollywood's Madcap Romantic Comedies.* New York: Crown.

Silverman, K. (1991) 'Back to the Future', *Camera Obscura*, 27, 109–32.

Sinclair, I. (1999) *Crash: David Cronenberg's Post-mortem on J. G. Ballard's 'Trajectory of Fate'.* London: British Film Institute.

Sklar, R. and C. Musser (eds) *Resisting Images: Essays on Cinema and History.* Philadelphia: Temple University Press.

Smith, D. F. (1986) *Nutrition in Britain in the Twentieth Century.* Unpublished PhD dissertation, Edinburgh University.

Smith, F. B. (1982) *Florence Nightingale: Reputation and Power.* London: Croom Helm.

Snowbeck, C. (2001) 'The mixed legacy of *Lorenzo's Oil*'. *Pittsburgh Post-Gazette.* Available at: http://www.post-gazette.com/healthscience/20010508hlorenzo1.asp (18 October 2003).

Sobchack, V. (1987) *Screening Space: The American Science Fiction Film.* New Brunswick, NJ: Rutgers University Press.

Sontag, S. (1978) *Illness as Metaphor.* New York: Farrar, Straus and Giroux.

____ (1988) *AIDS and its Metaphors.* New York: Farrar, Straus and Giroux.

Spurr, D. (1993) *Colonial Discourse in Journalism, Travel Writing and Imperial Admin-istration.* Durham and London: Duke University Press.

Stacey, J. (2005) 'Masculinity, Masquerade and Genetic Disguise: *Gattaca's* Queer Visions', *Signs*, 30, 2.

Swann, P. (1989) *The British Documentary Film Movement, 1926–1946.* Cambridge: Cambridge University Press.

Sweeney, L. (1968) 'Polanski's satanic parody', in *Christian Science Monitor* (Western edition; 22 June), 6.

Sweetman, P. (1999) 'Only skin deep? tattooing, piercing and the transgressive body', in M. Aaron (ed.) *The Body's Perilous Pleasures: Dangerous Desires and Contemporary Culture.* Edinburgh: Edinburgh University Press, 165–87.

Tasker, Y. (1993) *Spectacular Bodies: Gender, Genre and the Action Cinema.* London: Routledge.

Telotte, J. P. (1999) *A Distant Technology: Science Fiction Film and the Machine Age.* Hanover: Wesleyan University Press.

____ (2001) *Science Fiction Film.* Cambridge: Cambridge University Press.

Thumim, J. (1992) *Celluloid Sisters: Women and Popular Cinema*. London: Macmillan.

Tudor, A. (1989) *Monsters and Mad Scientists: A Cultural History of the Horror Movie*. Oxford: Basil Blackwell.

Turner, M. (1997) 'Sick: review', *Disability Now*, April, 22.

Turney, J. (1998) *Frankenstein's Footsteps: Science, Genetics and Popular Culture*. New Haven and London: Yale University Press.

Twitchell, J. B. (1985) *Dreadful Pleasures: An Anatomy of Modern Horror*. New York and Oxford: Oxford University Press.

Van Dijck, J. (1998) *Imagenation: Popular Images of Genetics*. New York: New York Uni-versity Press.

Vidor, K. (1952) *A Tree is a Tree*. New York: Harcourt, Brace & Co.

Waldman, D. (1981) *Horror and Domesticity: The Modern Romance Film of the 1940s*. PhD dissertation, University of Wisconsin-Madison.

Walker, A. (1976) *Evening Standard*, 29 April.

Waller, W. (1944) *Veteran Comes Back*. New York: Dryden Press.

Walter, T. (2003) 'Historic and cultural variants on the good death', *British Medical Journal*, 327, 218–20.

Weeks, J. (1985) *Sexuality and Its Discontents: Meanings, Myths and Modern Sexualities*. London: Routledge and Kegan Paul.

Wexman, V. W. (1987) 'The trauma of infancy in Roman Polanski's *Rosemary's Baby*', in G. Waller (ed.) *American Horrors: Essays on the Modern American Horror Film*. Urbana and Chicago: University of Illinois Press, 30–43.

White, D. L. (1987) 'The poetics of horror: more than meets the eye', *Cinema Journal*, 10, 2, 1–18.

Whittington-Walsh, R. (2002) 'From freaks to savants: disability and hegemony from *The Hunchback of Notre Dame* (1939) to *Sling Blade* (1997)', *Disability and Society*, 17, 6, 695–708.

Williams, L. (1994) *Viewing Positions: Ways of Seeing Film*. New Brunswick, NJ: Rutgers University Press.

Williams, L. R. (1999) 'The inside-out of masculinity: David Cronenberg's visceral pleasures', in M. Aaron (ed.) *The Body's Perilous Pleasures: Dangerous Desires and Contemporary Culture*. Edinburgh: Edinburgh University Press, 30–48.

Williams, R. (1983) 'British film history: new perspectives', in J. Curran and V. Porter (eds) *British Cinema History*. London: Wiedenfeld and Nicolson, 9–23.

Wilson, E. (1980) *Only Halfway to Paradise: Women in Post-war Britain 1945–68*. London and New York: Tavistock.

Wolkind, S. and E. Zajicek (1981) *Pregnancy: A Psychological and Social Study*. London: Academic Press.

Wood, A. (2002) *Technoscience in Contemporary American Film: Beyond Science Fiction* (Manchester: Manchester University Press).

Wood, R. (1984) 'An introduction to the American horror film', in B. K. Grant (ed.) *Planks of Reason: Essays on the Horror Film*. Metuchen, NJ and London: Scarecrow Press, 164–200.

_____ (1986) *Hollywood from Vietnam to Reagan*. New York: Columbia University Press.

Wood, S. H. (1935) *Intelligence and Public Relations*. London: Public Record Office, MH78/147.

Wright, T. R. (1986) *The Religion of Humanity: The Impact of Comtean Positivism on Victorian Britain*. Cambridge: Cambridge University Press.

Young, I. M. (1984) 'Pregnant embodiment: subjectivity and alienation', *Journal of Medicine and Philosophy*, 9, 45–62.

Index